OPENING TO GRACE

Learning to Be Me

PEGGY WRIGHT

WestBow
PRESS
A DIVISION OF THOMAS NELSON
& ZONDERVAN

Copyright © 2023 Peggy Wright.

All rights reserved. No part of this book may be used or reproduced by any means, graphic, electronic, or mechanical, including photocopying, recording, taping or by any information storage retrieval system without the written permission of the author except in the case of brief quotations embodied in critical articles and reviews.

This book is a work of non-fiction. Unless otherwise noted, the author and the publisher make no explicit guarantees as to the accuracy of the information contained in this book and in some cases, names of people and places have been altered to protect their privacy.

WestBow Press books may be ordered through booksellers or by contacting:

WestBow Press
A Division of Thomas Nelson & Zondervan
1663 Liberty Drive
Bloomington, IN 47403
www.westbowpress.com
844-714-3454

Because of the dynamic nature of the Internet, any web addresses or links contained in this book may have changed since publication and may no longer be valid. The views expressed in this work are solely those of the author and do not necessarily reflect the views of the publisher, and the publisher hereby disclaims any responsibility for them.

Any people depicted in stock imagery provided by Getty Images are models, and such images are being used for illustrative purposes only.
Certain stock imagery © Getty Images.

Scripture quotations marked (NIV) are taken from the Holy Bible, New International Version®, NIV®. Copyright © 1973, 1978, 1984, 2011 by Biblica, Inc.® Used by permission of Zondervan. All rights reserved worldwide. www.zondervan.com The "NIV" and "New International Version" are trademarks registered in the United States Patent and Trademark Office by Biblica, Inc.®

Scripture marked (NKJV) taken from the New King James Version®. Copyright © 1982 by Thomas Nelson. Used by permission. All rights reserved.

ISBN: 978-1-6642-9560-5 (sc)
ISBN: 978-1-6642-9561-2 (hc)
ISBN: 978-1-6642-9559-9 (e)

Library of Congress Control Number: 2023905098

Print information available on the last page.

WestBow Press rev. date: 07/06/2023

ACKNOWLEDGEMENTS

Thank you to my gracious husband, supportive family, and insightful friends that sustained and grew me through these healing years.

Thank you to my early readers who sharpened and refined my story with your input.

EARLY READER REVIEW

This book is such a beautiful story of a faith that perseveres. The author's writing is so beautiful, and the story so creatively told that it had me hanging on every word. Getting a detailed glimpse into the colourful inner world of the author was such a rare and wonderful experience, and I loved getting to explore her growth and healing along with her. This book will inspire you, bring up every emotion, and the story and characters are sure to linger in your thoughts.

—Alyssa Fleet

FOREWORD

This book has gone through several stages. I wrote the first draft in the third person as a novel, giving my story to a character called Grace. But I started to realize that I wanted to own and explore my story to gain self-understanding. So this is a true story, but I have intentionally focused on exploring the inner terrain of my processing. I have changed the names and context, and minimized the roles of others at times to protect their privacy. Where I have changed names, I have marked them with an asterisk* on first instance. I decided to take the character of my first boyfriend, Edward, and make it a conglomeration of experiences with different people, in order to protect their identities and help the story flow while making the points I was trying to explore about my responses. My writing efforts are not about exposing people in my life, but processing events that impacted my growth.

    I want to also give a trigger warning to those who are trying to work through their own painful parts in their stories. If this describes you, please feel free to skip over parts of the book that are not helpful. I hope to give words to those seeking to find language for their own experiences without burdening them with more emotional pain. Writing has been a celebration of life as well as therapy for me, but parts of it may not be helpful for where you are in your own healing process. Where I have recounted childhood sexual abuse, I have tried to be honest without minimizing it but chose to blur the experiences with poetry to spare my readers who may have suffered similar trauma. If you wish to skip over these sections, I intentionally used this font. Be compassionate with yourself while you read, and skip over details as much as you wish.

My healing journey has been one of moving from hiding, image management, shame, and secrecy to experiencing gracious, authentic connections with trusted family and friends. I believe that human stories matter. I love the exchange that happens when we hear one another's perspectives and experiences to gain empathy and understanding. This is not a road map, since there are many ways to heal that suit our individuality and circumstances. Trauma impacted how I processed my world, but grace has been a powerful force of healing. Offering my story is a redemptive step as I reclaim my voice to offer a glimpse of what God can do to create beauty from the ashes of our hard experiences. It would be an immense pleasure to me if God would use the winding, awkward path of my growth to ease the healing journeys of others.

PROLOGUE

I was twenty-two years old but felt as if I were ninety. Every day, I would get out of bed not knowing whether I could make it to my fourth-year university classes. Some days I would feel dizzy and achy by the time I finished showering, and my muscles felt like lead. On those days, I would be so weak that I would have to crawl on all fours back to my room to lie down again. I would get twelve to fourteen hours of restless sleep but still felt as though a truck had hit me. The body aches were like having the flu, and headaches became so common that I learned to tune out all but the worst pounding pain. I was really sick, and it wasn't getting better. Months stretched on without answers.

Some days I could accomplish simple goals like writing a paper, reading for classwork, and walking to school to attend classes. But even when I did make it to class, my notes could be crazy to read because my brain would fog over halfway through the lecture, and my hand would just slide down my page before I had to stop writing and put my head down. Great friends allowed me to borrow notes to catch things my mind missed.

I stopped playing guitar because my arm hurt when I strummed the strings. I stopped singing because my throat was often sore and I felt too weak to exert the effort. I stopped doing a lot of things!

But as my outward world shrunk, I was determined to grow my inner world, finish school, and choose life! Eventually I was given a diagnosis, but it offered no hope for recovery. According to everything I read, this fatigue and pain were my new normal. But I felt sure that God held good plans for my future. I wasn't ready to resign myself to a lifetime of lying on a couch. I trusted that there must be ways to help my body recover.

As I was praying one day, asking God to heal me, I got a picture in my mind of myself as a drooping flower bound tightly by weeds. A flash of understanding came with it. I felt as if God were saying, "Healing will be a slow process. As you trust me to lead you, I will show you part of the weed, loosen its hold, and remove its influence."

This image became the perfect symbol for my wellness journey. I was able to find healing steps and feel life and strength return. I've spent thirty years praying and following the nudges and illumination while making sense of what is healthy and determining where the weeds that were robbing me of life had crept in. This is the story of my roots, the places of entanglement, and the movement to spacious healing places of grace.

CHAPTER 1

ROOTS

I praise you because I am fearfully and wonderfully made;
your works are wonderful,
I know that full well.

—Psalm 139:14 NIV

I was a brown-eyed girl born in the summer of '69—July 4, to be exact. For a long time, I believed my parents when they told me that the fireworks in the States were launched to celebrate me. Growing up in the 1970s meant wearing wild geometric or flower prints, bright colours, and lime-green, orange, and brown plaid. I was often more comfortable in hand-me-down clothing from my brothers than the bright floral dresses passed on from female friends of the family. Maybe that is why the thought of dressing up still has me reaching for pants and a blazer rather than any kind of dress or skirt.

I started life as a free spirit. I liked my wavy brown hair long and untamed, resisting my mom's efforts to capture it into a ponytail or two. The elastics felt tight on my head. I preferred my hair loosely rippling down to the small of my back—even though it collected tangles that Mom would comb out at the end of the day.

I had a vivid imagination and an expansive inner world. I feasted on stories. My earliest memories of childhood are populated with heroes. I remember the rush home after school with my older brothers to see how Batman would find his way out of the mess that yesterday's show had left him in.

Paul and I would dream up our own Batman episodes at home on Stinson Street. Paul was my neighbour and first best friend. His mom often babysat us, and he was less fickle than the girls on my street. We found friendship natural and easy! We were Batman and Batgirl in our favourite playscape as we climbed over the side porch railings to hop on our bikes stowed below in the "Batcave." We would race around the block to defeat evil plots and keep the neighbourhood safe for all.

I mastered the skill of bike riding like most children do—by falling and getting up again. I had skinned knees for a month. But I also had a family who cheered me on. As I grew confident, I loved the thrill of speed with the wind in my hair as I flew effortlessly downhill. It is easy to feel powerful when you can fly! In my favourite dreams, flying was my superpower.

Visits to our grandparents would always include black-and-white episodes of Tarzan rallying the animals to defeat an evil plot or Zorro rushing to the aid of some oppressed victim. Heroes were celebrated with cuddles, comfort food, and cheers as evil plots were put down for another day.

My mom, Carolyn Hudson, grew up in a home where my grandma, Margaret Meyer, would take in children on short notice for foster care until the Children's Aid Society (CAS) found the right permanent place for them. They would move into high gear to prepare for, perhaps, a family of three children who would arrive in the next hour. Beds were made, clothing was found, and baths were drawn for the young ones, who would come needing refuge and comfort. Mom learned practical heroism from an early age!

Mom told me of one little girl who hadn't spoken a word since experiencing profound trauma. Children's Aid workers sent her to spend time in my grandmother's gentle presence in hopes that she could heal. Walking through my grandma's garden with the wonder of growing, living things opened a door to let light in. And it was in Grandma's kitchen, with her hands in cookie dough, that the girl broke her long silence and whispered words to explore her voice again. Miracles of hope and new life sprang from these labours of love. Grandma and my mom both naturally served others to enrich life and restore broken places.

My family fuelled my appreciation for the natural world. My grandma had a porch full of planters with colourful flowers spilling over the edges. Her garden in the backyard was always bursting with healthy-looking vegetables to feed her family and share with neighbours. As a carpenter, Wesley Meyer, my grandpa, knew the texture and grain of every type of tree. When we took family walks together under the forest's tall arches, he would caress a trunk and help me see the tree's majestic beauty. I could almost see how they would move and laugh if they were infused with personality. Grandpa Meyer expressed his appreciation for the woods around his home by turning dead wood into artistic creations. He demonstrated a partnership with creation as he supplied birdhouses and shallow bathing pools to create a haven for birds.

I best remember Grandpa as he worked in his backyard woodshop in Peterborough with the scent of sawdust lingering, or surrounded by blue sky and green grass while coaxing small chipmunks and squirrels to take a peanut from his hand. He always carried peanuts in his pocket so he could crouch low and offer one while making a clicking sound. I would hold a nut, squat down beside him and try to imitate the sound, but the chipmunks would just look at me from a distance and wait for Grandpa to crouch again. I often watched in amazement when a chipmunk grew bold enough to run up Grandpa's leg and peer out from his pocket with a peanut in each cheek. One even perched on his shoulder, nibbling a nut clutched tightly in its paws, watching without fear as Grandpa gently sanded the wood on a carpentry project.

Grandma fanned into flame my deep love for redemptive stories. She was always gifting me her favourite childhood classics: *Trumpet of the Swan*, *Stuart Little*, *Anne of Green Gables*, and *The Secret Garden*. I loved getting swept up in a story, though I often felt compelled to peek ahead to be sure of a happier outcome before I could leave a character and put down a book. I had to know whether Anne finally forgave Gilbert. Did the swan survive without a voice? One glance at a later part of the book would provide the reassurance I needed so that I could move from Book World back to this one.

Stories had to have happy endings to become my favourites! As a child, I could never have put this into words, but stories where wrongs were made right, where one character enriched another, or where brokenness was restored evoked tears of relief and joy. They would trickle down my cheeks, and I could go to bed content with the world. It was as if my soul needed fuel for my faith that 'all is well - and all will be well.'

When I was around four years old, my parents decided to open a room in our home to continue Grandma's tradition of providing foster care to a child who needed a kind place to grow up.

Simon* was eight years older than I. He was artistic and funny, and mostly kind. As I learned more of his story, surviving on the streets with a younger brother, I could not imagine such a dangerous beginning. It left my soul with a chill that the world could be so cruel.

It must have been an adjustment for Simon as he became part of daily family dinners and joined in watching our favourite TV shows. Every night, Steve and I would climb onto Simon's bed for a story and devotional from a book Mom would read to us. I loved the simple examples about how to live out the best version of ourselves with God's love to guide and empower us. Steve and I would talk with Mom about things like kindness, selflessness, love, forgiveness, and second chances—life things. Simon didn't say much. I, however, was always eager to answer the questions and ask some of my own as I leaned into my mom's softness. Mom was a gifted teacher and enjoyed sharing what she knew of God and how to make wise choices every day. I loved ending the day holding up our ideals and snuggling into the family closeness of it all. It fuelled my faith in the kind of world we could create if we learned how to love well.

We didn't have to be perfect, but my parents valued good intentions and efforts to make things right. We were taught important words, such as "I'm sorry," "thank you," and "I love you." My mom and dad modelled love for our neighbours and connected it with their knowledge of God's love for all of us. They affirmed that we were each seen and valued by the creator who formed us. It appealed to me to see the world as a place God watched over and tended like a garden, even as I trusted that my parents would do their best to watch over and lead us. They fuelled my faith in goodness.

My parents made it clear that our home and yard were always open to our friends. Mom loved children, and I think the kids on the block could all feel it. Our backyard became a gathering place for play. It was also the setting for neighbourhood carnivals. We kids would practise swinging from the top bar of our swing set, hanging by our knees, and letting our arms hang wildly. Then we would pull our bodies up to look over our stiff arms from the heights before somersaulting around the bar to land on our feet. Ta-da!

When our acts were ready, we would make tickets out of slips of paper. We would go around to the neighbours, inviting them to come to our yard at the appointed hour. My parents were supportive of us putting on our shows. Once, Mom helped us host a more organized version of a kids' carnival to raise funds for muscular dystrophy research. But our regular shows were much less elaborate. My parents would act as greeters. They bought us a small pop dispenser. We filled Dixie cups for a dime. One kind senior gentleman down the road never missed a performance. Lawn chairs formed a circle of visitors who would linger when the show was over to talk and laugh together. I was developing a sense of how a community could form over invitations, silly acts, and Dixie cups of sparkly bubbles.

Living in a world of imagination was so natural for me. Often Paul and I would climb the apple tree in the empty lot across from our houses and pretend to look down onto the grasslands of a far-off place. We were not sure yet where jungles could be found on the globe, but just the word "jungle" held an exotic thrill and intrigue that lifted us far beyond the ordinary days on Stinson Street.

One day I lost a front tooth when I swung down too quickly from my perch in the apple tree and my mouth hit a branch. But no matter the injury, I learned not to cry in front of the other kids. "Crybaby" was a scorn-filled label I heard from the boys at an early age. I was determined to earn the respect of our neighbourhood tribe. I internalized early the message that tears and emotions were best kept to myself.

Paul was a great companion. He never made fun of me; he was brave and kind. I enjoyed the presence of a steady, trustworthy friend at my side amidst a large playgroup. Larger groups meant navigating many opinions, many emotions, and many ideas. Paul was a comfortable friend who augmented play by adding to my ideas without overshadowing them. For some games, though, we included all the kids on our block. We would gather in my family's backyard or the grassy lot across the street. Our imaginative play turned the empty lot into many worlds.

It was normal in the '70s to spend a lot of each day outside when the weather was nice. We were told to come in when the streetlights turned on. I remember those days as adventurous and free. My personality seemed unrestrained, and my days held a general air of happiness. I was rooted in family, friendship, and a sense of the world as a place where heroes triumph and we all look out for each other.

CHAPTER 2

FAITH COMMUNITY

> All things bright and beautiful
> All creatures great and small
> All things wise and wonderful
> The Lord God made them all.
>
> —Mrs. Cecil Alexander

From my earliest memories, I saw nature's beauty as a reflection of God's artistry. Deeply breathing in the fresh air and fragrance of trees and wildflowers in wide, spacious places was a delight that fed my soul's lungs.

This love of natural beauty was fuelled by family camping trips, hikes, and visits to my grandparents. Nature became the vast cathedral for my faith roots. Time outside fuelled wonder to refresh my spirit and never failed to make me feel connected to my Maker.

Faith was as natural as breathing for me. I often memorized and recited my prayers as if they were a talisman against harm, but I found comfort in knowing there was one who could reach my mind and soothe my heart. I pictured God as the most perfect Hero filled with light and goodness. There was one who loved me and never grew tired or weary, watching over me even as I drifted off to sleep.

Behind the veil of Nature's beauty, I would sense the Creative Genius in the blended colours of a sunset or the detail displayed in a delicate flower swaying in a fragranced wind. The sky became a window into heaven's colourful glory, filling me with gratitude and a sense of "God-with-us."

At one summer visit with cousins, one of the older boys assembled the group of us in rows of chairs to play church. We started to sing a worship song together. Our voices blended beautifully. We are a family of singers. The day had been cloudy and grey, but suddenly I felt sunlight kissing my cheek. I looked up just as someone called out, "Look, God is listening!" The clouds above us had parted, and the sun shone on our faces as if God were smiling down on us. I was filled with a sense of wonder as the sun's rays accented the warm liquid peace that poured over me from head to toe. Moments like these became anchors for my young faith.

I loved my family's regular trips to Colborne Street United Church. My mom led the Christian education that shaped the activities of our weeks. My dad was an elder and regularly attended evening meetings. The church community formed the centrepiece of family life. The only drawback I remember is how hard it was to keep still in the pews during the long services. Mom had to frequently remind me with a gentle hand on my knee to stop swinging my legs, which couldn't yet reach the floor. I didn't mean to whack the pew in front of us on one of my arcs. My swings were just a little too enthusiastic sometimes as they moved to the constant music soundtrack in my head.

Being released to Sunday School was my favourite time. We started all together in the gym, singing simple melodic songs that expressed beautiful thoughts that appealed to my mind. A special version of "Happy Birthday to You" was sung each week for the children who were called to the front to have their day of birth recognized and celebrated: "May God's richest blessings descend upon you." I loved to picture blessings falling like drops of sunshine full of love and goodness on the birthday girl or boy.

Attendance was celebrated each week with a chart where we could add stars beside our names. I loved collecting my row of stars. Then we would split off into classes where the kind teachers prepared games, crafts, and, best of all, inviting stories.

The Jesus stories became my lens for picturing God's heart and care. The leper who was despised and ignored by others was touched and seen and healed by Jesus. The shepherd who searched for the lamb that wandered and got lost made me confident that God saw me and would never leave me alone and forgotten.

Jesus welcomed the little children and spent time with people that were often ignored or despised. Jesus defended the woman who was accused, her shame exposed, by reminding all who pointed a finger at her that they were also broken and guilty of wrongs. Jesus talked of God as the father who welcomed home the wayward son and ran to meet him when he returned.

By the age of five, I knew I wanted to have God living in me to guide and fill me with goodness and love like Jesus. I asked God to come into my heart. This invitation was the prayer that influenced the direction of my growth and becoming.

Stories of Jesus gave me pictures of how God cares for all people, animals, plants, and works of creation. Jesus's life of restoring and making things right gave me the clearest images to hold as I talked to God as Shepherd, Father, Healer, and Light. God held all things together and was bigger than my fears. God could be with me even when my parents were busy at work or with adult responsibilities. I had an ever-present friend who understood me even when I didn't know the right words to explain how I felt or what I was thinking. Talking to God became my safe place, my refuge throughout the years. I found that my talks with God became a way to gain perspective and insight. My early faith coloured all the ways in which I saw the world.

Just as nature and Jesus's stories gave visuals to my faith, church music supplied harmonic soul food. Melodies came so naturally to me. Lofty ideas expressed in hymns shaped my understanding of God's love and formed the soundtrack of my memory.

I joined the junior choir when I was old enough and loved learning the complicated melodies of the old hymns. As my ear grew to learn the harmonies, I delighted in singing the layers that moved from discordant to harmonic intervals. I developed a good ear for parts and often was asked to help anchor the alto section. It filled me with wonder to take part in a sound that was so much bigger than one voice as we listened and blended to make a resonant chorus.

Music's rhythmic percussion and layered tones always made me want to move to express the emotional soundscape I felt vibrate in the strings of my soul. I remember Simon smiling as I danced and sang the Sunday school songs with sincerity and enthusiasm. This may have been what encouraged me to branch out into full choreography.

One summer holiday with extended family when I was around five years old, I wanted to impress my older cousins with the dance moves I'd created to the song "(Shake, Shake, Shake) Shake Your Booty." I was a little puzzled by their laughter as I shook my foot with its imagined boot every time it came up in the song. It was several years before I realized the song was referring to another kind of booty.

The church continued to be a joyful space for me. It gathered people together for shared meals, carol singing, Christmas concerts, and plays. It felt like an extended family where everyone knew my name and smiled when they saw me.

As a sensitive child with a vivid inside world, I was generally more reserved and cautious in new situations. I liked to observe before trying something new because I liked to get things right the first time. But at church, I found a place of expression and freedom. My memories of church are precious to me because they were my first and lingering taste of a caring community made up of all ages and backgrounds. I "belonged" in a way that was helpful to me throughout the years as other things around me shifted.

CHAPTER 3

A WORLD OF FEELINGS

> When I think something nice is going to happen, I seem to fly right up on the wings of anticipation; and then the first thing I realize I drop down to earth with a thud ... the flying part is glorious as long as it lasts ... it's like soaring through a sunset. I think it almost pays for the thud.
> —L. M. Montgomery

Having a vivid imagination and a sensitive soul helped me to connect to God and friends, but these qualities could also fuel fear.

I remember a gathering of my dad's family where a ghost story was being told upstairs by my aunt Phyllis, who was an amazing storyteller. She used her guitar and voice to enhance her story with sound effects. I was sitting on the bed with a group of cousins listening to the story, and it started to get too creepy for me. Finally, I couldn't stay any longer. I could feel fear coursing through my veins and crawling like a spider down my back. All my hair felt as if it were standing on end.

I slipped out of the room and headed downstairs to where all the adults were gathered and having a loud conversation. The door at the bottom of the stairway was closed so that another chair could be placed in front of it for seating. My dad had six brothers and six sisters, so when the family gathered, we made quite a crowd.

I quietly knocked on the door to be allowed to join my parents. But a roar of laughter drowned out the sound of my soft knock. I decided that I couldn't go back up to join my cousins and the scary story, but I couldn't open the door to join the adults. So I plunked myself on the stairway to wait for something to change.

I had been there for only about two minutes when my older cousin, Paul, came down to check on me. When he got close, he whispered urgently, "Peggy, don't sit there!"

"Why?"

"See that hole in the step beside you?" Dramatic pause. "That's where the bogeyman lives!"

I jumped up, screamed, and started pounding on the door. The adults heard me this time!

The door flew open, and I was quickly enfolded in my mother's hug and the concern and safety of the adult clan. Paul knew enough not to wait for judgement from the adults and scooted back upstairs.

I'm sure it took a long time to calm me down, even after my dad explained to me that the hole in the step was left over from a furnace pipe that used to pass through there. It wasn't that I didn't believe his factual logic; I just had a tough time shaking the pictures created by my imagination of a wispy wraith that reached up to take hold of unsuspecting little girls. How could cold facts dispel the fearful images that seemed much more real to me? The solid presence of so many caring adults finally restored my sense of security, and peace returned. I found refuge on my mom's knee and snuggled in.

Another time, Simon fuelled my fear with his love for the sensational and spooky. He was good at building just the right amount of mystery and suspense. I think I was around five or six years old when Simon told me that there was an old lady who ate children who lived in the big, dark house by the park. I couldn't sleep that night as a leering face haunted the edges of my dreams. When I tried to cry out, my voice was gone. Nothing would come out of my mouth. I was on my own against a suffocating fear that loomed and lived inside my head where no one could reach me.

Night after night, I relived the dream of biking down a dark street and wiping out right in front of a home with two windows. In one dimly lit picture window was the child-eating witch, moving swiftly to the door to get to me. My scraped knees trembled weakly making it impossible to hop onto my bike or run away. In the other window was a kind-faced grandmother who was moving too slowly to save me. I always woke up with my heart racing and a prayer on my lips before either woman reached my side. Faith and fear were equally strong in me.

I had to be careful what I watched. Scary characters like the Wicked Witch of the West from the film *The Wizard of Oz* gave shape to my fears and made me afraid to close my eyes each night. The images were stamped on the screen of my mind. I would jump into bed from several feet away so that anything lurking in the darkness under my bed couldn't grab at my feet.

My mother's comforting presence, loving songs, and prayers were the tools I learned to use to fight fear. The soft glow of a nightlight and holding tightly to my favourite stuffed animals helped too. Many nights, my mother would sit on the floor by my bed and hum Brahms's "Lullaby" to quiet my mind and heart after bedtime prayers. It was this melody that I often rode to the Land of Slumber.

Sometimes at night when I would wake with fear, I would creep to the open door of my parents' bedroom for comfort. Usually before I even called my mother's name, Mom would sense my presence and ask what was wrong. I was sometimes allowed to crawl into bed between my parents' warm, solid presences to fall back to sleep. In these rare moments, Dad's snores and Mom's deep breathing created a soundscape of security. Most of the time, my mom would walk with me to my room, praying the fear away as she rubbed my back to help me settle in my own cosy bed.

There wasn't a clear roadmap for how to navigate big feelings. Fear was an inconvenient impulse that often felt beyond my control. And generally, life rewarded me when I would manage or downplay emotions. Reason and logic were prized over any emotional responses.

It must have been my fourth birthday party when I was confused by feelings of disappointment in the middle of a joyful day.

It began with big plans. I was a natural programmer like my mom. I would spend weeks living in the future, envisioning and preparing for life's big moments. Anticipation held half the pleasure as I played out all the details in my mind.

On this occasion, I had decided who would most fit with which animal party hat that we'd purchased, and I carefully arranged them around the table in the order in which I wanted everyone to be seated. I planned who would sit beside me, which princess hat I would wear as the birthday girl, and which less-favoured neighbourhood boy would wear the monkey hat. Since I couldn't write well enough to make place cards, the hats played that role.

The problem was that I didn't communicate my plans and preparations to my mom. She was very busy with tasks of her own. She bought special patterned paper plates, balloons, streamers, and gift bags with treats and toys for each guest, and prepared my favourite meal with a homemade cake, in the shape I chose, for dessert. She filled the day with special attention to celebrate me.

On this party day, the house was clean, the table was set with the hats as placeholders, and Mom invited all the children to come in and be seated around the table. The rush of guests moving to the table happened before I could say a word. I couldn't explain my teary eyes when the princess hat—my princess hat—was claimed by another girl and everyone sat in the wrong place. When the only hat available for me to wear was the monkey hat, my least favourite, I was close to tears. I made myself swallow down my disappointment and tried to enjoy the party. I felt keenly the sting of having my plans dashed—especially on my birthday. I knew enough not to bring unpleasantness to the moment. It would be babyish and insensitive to my guests, but I couldn't turn off my disappointment or explain it. So I swallowed my negative reactions and felt a little flat as I played the role of the birthday girl. But when we got up from the table, I saw that the princess hat had been left behind. I claimed it as my own and threw the monkey hat in the garbage before I went to the living room to open gifts. This small corrective action did a lot to shift my mood.

As an introvert, my feelings were not often evident to others, but they beat strongly inside me. It was only when I wrote about this incident that my mom had any idea that it happened. It's strange how the things that leave imprints on us are often not of our choosing. But it's clear that learning to exert my reason over my emotions became a well-established pattern. It was many years before I learned to value deeply the wisdom that emotions can hold.

CHAPTER 4

ALLIES

A sorrow shared is but half the trouble.
And a joy that's shared is a joy made double.

—adapted from a Swedish Proverb

I was six when my mom was expecting a new baby. Though I preferred playing with the boys on the street and was used to being with my older brothers, I was secretly hoping this baby was a sister. I think the boys were voting against me, but I was praying hard for a girl. Without the benefits of ultrasound, nine months felt like a long time to wait to find out!

When the new baby was about to make an entrance into the world, Dad took Mom to the hospital while we waited with a neighbour. The baby was six weeks early! Fortunately, the boys had already moved into one room in preparation for the new little one. I remember that day being surrounded by an air of anticipation and excitement.

The phone rang, and the babysitter shared the news that our baby had been born.

It was a girl!

I felt a glow of satisfaction and anticipation.

Being a future thinker, I could already picture reading my favourite books to my sister, puddle jumping on rainy days, exploring the world together, and passing on life lessons I'd been storing up diligently in my memory.

Katherine Leslie was not able to come home from the hospital for several weeks because she had lost some weight and had elevated bilirubin levels, which made her look a bit yellow. My mom always said that Kathy was the best Christmas present ever, since we were all finally able to celebrate her when she was released to come home on the day before Christmas.

Kathy was so tiny and fragile, yet absolutely perfect. I couldn't believe how tiny and exquisite her hands and feet were. As a six-year-old, I already felt so grown up, and I was eager to help. I will never forget the first time Mom let me sit with Kathy alone in my lap while she went to heat a bottle. A protective impulse towards my little sister rose in me. I had never known what it was like to be the big kid. My brothers were always the older, bigger guys who led the fun or talked me into their crazy experiments.

But I was no longer the youngest. I loved the peacefulness of cuddling my tiny baby sister. I could be a heroic shield for her! I was wiser to the boys' sometimes reckless planning. I'd warn my little sister of the time the boys slapped together boards on wheels for a go-cart and talked me into testing it out down a big hill with a helmet on. The helmet didn't protect me from skinned knees and a huge welt when the go-cart rolled the wrong way and tipped over at high speed. There was no way Kathy would be a crash test dummy with me there to watch out for her! I loved the idea of growing up with my little sister.

Our family expanded with my baby sister, and then we also got a dog. Buffy looked like a small collie with pointed ears and a soft brown-and-white coat. She had this tidy eating trick where she would pile the little pieces of food that she didn't like next to her dish. She was a faithful companion and loved to play in the yard with the kids on the block. Buffy was everyone's favourite. But the gate had to be kept tightly fastened because Buffy was a runner.

My first big sorrow came when she got loose one day while we were at school. My dad told us that Buffy had been hit by a car. The driver didn't stick around to see whether she could be saved or fill in the details. All we knew was that Buffy was gone.

I felt a hollow sense of grief. It was a dark cloud that shadowed my days for a while. No little dog to cuddle beside us on the sofa. No eager greeting at the door. It was my first experience of loss. Shortly after the accident, I had a sleepover with a few neighbourhood friends in a tent trailer parked in our driveway. As darkness fell, we took turns talking about the things that made us sad or mad or scared. We were exploring the language of the heart. I shared my sadness with these few, who knew and loved Buffy as I did. We all cried together and somehow felt better. Our shared sorrow connected us in a way that all our days of play and laughter never had before. This first taste of sorrow taught me that burdens could be lightened by sharing them with friends.

CHAPTER 5

WEARING STRENGTH ON THE OUTSIDE

> Fitting in is about assessing a situation and becoming who you need to be accepted. Belonging, on the other hand, doesn't require us to change who we are; it requires us to be who we are.
>
> —Brené Brown

I've always worked hard to avoid embarrassing behaviour. The boy in preschool constantly crying with a runny nose was not attractive to me. I placed a high value on self-control!

Though I could be vulnerable with close friends, I was wary and careful on the school playground, where name-calling and judging were everyday norms.

Generally, if I had an embarrassing moment, I would quickly pretend it didn't happen and look as normal as possible. It never occurred to me to simply laugh at myself. I determined it was better to just erase the mistake and hope nobody noticed.

I remember a time when Paul and another guy friend were

taking turns doing straddle vaults over the fire hydrants on our street. I wanted to prove myself a brave equal to the boys. I followed their lead and successfully cleared the first two hydrants. I was gaining confidence. I didn't notice that the next jump had to be higher to accommodate an extra nut on the top of the pipe. My pelvic bone slammed into the top of the hydrant, and I kind of crumpled the rest of the way over. I wanted to fall to the ground doubled over in pain, but with the boys watching I made myself walk as normally as possible while shrugging away any attention as they asked whether I was all right. I would not expose weakness to the boys. I managed a laugh outwardly so no one would notice how much I had hurt myself. I developed a pattern of trying to cover my hurt with a shield of dismissal.

By the time I reached grade one, my foster brother was in high school. He was becoming increasingly troubled and unpredictable. One day after school, he was gone. It was strange how this boy who had shared our home for several years suddenly disappeared from my life. He got in trouble with the law and was sent to a juvenile home. I remember feeling sad that he had made choices that took him away from us. I saw him only once after that, as our parents kept in touch with Simon's caseworker, but he was no longer in our care.

The summer before I entered grade three, Mom, Dad, Stephen, Kathy, and I moved to a white brick house on three-quarters of an acre just beyond the city limits. The backyard was filled with unkempt weeds that rose above my head, but Dad assured us that once it was mowed it would be an awesome space to play. We settled into our new rooms and ran all over the house, exclaiming over the lever faucets and large stone fireplace. It was all so wonderful and new, with lots of space for all of us!

The best thing about our new house was the forest on one side. I loved strolling as a family through the woods in the spring, looking for trilliums as Mom pointed out trees and flowers that we had learned to love. On the edge of our country property, wild sweet peas grew in every colourful shade from white to brilliant pinks and purples. Seeing them among the lupines on the hill made me happy. It was fuelling to be surrounded by such spacious loveliness.

When fall came, we had to go to a new school. Being the new kid was an anxious reality for me. I had felt so at home on Stinson Street among all my friends. I was a leader there. Now the hard work of fitting in had to begin on a new playground where I knew no one. My brother treated the changes so much more casually. He was usually quick to find a group of guys to laugh with. It took longer for me since I was looking for kindred spirits.

On the first day, I wondered whether I would find a friend. I wondered whether I would like my teacher. And, most importantly, I hoped I would be liked. As an eight-year-old, I was embarrassed when my brown eyes filled with tears and my heart raced. But there were so many unknowns I couldn't prepare for. There was no avoiding the first day at a new school.

My mom walked with me from the car over to the lines of children waiting to go into class for the day. I was told which line to stand in, but I didn't seem able to pull my hand from the secure warmth of my mother's connection. I couldn't just hang there driftless. I needed a new connection to allow myself to let go of security.

"Crybaby!" a boy from my line said just loudly enough for the kids around us to hear. Some boys chuckled and girls whispered as attention shifted in my direction.

I swiped at the tears that were trying to squeeze past my self-control. Just then, a grade-four student stepped out of the line to put her arm around me and introduce herself. The girl shot a look of contempt at the boy and then turned to say, "Don't listen to him. I'm Tammy, and we'll be in the same class. It's a grade three-four split. Why don't you stand in line with me?"

That lifeline was all I needed to give Mom a reassuring smile and let her go off to work.

Tammy never moved from my side until we both found seats in class. I was so relieved to have someone kind to stand with and show me where to go. It made me feel more positive to meet compassion in this new place.

The familiar classwork was perfect to settle the butterflies in my stomach. School was well suited to my abilities. The routines were comfortable, the work simple, and the teacher friendly. Math questions added and subtracted, as they always did. Printing, reading, and creative writing were a happy world in which I could immerse myself. But even if I thought I knew the answer to a question in class, I would offer it only if my teacher called on me. I didn't want to draw any attention to myself. I was all for minimizing social and academic risks.

Art lessons felt risky to me; it was hard to know how to succeed, because the rules were less clear. Success and "pleasing" were important to me. I often chose things I knew I could succeed at and avoided anything that could lead to failure or embarrassment. That summer I had been practising and learned to make copies of Snoopy from Charles Schultz's cartoon *Peanuts*.

So, in every art class, through various media, I would make Snoopy. I was all about playing it safe and making something recognizable and popular: a Snoopy drawing, a Snoopy painting, a Snoopy mosaic with tissue paper. Finally my teacher asked me to find a new subject for my artwork. She was kind about it, but I still felt the sting of correction from my beloved teacher. It was hard to win the game of pleasing and perfectionism.

One day, my teacher asked me whether I would lend my pencil crayons to a classmate in grade four who had forgotten his. Did the teacher realize what a bully this boy was? How he terrorized us girls? But I knew I had to do the right thing and give when asked. So my perfectly sharpened pencil crayons were passed in the like-new box to a boy I feared.

The class went on, with our two grades working on different

subjects. When recess came, I had to go to the boy to ask for my pencil crayons back. Without a word of thanks, he gave me an annoyed glare as he handed me the box. I had to quickly turn away because I felt tears rising behind my eyes. The box had been squashed, the pencil crayon tips were worn down or broken, and, horror of horrors, they were all out of order. When I reached my desk, before going out to recess, there was something that needed to be done first. I had to do what I could to restore order to my small universe. I put every pencil crayon back where it belonged and tried to fix the shape of the box. Only then could I face the playground social scene.

It didn't take long to find a girl group to hang out with. Tammy, being a grade older, gradually drifted away from me to her peers in the class. But she had played an important role in helping me transition to this newness, and I always thought fondly of her.

With a new group of girls to adapt to, I watched and learned. I often rehearsed how to avoid repeating missteps. A mannerism or phrase was quick work to alter. I studied people's reactions and prepared so that I would avoid negative remarks, a roll of the eyes, or the shared significant eyebrow raise that would exclude me.

A snide comment about a piece of clothing was easy to manage. I would bury the offending piece in the bottom of my dresser drawer. It could become painting clothes!

I was teaching myself to blend in and earn a place in the tribes of public school without compromising the inner ideals that functioned as my guide. I learned to avoid attention and purposely dressed and spoke in ways that allowed for general acceptance. I was determined not to be a target. Gradually I felt accepted in this new tribe and contributed to our imagination games fuelled by the dragon shape of one of the playground structures at recess.

Living to avoid conflict and please people got more difficult as we all got older in junior school. The schoolyard could be a cruel place. Even as a child, I was wired to feel deeply and pick up the fears, hurts, and longings of those around me. So the social scene of school was a trial for my developing sense of fairness and kindness. When a little girl in my circle of friends was excluded from a game, I had to decide whether I could manage the disapproval of my classmates to extend the sympathy I felt.

Often, I would go home and cry with my mom over the impossible demands of competing friendships. One girl would play with me only if I wasn't friends with another girl. I was asked to choose between two girls I liked, because they didn't want to be around each other. Mom was a patient listener and advised me to pray for my friends and look for ways to care for both girls, even if I had to be with them separately.

Power plays, manipulation, and coercion were abhorrent to my young soul, though I wouldn't have known what words to use to explain what I saw and felt so keenly. I wanted there to be a place for everyone to be valued and to belong. I wasn't immune from feeling a distaste for certain people's actions, but I didn't ever feel the need to be cruel to them.

My zest for superhero dramas fuelled my dislike for any kind of meanness. The injustice of labels and dirty names tossed like grenades out of earshot of the adult lunch supervisor really bothered me. I would feel a fury rise in me when a group of boys would steal a hat from a weaker child for a game of keep away while ignoring his protests—or, worse, being fuelled by them. Moments like these made the world feel like a hostile place. And when mean words and actions were aimed my way, I felt helpless. I could never think of a good response in the moment. On the nights following such incidents, I would lie in bed trying to think of what I could have said or done to turn the tide of events.

This debriefing and editing process became a nightly habit. After the day's activity stopped, my mind was free to roam, and I would replay the discordant notes of my days and rewrite them. I would imagine a way of deflecting so that I could avoid being labelled or embarrassed. I was rehearsing for the next time it happened, but it didn't really help. In the heat of the moment, I would always freeze and see only a blank screen in my mind. All my well-rehearsed thoughts escaped me.

Unfortunately, negative remarks shaped my self-perception. Two boys were laughing at me and said my long nose and pointed chin made me look like a witch or a grandmother! I internalized that I wasn't one of the "attractive" or "pretty" girls. I felt some satisfaction that one of the confident girls put the boys in their place with her disgusted retort: "Don't be so mean!" The tribes of girls had divisions, but against the boys, we stuck together.

In grade school, I began to practise how to look and act to appear strong and invulnerable. I even coached myself to look confident in places where my skills were low, such as in gym class and during recess sports. I imitated the look of an athlete. I would crouch attentively in the net or take a casual stance with a soccer ball tucked under my arm. I could look the part, even if it was just a smokescreen to hide how uncoordinated I really was with a ball or stick.

I discovered a way to influence the social dynamics at recess. Owning a soccer ball gave me bargaining power. Because it was my ball that was used for our games, I was able to decide that anyone who wanted to could play! I liked being an includer.

Summers were a break from the hypervigilance of the social scene.

The Sunday school picnic would mark the beginning of spacious summer days! It was my habit to lie awake the night before the picnic, picturing all the details of what I would wear and how the day would unfold, and making sure I had thought through everything I needed to pack to enjoy this special event in our church life.

Family camping adventures, visits to a friend's pool, and day trips to places like the African Lion Safari and Storybook Gardens punctuated the long, lazy warmth of summer. At home, I would soak in the unhurried quiet with time to read, unwind, and enjoy my family. Summers were a wonderful break from the social scene, where I worked hard to fit in.

CHAPTER 6

LIFE CAN HURT

In the same way, the Spirit helps us in our weakness. We do not know what we ought to pray for, but the Spirit himself intercedes for us through wordless groans. And he who searches our hearts knows the mind of the Spirit, because the Spirit intercedes for God's people in accordance with the will of God.

—Romans 8:26–27, NIV

Grade five began with school days that played out one after another like beads on a string. Then, just before Christmas, I had an accident sliding on the icy playground at school. When I fell back, I felt a serious jolt of pain as I tried to catch myself with my arm. The sharp waves rolling through my shoulder told me that this was serious. But for some reason, my response was to laugh—a high-pitched, nervous-sounding release. My friends laughed with me until they noticed that my laughter had turned to tears. I heard their voices as if they were far away.

"I think she's hurt."

"Should we get the lunch mom?"

"Peggy, are you okay?"

The lunch mom came. I was in a haze of pain as I was tenderly helped to my feet and taken to the office where adults made a sling out of my scarf. The secretary was kind and sympathetic as she guided me to a bench in the hall and called my mom.

When Mom arrived, she drove straight to the hospital's emergency room. As we walked from the car up the long hill to the door, I was stepping gingerly, trying not to jostle my arm. Any motion sent stabbing pains through my shoulder.

When the doctor looked at the X-ray, he didn't see the hairline fracture. He surprised me by grabbing my arm and pulling it up over my head to show me the physiotherapy movements he wanted me to do to strengthen my shoulder and keep it from stiffening.

I was seeing black spots, but I never screamed. My pale face and quick inhalation alerted my mom that the pain was higher than I could express verbally. As an introvert, whenever I was most in pain, I went inside myself to cope. I was not demonstrative. The doctor continued his torturous movements for a minute, but I just blocked him out. I was inside, trying to cope with the stabbing jolts that made me feel sick to my stomach. I felt helpless and small as the doctor made me feel as though I were being dramatic and overreacting. How could I let him know I wasn't faking the pain?

Finally the doctor released me. Only when we got outside and I finally felt safe again did the tears quietly course down my cheeks. In the car, every bump caused a fresh flow of silent tears. In the driveway at home, I couldn't rise without help from the car's front seat. I whimpered with each step up to the front door. I made it to the chair at the kitchen table, throbbing and sobbing.

Mom quickly called our family doctor. His words to her were "Carolyn, if it hurts that much, it must be broken. Just put her to bed and alternate ice and a heating pad as needed for the swelling. Pain medications should help her as she tries to find a position she can maintain. Tell her to be still and rest." There wasn't a cast or brace for collarbone fractures in 1979.

I was so relieved to be believed. I knew the pain of a broken collarbone from an earlier experience—and this was it. I rested and mended for the last few days of classes before Christmas break.

I spent the week before Christmas mostly in bed. In the first few days of mending, I had to have Mom or Dad sit me up in bed. Mom was the one we naturally looked to when we were sick or in pain. Some days I felt well enough to have Mom help me change clothes to move to the living room to watch Rudolph, Frosty, and the Grinch while enjoying some buttercream mints, shortbread cookies, and peanut brittle. These were our family's favourite festive homemade treats. Christmas morning was the first day I was able to sit up on my own. Getting dressed was tricky. Fastening buttons was the hardest. I kept my arm in a sling under my shirt. My left sleeve hung limp at my side.

Each year in late November, our childhood tradition was to form wish lists by studying the Sears catalogue. My biggest wish for Christmas that year was the gift of a Barbie motorhome. My siblings and I could create adventures for hours with Barbie and Ken: concerts on a stage with a curtain, drive-in movie dates in the Barbie car facing the TV, Olympic stadium gymnastics, Batman in his Batmobile saving Barbie's little sister—anything could happen! The motorhome would widen the possibilities to play in the great outdoors. We already had a zipline for GI Joe and a Barbie-sized inflatable pool!

On Christmas morning, as I lifted off the wrapping, there it was: a Barbie motorhome! I was full of excitement about this addition to our Barbie world. What I didn't count on was the assembly required!

This was where Dad's heroism shone! He sat with me patiently for three hours, taking tiny plastic pieces from the packaging frames and putting them where they belonged in the camper to create a kitchen, shower, bunk beds, and steering wheel console. Dad did not stop working on the project until the last decal was fixed in place. I could do so little of the actual work with my arm in a sling. My dad became my hands as he listened carefully to each step that I read out to him from the instructions. He let me direct him so I could be active in owning the gift. My parents always made Christmas special. Singing along to records of Christmas music added to the feeling of festivity. Even though my shoulder hadn't yet mended, my love tank was full.

I healed up quickly just in time to return to classes after Christmas break.

I loved my grade-five teacher, Miss Craig. She led the school choir, where we were learning a magical-sounding song: "Pussy willows, cattails, soft winds, and roses, / Rain pools in the woodland, water to my knees. / Shivering, quivering - the warm breath of spring."[1]

That spring, however, brought with it a deep sorrow.

My siblings and I were called over the PA system to come to the office shortly before lunch one day. I knew something was wrong. My mother's eyes held a sadness as she met us. When we reached the car, Mom explained that Grandpa's fight with cancer was over.

We knew for a while that Grandpa's lungs were not working well. His years of smoking caught up with him, I guess. He had been diagnosed with cancer many months before his death. But just a week prior, he was declining in the hospital, and Grandma told Mom that we should come. We drove to Peterborough, and our visit with him was full of laughter and connection. He was clear-minded and present in a way that he hadn't been for a while. I had sat on his hospital bed beside him while he pulled me close to his side and called me "Punkin." And I said what I always did: "I'm not a pumpkin; I'm a girl!" And we smiled as I leaned in. We didn't know that would be our last visit.

It was hard to fathom that he was gone. A blankness opened where Grandpa had always been.

A solemn silence filled the car as we were each lost in our thoughts. I didn't feel like talking. My mind was trying to picture Grandpa's spirit in heaven and what it might be like to be so close to God. My memory replayed moments when I knew Grandpa's sacrificial love personally.

My ninth birthday flashed on the screen of my memory:

As we arrived at their house, Grandpa called out to me with his special greeting: "Hi, Punkin!"

I responded with my usual: "I'm not a Pumpkin; I'm a girl."

"Well, what does my birthday *girl* want for a gift this year?"

"Well ... I have a lot of books that I love, but I have no shelf to put them on. I really could use a bookcase of my own someday."

The next morning at breakfast, Grandpa set up his surprise in the kitchen. It was a perfectly sized bookcase for my room. He had risen before the sun to craft it for me in his woodshop!

I was stunned and moved by such a personal gift! I felt so understood and loved by his sacrifice of sleep and his hand-crafted labour of love.

My mind shifted back to the present.

The funeral would be in Peterborough, three hours away. Dad was coming home early to meet us. We would drive up together to be with Grandma.

That funeral was my first.

During the service, tears kept rolling down my cheeks as my mind replayed memories and images of our times together: seeing the Royal Botanical Gardens with Grandpa pointing out his favourite flowers; walking the park path by the fenced-in animal areas and hearing Grandpa's laughter when Dad got spit on by a llama; seeing the chipmunk perched on Grandpa's shoulder in his woodshop.

While the minister was talking, my mind went back in time to when I could still feel his arm around me as we watched Tarzan on TV at Thanksgiving before his sickness got so bad. As I stood missing him, I was aware that so many moments of my childhood held the grand presence of this gentle man. It was impossible to imagine life without him. I drank in the beautiful reflections, tributes, songs, and prayers from the service, thirsting for peace. I remember his Bible, all marked up with underlining and notes. I coached myself to remember that Grandpa wasn't in pain any more—that his spirit was free.

My Peterborough cousins wrapped me in big hugs afterward while I let myself cry. The large box holding Grandpa's body felt as if it held only the shell of the man I knew. His body lacked the animation of his lively spirit.

I wasn't sure what to do with the sadness sitting inside. I was trying to let it leak out of my eyes so that it wouldn't stay in and hurt. I knew we all felt the weight of loss. There was no script to know how to manage it. My instincts were to try to be helpful or stay out of the way and not add to the burden Mom and Grandma must have felt. The impulse to make my needs small and to turn down my sensitive heart became a pattern that grew to shape me. Helpful activity seemed to be the natural path forward to swallow up the pain.

CHAPTER 7

LOOKING FOR CONNECTION

Looking for significance and worth from people put me in a posture of pleasing, where I was afraid to make a wrong move and be rejected. I needed to internalize God's unconditional love and let that fuel my love for others.

After Grandpa's death, someone bought Grandma a toy poodle to keep her company. Though Grandma enjoyed his companionship, she found the level of care he required too demanding. So my family inherited a new dog. Buttons was a great cuddler and loved to be at the centre of things. He followed me around whenever I was home to wait for the moment I would settle. He always sat with me: on my bed amidst my books and papers, on the couch watching TV, and he even wiggled his way onto my lap under the desk while I sat to do homework. We all loved Buttons! He gave the best enthusiastic greetings! He made us all feel like celebrities when we walked in the door.

Celebrating people was a rare experience at school. I did enjoy my peers, and socializing at school could be fun, but the atmosphere felt more competitive. Thinking ahead and dreaming of outcomes, both positive and negative, was a natural defensive move for me.

In grade six, tight jeans were in. I convinced my mom to buy a fashionable pair for me rather than wear the hand-me-down boy jeans from my brother. I was ready to own my style.

I lay in bed that night dreaming about my reception the next morning when I arrived at school with the fashionable new jeans. The girls would all compliment me and usher me into their midst now that I had joined the popular trend.

In reality, my new jeans didn't make a blip on the day's news meter. Nobody commented or seemed to notice. But I felt the power of conformity without anything being said. The girls had simple ways to show acceptance and admiration. And I was so tuned into it.

Later that week, when I was running back from the fields at the end of lunch, one of the boys bumped into me on the pavement. I fell and scuffed the knee of my new jeans. Sadly, they were no longer unspoiled and new. There was a whitened spot and the glimmer of a hole just below the left knee! I'm confident the girls around me helped me to display proper disgust at the boy's roughness. Girlfriends are great for expressing sympathy!

Just as I hid the ache of my scraped knee and rumpled emotions, I learned to downplay accomplishments. I worked hard to avoid labels like "stuck up" and "know-it-all." When my paper had an A+ at the top, I was quietly thrilled. I learned it was best to focus on encouraging and consoling the students around me, and I shared my mark only if someone asked. Even then, I learned to couch the information with some sort of dismissive comment that put the asker at ease. It was important to me that people felt good around me. I didn't mind making myself small to help others feel better.

I also learned that if I said something about my mistakes or criticized myself first, I was met with reassurance or understanding.

It was easier to critique myself than to endure negative comments from others! My natural inner critic was affirmed, and I mistook it for humility.

The social world took a lot more study than the schoolwork I was assigned. The enrichment classes I attended offered some fresh stimulation, but my teachers often wanted to fuel the interests of their students, and I had become conditioned to deliver what the teacher wanted. Leaving projects and topics up to me was just a vast guess at pleasing them. I had become disconnected from my curiosity, interests, and preferences. Fitting in and pleasing my teacher to earn top grades consumed my academic energy. Even in my daily school journal, I wrote what I knew would get a chuckle from my friends instead of offering true impressions. I laugh now when I read what is written there. It was so obvious that I wrote knowing that my friends would read it. It doesn't resonate or sound like me at all. I was aware of the need to act, please, and achieve in my school days.

Performing and pleasing others caused me to unwittingly shut away many unique passions that could have fuelled my creativity and study. My inner world was big and complex but was tucked deeply away—not easily accessed or shared. Honest reflections and feelings often surfaced at night when the external world got quiet.

By nature, I wasn't a quick decision-maker. There wasn't enough time to explore my thoughts and interests before we had to decide on a topic or a focus for speeches and projects. I learned to borrow ideas from others' passions for my school presentations and papers. This worked well because it wasn't hard to capture my interest once I started to explore any topic. With every bit of knowledge unearthed, a door opened to new possibilities and wonderings. I liked to spend hours drawing and colouring a title page or taking time to use a thesaurus to find the exact word to express a thought. I didn't mind spending extra time to please my inner sense of rightness and to get a good mark or a positive comment.

My class peer group was full of bright, motivated girls who generally scored top marks in various subjects. I found it stimulating to talk to them and learn from them. I borrowed and mimicked their handwriting techniques, learned from them about wider news events, and caught on to qualities I admired. Some of them were so brave at standing up for things and people. I consistently stayed near the top of my classes, even though my marks sometimes depended on having a good memory rather than deeply understanding a subject. We studied topics like Ancient Egypt alongside pioneers. It was only much later in life that I gained a sense of history's flow and realized that these subjects were separated by a few thousand years.

I was not keen on class participation marks. I liked to listen and observe before forming my own thoughts. Generally, I liked the pace of life to be slower. I liked to have time to think and prepare before giving a response. Under pressure, I would just defer to others or stay silent. This could be why I felt uncomfortable speaking up in large groups and in public.

My mom tried to help me overcome my shyness by motivating me to talk to salespeople when we went shopping. Sometimes Mom would offer to stop for doughnuts for supper if I would go in and order them. At this suggestion, my heart would start racing and I would feel my chest tighten. To place an order for a dozen doughnuts meant that I would have to remember and communicate every family member's doughnut preference. Twelve different times, I would have to verbalize a choice to fill the box. I knew I'd get tongue-tied and nervous. My voice was soft, and I was often asked to repeat myself. I usually chose to shed a few disappointed tears in the back seat of the car rather than face the doughnut lady. My family would just have to live without a dessert that night. My natural reserve was not easy to overcome.

My "safe place" was in the world of print. I read everything in sight—even the cereal box at the breakfast table. But I was drawn to beautiful thoughts that lifted my imagination to new heights.

My inner world was bigger than my outward expression hinted at. I've always wondered deeply and widely about subjects like good and evil, the nature of God, and what motivates and shapes people. "Book World" was my escape and instructive refuge.

I admired protagonists in novels who worked for good in their home lives, school, and the world. Heroes can have supernatural abilities or just live with intentional bravery and kindness that mark their path with restoring care. These became my ideals—the ones I wanted to be like. Goodness drew me like a bright light!

Evil seemed so easy to recognize and avoid in books. I would always tell the protagonist what the right choices would be. But by adolescence, I was learning that we all have a mixture of good and bad in us, and that can make life complicated.

CHAPTER 8

DISSOCIATION

Dissociation is a coping mechanism allowing a person to function in daily life by continuing to avoid being overwhelmed by extremely stressful experiences, both in the past and present.

—Robyn Brickel

Mom was one of my heroes! She earned it with her boundless energy for pioneering new ways to meet the needs around her. Ever since Mom's parental leave with Kathy was over, she had gone back to the classroom to teach. She was great at her work; she discovered new ways of reaching children with special learning needs. I loved hearing Mom's stories of a child saying a word for the first time after working long and hard in speech therapy. Mom celebrated every student's success by inviting each one to share a hard-won victory with the others. These students knew how to applaud one another's efforts. Everyone should have such a cheering section.

One of Mom's church projects was a chapel service where families of children with special needs would feel welcomed and included. Their vocalizations could be disruptive to regular services, and many churches weren't wheelchair accessible. But meeting in the main floor chapel after our regular church service became a loving way for families to connect and overcome the isolation that often went with their children's diagnoses.

I remember joining the families in the chapel one week when Mom was sharing about the gift of communion. She passed around a large loaf of bread, symbolic of Jesus's sacrificial love and provision. I had been to church every week and knew exactly how this worked. I pulled off a small, tidy piece of bread and sat quietly, waiting to be told we could eat it. The girl beside me from Mom's class grabbed a big hunk of bread and started chowing down before grabbing a second piece. I was horrified and full of indignation! This wasn't how communion worked in church! The rest of the service was lost to me. But I dutifully helped clean up before voicing to my mom the outrageous behaviour of one of her students!

Mom turned to me and wisely said, "Don't you think God wants us to take in everything He has for us? I think the girl you refer to got it right. She was hungry and turned to the bread of life to find fullness. 'Take, eat in remembrance of me.'"

That lesson lingered as a reminder that religion isn't as important as love. God cares most about the heart.

Mom was the Christian education coordinator at church, worked full-time, and was still the manager of the household. There were many people in the late 1970s that felt a woman's place was at home. To please the voices from her parents' generation, she had to cook healthy meals, tend a garden, preserve and can produce, keep her home organized, and be present for her family to prove that a working mom could cover all the bases. I would often read aloud my homework to her for feedback while she was cooking dinner.

To juggle all the demands, she would include us in her household and work projects. I thought it was fun to trace pictures on carbon paper so that Mom's lessons could be rolled on the Gestetner copier in the morning. Mom was committed to bringing home any special crafts she did with her students to share the activity with us. I have lots of fond memories of painting plaster of Paris figurines from moulds we poured together or doing a paint-by-number art piece beside Mom while she checked the boxes of her long to-do list. She gave freely and worked hard to supply whatever she could give.

On top of parenting, working, and volunteering, Mom also had to upgrade her teacher's certificate to a university degree to grow professionally. It's not hard to see why Mom was my hero. Her energy seemed boundless! She was the planner and engine in our house. I felt lazy in comparison. I loved time to dream and reflect. It was clear that she was giving her best to all of us at church, school, and home.

My parents were very different. Dad kept a patient pace in his activity. He got things done, but he was a problem solver who took the time to do things methodically. He seldom seemed rushed or busy, perhaps because he always made space for downtime.

It was often my dad who had the extra time to drive us to activities or quiz me to see whether I was ready for a test. Once he paraphrased a book that was too hard for me to read so I could get information on Beethoven for a speech I had to write in grade five. Dad had the patience to play backgammon with us or untangle a fine chain that became knotted. He was naturally the one we all looked to for board games and snuggles. He did up the bows on the back of my dresses before church while everyone else scrambled with last-minute preparations. He was a gentle and patient soul.

At work as an electronics technician, he had the skill and perseverance to figure out what was wrong with the most challenging, finicky televisions and small appliances. Dad was an introvert who spent much of himself working in a job where he was surrounded by people all day. He was also a creature of habit. Every day, he would walk in the door, unpack his lunch box, and sit down at the table with the newspaper and read. His familiar ritual would end with the daily crossword puzzle and a cigarette. The smoke moved us away. Dad created a daily cave time. Dad loved to read or to get lost in solving puzzles. His favourite gifts were a Rubik's Cube and brain teasers with complex parts to assemble. He lived largely inside himself and didn't often share his thoughts out loud. When he wasn't working, Dad had few plans. He knew how to relax.

Mom would come in the door an hour after Dad got home and would comment, "I don't suppose anyone thought to start supper?" When it was obvious that nothing was cooking, baking, or bubbling, Mom would sigh deeply and pick up the slack. Kathy and I were sensitive to girl cues. We felt for our mom and made efforts to help with dinners and housework.

My dad didn't do subtle cues. The offhand remark was seen as implied criticism that caused him to get defensive and stubborn—less willing to hear the plea for help. He would defend his need for downtime. He felt he had a right to read the paper to see what was going on in the world. There was nothing wrong with that!

Mom would predictably bristle at the lack of sensitivity that failed to recognize her need for a break. She worked long, hard days too. "He has been home for an hour already. Can't he do something to help around the house?" It was assumed that Mom was responsible for the household. Though she was good at it, motivating our family to contribute to cleaning and maintenance while managing the planning, shopping, and preparing meals could be exhausting. Yet order and design at home were seen as a reflection of her abilities as a homemaker, parent, and wife. So she swallowed her frustration and fatigue while she dug deeper to make things happen.

As a child, I didn't recognize the larger context of this scenario as men and women were renegotiating household norms and responsibilities. Instead I perceived only tension between my parents, and I would try to fix it. I would quietly step into the gap between them and ask, "So what do you want for supper? I can help."

I was an observer and made it a habit to study people and try to understand their motivations and deeper feelings. As a peacemaker, I took on the role of creating household harmony. I was unaware that my tendency to take on other people's emotions and stresses to restore peace pulled energy away from the tasks of personal growth and self-care.

It felt normal to try to ease tensions between my siblings, since we were each other's first choice of playmates, our family having no close neighbours. In winter, we would toboggan down the small hill in the backyard together or play indoors near the fireplace to get warm. Mom fuelled our fun with balls, badminton racquets, and eventually cross-country skis to help our family enjoy the outdoors. She would make chores a game when she would pull out the rakes to make huge leaf piles for us to play in each fall. She would pay us a small allowance for helping gather the walnuts that fell plentifully from the tree beside the house.

In baseball season, my brother Steve played catch with me while Kathy got her exercise running after the balls we missed. Soccer was a favourite pastime as we practised passes and dropkicks and tried to score on each other.

The piano often filled our home with music, as Kathy and I both took lessons and loved to sing. We memorized all the songs from records Mom bought. The soundtracks to *The Sound of Music* and *Annie* were favourites. Steve was more experimental and tried lots of instruments before joining an orchestra with his viola. The drum phase was his loudest trial, but he had great rhythm and enthusiasm. Our whole family was naturally musical. My siblings often sang with me while doing the dishes. It was better than arguing over whether a dish was clean enough!

For years my siblings and I enjoyed using our imaginations to create adventures, concerts, and life dramas. I loved sharing my favourite books by reading them aloud to Kathy. We also cuddled together while listening to the Disney read-along books where the page turn was signalled by "when Tinker Bell rings her little bell, like this."

Our life in the country was full of simple pleasures, ordinary school days, and lots of time watching TV or doing homework. Our large property became the new backyard space to share with friends. My parents hosted an annual fall hike followed by a barbecue and games at our home afterward. We often had Bible studies in our house. In turn, we would go to the homes of our parents' friends for meals and pool parties. Many people swirled in and around our family circle with dinners, church events, gatherings, barbecues, visits, and sleepovers.

Sadly, even great families can have cracks that allow trauma to slip in.

My family wasn't there on the days "it" happened. When I was between the ages of eleven and thirteen, my siblings and I were often left in the care of a close friend of the family. He was closer to my dad than my mom, but they both trusted him implicitly.

When I hit adolescence, this caregiver began to create spaces to be alone with me. I felt special. He gave me special gifts and attention. But then he crossed a line.

> He used his power to hurt
> instead of caring for me.

> When my developing body was an object of interest, I froze.
> My trust was weaponized. This was bad.
> A voice inside my head was insistent:
> 'If you tell, it will break your life apart.
> Just stuff it down and forget."

> I tried to wipe away the dirty feeling with lots of toilet paper.

I started to have dreams of a looming shadowy figure pursuing me.
I would shrink, hide and try to disappear.
My voice never worked when I would try to cry out.

Shame and self-doubt became ordinary.
Being female meant hypervigilance.
The last time it happened, I was thirteen.

I knew it wouldn't happen again:
He stiffened and left the room when he heard me softly crying.
The door closed.
The door cracked open again and the light shone in.
"I'm sorry," he said.
I wiped away my tears and launched into activity.

I erased it as if it had never happened.
But it changed me.
I lived a splintered life where pretending was necessary.
I became an actor on the stage of the everyday.

I convinced myself that this man would drive my parents apart if they found out. There would be blame and tension, and I would be the cause of it all. So I hid instead. I put on a smile for the world's benefit. But my body became my enemy.

Already I had learned to contain emotions to avoid embarrassment and fit in. Now my emotions had to detach completely so that I could enter a room and act normal. I learned to dissociate from myself. My complicated feelings didn't have a place. I started to get bad headaches, period pain, and muscle tension that never eased. They became my normal.

I saw a path forward by spending all my energy on "doing good." Busy days became a way to leave the hurt behind. Dissociation—I could just pretend it never happened! Forgive and forget, right?

However, despite my school success and growing list of achievements and recognition, I felt constant tension and a feeling of disappointment in myself. I found it easier to forgive my abuser than myself. I wasn't mad at God, so the anger could only turn inward. I felt self-contempt grow in me. I judged only myself.

I didn't recognize that a schism formed inside me between the parts of me that the world saw and the parts I silenced and kept buried. I didn't know that the secret had the power to shape me even as it was rejected, contained, and denied. It didn't disappear as I had hoped.

CHAPTER 9

DRIVEN

> The Controller's strategy is to manage the inner sense of not feeling safe in the world by controlling themselves and their environment ... Perfectionists define their self-worth and create a sense of safety in the world by getting things perfectly right.
>
> —Alex Howard, *Decode Your Fatigue*

By grade eight, I prized my ability to discern what would be admired by others and to perceive feelings below the surface of a conversation. At the same time, I rigorously policed and contained my own emotions. Being a victim made me feel unworthy and ashamed of my needs, since they made me vulnerable. I learned to bury shame beneath success, pleasing others, or being productive, but the sense of being stained didn't go away.

I was gaining confidence as a performer at church events and school. Taking on a character was a way to explore feelings without being vulnerable. My faith community encouraged my gifts of creativity, storytelling, writing, music, and drama. I helped a Sunday school teacher rewrite the words to "'Twas the Night Before Christmas" for our Christmas pageant. We borrowed the poem's metre and rhyme pattern to tell the story of a family that grew closer and less selfish as they allowed Christmas to impact their character and connection. Jesus was God's gift of love, inviting us to draw near and be transformed by the encounter. It was satisfying to use creativity to create goodness and beauty to enhance life. I experimented with acting and loved stepping into a role. With enough practice, I loved to sing, act, or play piano for a safe audience. My security rested in having time to prepare.

I was still taking piano lessons, I had started babysitting, and homework was getting heavier. The demands on my time were growing with my abilities. I learned that productivity could quiet my inner critic and that there were great rewards in being helpful and pleasing to others.

People at church were good to me. As I grew older, I was given responsibility. I helped wait tables, decorate, cook, and clean up at spaghetti dinners and pancake brunches. I was encouraged to learn and take part in the community. There were lots of ways to help and give, and I hadn't realized yet that I couldn't stretch enough to do all of them.

At school, I took on new roles. I helped the school librarian at recess or lunch, mending or shelving books. I volunteered as a reading partner with children from a younger grade. I was chosen by the principal to be the bell ringer for recess and lunch breaks. I felt honoured to be chosen for this task but also felt nervous about it. If I made a mistake, I could be publicly embarrassed since the whole school would witness it! I generally didn't like that kind of exposure, but I couldn't say no to my principal!

I was part of an enrichment group that often worked independently in the library while the class worked on concepts that we had already mastered. I never advertised my marks, but I liked to do my best to stay near the top of the class standings. Perfection was the goal, and I hated losing a mark or two. My perfectionist streak had me spending many hours on assignments to get a top grade. I would rewrite a whole page rather than submit a messy one marked up with liquid Witeout. That's how we did things in the 1980s before home computers became the norm!

I was growing and experimenting and pushing myself to succeed in and beyond the classroom.

I wanted so much to do what was right and good in the eyes of everyone! I gained a radar for the feelings and expectations of those around me. I would read those messages to guide my decisions. But the voice that was hardest to please was my inner measuring stick. I could never quite rise to the vision of my ideal self.

I learned early to love and treat others as I would like to be treated. I thought carefully about how my actions would affect others. But I didn't know what to do when others' choices impacted me.

Gradually I started to feel the pressure of too many different expectations that competed for my time and energy. Being a pleaser often led to overcommitment. I hated to disappoint anyone. I was terrible at saying no to anything.

My growing stress and pressure would spill out in crazy dreams of being late for a deadline, or of a command performance where I was dressed in my pyjamas and didn't know the words to the song playing on the piano. Somehow, even in my dreams I couldn't be honest and admit that I didn't know the words or try to stop the show. I felt as though I had no choice but to fake it and "play on!" I was on a hamster wheel that had to keep turning or I would fall apart. My body felt constantly on high alert. Even at night, I found it hard to wind down my mind and body for rest.

Nobody noticed the deep pressure that was building beneath the surface, although my health was giving clues. My immune system seemed to be weak. I caught every cold around me, which often turned into a secondary infection in my sinuses. My list of allergies was growing to include many tree pollens, pet fur, feathers, dust, mould, and different environments. My need for Kleenex in my pocket was a daily reality. I never left home without a neat stack folded and ready! But these symptoms were easy to label and dismiss.

Under the surface, I was unaware that I was trying to silence the feeling of being dirty and used by propping up my identity with perfectionism and image management. My self-worth was in question daily. I was only aware of a vague sense of being pulled in many directions without knowing what to do about it. I often felt out of control and exhausted. Taking on responsibilities at school, church, and home was a great distraction to turn off painful thoughts and feelings. Beneath the busy days, I felt the pressure of performance. Sometimes when I turned out the lights at night, I would take huge gulps of air and cry alone in my room without any clue as to why I felt so drained.

Amid the pressure I put on myself or absorbed through my desire to please others, faith in God was my anchor. I experienced God as a very real companion, a kind counsellor, and an unwavering, loving parent. Often in the quiet, I would seek the light of God's goodness. Walking through the woods or alone in my room, I would feel a warm presence holding me. In my connection with God, I felt completely known and understood. The nourishment from these anchoring roots sustained me even as the weeds of image management propped up my sense of identity. Love was real: I had encountered it.

That summer, our family took a wonderful vacation driving and camping on the way to the west coast of Canada. We were introduced to Amy Grant's *Age to Age* album, and it became the soundtrack of our trip. She was young when she compiled her songs, and I felt encouraged to find creative expression for my reflections and inner music.

I wrote my first song within the year. The firm roots of God's knowledge and care were a gift I wanted to share with others who longed for a stable place to stand.

I'VE FOUND IT

All my life I've been searching
for a love that will never end—
a love that's kind and forgiving,
and never fails.

CHORUS:
I've found it;
no one can break it.
I've found it;
no one can take it away.

Jesus loves us just as we are, His love lasts forever.
We will live eternally, Help us to live in harmony

CHORUS:
I've found it;
no one can break it.
I've found it;
no one can take it away.

The knowledge that I was seen and known and loved didn't always sink past my head to my heart, but it was a firm soil in which to root my fragile identity.

CHAPTER 10

ALONE IN A CROWD

> I'm gonna fly, no one knows where
> But I'm gonna fly, I'll soar through the air
> 'Cause all my life seems I've waited for the time to start
> Being the person inside of me unafraid of being me.
> —Amy Grant, "I'm Gonna Fly"

I started high school full of hope for a new beginning. My heart moved between faith that all would go well and a looming fear of failure. I found some of the older students quite intimidating and was thankful that many of my junior school friends came with me to this new place. They were a comfort amidst so much that was new. I decided that I would be more outgoing. I knew instinctively that we all mask insecurities, and so I let that embolden my efforts to be friendly. I swallowed my fear and chose to smile and be open to making new friends.

On my first day, I walked into my geography class while a friend was telling me a story. Naturally, we sat down next to each other. When the bell rang, the teacher explained that there would be no talking during class. My friend leaned over to whisper something.

I whispered back that she could tell me later—we had to be quiet. But it was at that moment that my teacher turned to the source of the disturbance and saw me talking.

He made me an example for the rest of the class.

"Stand up! What is your name?"

I managed to squeak out, "Peggy."

"You will remain standing for the rest of the class as a reminder that I mean it when I insist on no talking."

I wanted the floor to swallow me up. I had never met most of my peers whose eyes were all looking at me. I tried to look confident and to take the punishment in stride. But I hated being centred out and felt the sting of injustice over being corrected for talking when I was only trying to quiet my friend. My cheeks were flushed with embarrassment as I stood through the entire class period. On the way out, my friend tried to cheer me up and laugh about it. I wasn't ready to let it go, and I wore the shame and indignation for the rest of the day. It took time for me to wear an emotion before I could release it!

Beyond these bumpy beginnings, I was determined to succeed with hard work! Grade nine became a succession of good, yet ordinary, days. Sometimes high school drained me with its competitive, negative environment. But I was working hard on remaining optimistic and hopeful.

I excelled at schoolwork but disliked the stress of deadlines and resented mindless assignments that necessitated homework after already spending a whole day at school. I felt the pressure from having very little downtime. I still had constant neck and head tension. My recurrent sinus infections and allergies were accompanied by painful periods with vomiting that would cause me to miss a day of classes every month. I didn't understand the signals my body was sending to alert me to take care of myself. These symptoms had become normal to me. I easily dismissed them.

Despite the pressure, I was still enthusiastic about learning and generally enjoyed school. Appearances were important to me. I would never walk out the door without taking time to carefully shower, style my hair, and put on makeup. I was so focussed on my external image and accomplishments that I was only occasionally aware of deeper feelings of loneliness.

No matter who I was with, I remained detached from the inner terrain of my heart. It was hard to feel close to someone when I wasn't even close to myself. My wounded heart had no space to process and explore in safety.

So instead of trying to invite others in, I looked for beautiful thoughts to lift my soul—truths that held up over time and were expressed by poets, novelists, historians, and the scriptures. I began collecting quotes and thoughts in journals to capture an ideological world that was vivid, lovely, and real to me. Beautiful thoughts lifted me high above the unexplored physical and emotional undercurrents inside me. I clung to ideals of selfless compassion and the restoring dignity of forgiveness.

Books became a point of connection with a deeper world that satisfied my search for understanding and beauty. As a teen, I would take breaks from the demands I placed on myself to be successful, productive, strong, and likeable by retreating into Book World. I loved glimpses of different lives and possibilities. My mind became populated with characters that felt like friends—often brave females who lived intentionally in righting wrongs, caring for people, and living from their convictions while growing from their mistakes.

I was drawn to stories of reformed drug addicts and prostitutes who left behind their failures and lived meaningful lives. It was beautiful to see people heal through loving support systems. I identified with their stories and became hungry for an authentic place of connection and healing, too, while paradoxically telling myself that I was fine now that the man left me alone. I had learned to minimize what had happened to me.

I had concluded early in life that emotions were to be governed by the mind. I could force them to be quiet so I could be productive instead of indulging them. I still felt things deeply, but I didn't allow space to process or try to understand my emotions. The only place I felt free to express them was in tears of empathy while watching a movie.

Instead I did my best to live up to all the ways I thought would please God. I felt like anger, fear, doubt, and resentment were marks against me. I was sure these feelings disappointed God. I tried to turn off these human responses to life.

Yet God remained my most honest attachment. I could say things to God and in my journal that had no other place of connection. My faith was essential to holding life together. But I also created a religious standard of perfection that fuelled my inner critic to be incredibly harsh and demanding. "Only Wanna Do What's Right" was a Bryan Duncan song I would thrash to when I was frustrated at my inability to feel pure.[2] I felt tainted and dirty beyond my control.

I found a path forward by living in my imagination and ideal visions of life. I believed in second chances and transformation that birthed new directions and possibilities. A steady diet of redemption stories fed my convictions that brokenness could be restored and that there was no darkness that the light could not enter, illuminate, and change. Divine light could change evil shadows into bright goodness. This spirit of transforming light and love was humanity's greatest hope—my greatest hope.

Hope fuelled me and helped me to cope—or to forget the imperfection that marred my ideal vision of what life should be. Inspiring thoughts fuelled my inner life and made me long to do big, loving, healing, world-changing things. I aspired to rise and live beyond my hurt. Like the phoenix of the old classics, my spirit was determined to soar out of the ashes of my wounds, failures, and disappointments. I wanted to fly.

CHAPTER 11

DEEPENING FRIENDSHIP

This is my Father's world:
O let me ne'er forget
That though the wrong seems oft so strong,
God is the Ruler yet.

—Maltbie D. Babcock, 1901

It was in the next summer that life shifted. The wisdom of Providence turned a long-time friend into a kindred spirit. In the middle of the summer, my neighbour Stephanie reached out to ask about attending church and youth group together in the fall.

Steph had just returned from a Christian camp where she had deepened her experience of God's love. Steph had been a friend for a long time. We were bus buddies and often saved seats for one another. Though she was my nearest neighbour on the other side of the forest, I seldom noticed the hints of a deeper life beneath the light, giggly chatter we usually shared. My daily exercise of emotional control and self-protection diverted my energy from noticing significant things in the people around me.

Steph began campaigning to convince me to share a week at camp with her. Steph insisted that I would love it. I listened to her enthusiastic stories and enjoyed her growing faith that had been fuelled by her experience. It sounded inviting, but also scary for a young girl who preferred books to large groups. We would have to sleep in a cabin with eight other people, share meals with fifty, be involved in programming from morning to night with no space to be alone with our thoughts or read books. As an introvert, I had always refused to go to a camp before. But Steph could be persuasive, and I found myself agreeing to go—as long as we went together.

It was a musical drama camp. I had enjoyed acting in Sunday school concerts and singing in school and church choirs. But this camp was different. We would create the drama, learn the songs, and perform it by the end of the week—for an audience. It sounded crazy and risky, like a social nightmare to navigate twenty-four hours a day for a week.

On the other hand, I enjoyed structured times like youth group, which gave safe space to explore faith and meaning with peers. The creativity was appealing. It was bound to be more meaningful than the rest of my summer: trying to coax out a tan instead of freckles from my white skin while cutting the lawn, playing catch, scraping the paint off the fence with my brother for a few dollars, and occasional visits with friends. This could be the perfect adventure to spice up an otherwise ordinary summer.

When my parents dropped us off at camp, I was struck by the natural beauty and simplicity of the site and the open friendliness of the staff and campers. The air vibrated with positive energy. The games were designed to help campers get to know each person in the cabin and prevent exclusive cliques. Small group games and discussions helped us to learn each other's names and to create deeper connections within the larger group. Campfire's silly action songs broke down the "cool factor" that locked people our age away from each other. I found that camp could be a place to try new skills and take risks alongside supportive peers and leaders. Failure was met with encouragement and cheers instead of ridicule.

There were parts of each day set aside for reflection and sharing. Beautiful stories and thoughts fuelled wonder in me. There was session time each day where songs full of faith and honesty gave my heart words to express what had remained unspoken. I started to find a voice and feel at home in these spaces.

Jesus's compassion and example were explored, allowing them to become a compass for how people were meant to care for one another. God's spirit was like the wind in the trees, available to blow through each life to comfort, heal, guide, and enable all of humanity to love better and to plant peace, kindness, patience, joy, goodness, and self-control.

Perhaps this was a place where my inside and outside worlds could merge. Could it also be the place where I could be honest—where deep wounds could be touched and healed? The songs spoke of God seeing our tears fall in the dark and asked us to trust and cast our burdens on Jesus to find rest for our souls. It filled me with hope and joy.

Each day, there was a camp swim in the lake. The water was refreshingly cool, and that year there was a large mud pit at the base of the cliff. There were only four of us fifteen-year-old girls at the camp, and we hit it off right away. Sam* was a redhead with a short haircut and heavy bangs that accentuated her quick humour and sparkling eyes. Janice* was tall and friendly with creativity that flowed out in the songs she liked to write. Steph and I found great companions in these girls. We bonded the first day in the mud pit, giving each other facials and pretending to be at a high-end spa where only foreign accents could be used when speaking. I couldn't remember laughing with friends so much. By the time we had cleaned off in the water, we had become "The Mudsketeers," bound together by exuberance, laughter, and the determination to create something wonderful in our week together.

The counsellor in our cabin was only a few years older than the Mudsketeers. She seemed tired of her job and impatient with the only nine-year-old in the cabin. When night came, this young girl was frightened and homesick. The counsellor yelled at her to "be quiet and go to sleep," before she turned over and followed her own advice.

This comforting strategy didn't seem to do the trick. I could hear the young girl crying. So I quietly climbed to the top bunk to perch on the edge of the girl's bed and whispered with her to find out more about what she was thinking and feeling. I resonated quickly with the fear she spoke of. I used my mother's comforting methods—a quiet prayer, then a song, and a soft hand to rub the younger girl's back. I was surprised at how quickly the girl responded to care and attention, and I thought that I would enjoy being a counsellor someday. By the time I found my bunk in the dark, I fell asleep knowing the sweetness of overcoming a common enemy—fear—and helping a younger version of myself find peace.

By the end of the camp, Steph and I had become inseparable! And under the guidance of staff, we campers had indeed created a play; it was definitely not a five-star performance, but a story nonetheless of courage, faith, compassion, and possibility. We worked together on our pieces to make a whole play that was very satisfying to all of us. Our songs rang out with simplicity and confidence, and the parents clapped loud and long.

The partings at the end of the week were tearful and full of promises to stay in touch. But even if we didn't, these friends had opened a satisfying way to connect the surface and playful parts of me to a shared deeper life. It birthed hope that my inner world of faith and fear that hid away so often from the light of relationships didn't have to remain disconnected. The belief that I could connect deeply, be known, and be enjoyed authentically awakened.

CHAPTER 12

ANCHORING

Love is patient, love is kind. It does not envy, it does not boast, it is not proud. It does not dishonor others, it is not self-seeking, it is not easily angered, it keeps no record of wrongs. Love does not delight in evil but rejoices with the truth. It always protects, always trusts, always hopes, always perseveres. Love never fails.

—1 Corinthians 13:4–8, NIV

By the time grade ten came around, Steph and I had become best friends. She gave me confidence and made me feel valued.

Steph was great at thinking up adventures and activities. Though we both could dream together about beautiful ideas, Steph was quick to laugh at herself and didn't seem to waste energy on being embarrassed. She would process out loud the shows that she watched and the plans for exciting outings we could do together. She could give amazing play-by-play accounts of conversations and events at school. Steph brought me out of the world of introspection and into the world of social activity. She was the perfect companion to help me feel comfortable going to dances, film nights, youth retreats, and special events.

High school days stretched on much as they began—one day like any other. Except now I had a friend who would wait for me by my locker after class, pass me notes, save me a place at lunch, and always hold a seat for me on the bus. Steph's friendship was the steady constant that made me feel known and cared for. Steph was also great at including others in her infectious sunshine. People generally felt relaxed and safe around Stephanie, and so I found that my circle of friends naturally expanded.

I enjoyed, largely as an observer, the relaxed, often funny banter of the lunch crowd. Bonding often happened through complaining—about a teacher, the cafeteria food, the weather, a bad hair day ... There were endless sources to fuel such communication. I sometimes tried to influence the direction of a conversation. I looked for the good in others and liked to offer encouragement. If someone criticized a fellow student, I would think of something kind to say about him or her to try to change the channel to a more positive flow. I wanted people to know they were safe with me.

I was learning how to listen not just to words but also to the emotions beneath.

In a communication exercise in class, we were taught to ask questions to clarify and draw people out instead of just planning our next contribution to the discussion. I recognized the tendency in myself to want to say things that would earn a laugh or a positive response. But I wasn't good at thinking of sensational or clever things to say. My best responses came hours after a conversation was over and I was reflecting on it in solitude. So instead of formulating responses while my friends talked, I began to quiet my thoughts and feelings to be attentive to others. I learned to rephrase what I was hearing to be sure it resonated with what my friends were trying to convey.

I was surprised when friends started to confide in me. I was starting to see beneath the surface of my cool teenage peers. I was drawn to understand the heart places and probe them for meaning.

As a culture, my peers sometimes came through with encouragement and reassurance, but sometimes a sarcastic word could cut and wound. I became convinced of the power of kindness and compassion to create safe spaces to grow and to help one another learn about ourselves.

I was still a sensitive soul who was hurt easily. Habitually, I pushed away my inner drama because I couldn't yet deal with it. I just swallowed it down deep to my toes, where it couldn't interfere with my days. I was unaware of how my traumatic experience drove me. I flinched at the word "body" and found the crude jokes at the back of the bus unsettling. How the boys could find a sexual innuendo and a base laugh in any phrase astonished me. I coached myself to imitate the other girls' responses. I acted casual and never acknowledged the pain and confusion their jokes triggered. But I decided to keep some relational distance from guys.

Instead I learned to focus on trying to help others whose hurt I could sense. I found that empathy came easily, and somehow I lost my sense of woundedness in trying to help someone else. It always surprised me when other girls would ask me for advice—especially about relationships with boys—since I rarely even talked to guys at school.

When my friends complained that all their boyfriends wanted to do was get physical, I asked them what would happen if they put strict limits on the physical side of the relationship so that the friendship and emotional side of the connection could grow. If the relationship died, then it was not worth the emotional attachment. It seemed like solid advice, but I had never had an opportunity to use it myself.

I did notice that girls seemed so quick to commit to relationships emotionally. They were tied in deeply, while the guys seemed to stay loosely connected and moved on faster after a breakup. I thought it was safer to avoid the romance roller coaster that I watched my friends ride. In high school, I barely knew myself yet. I wasn't ready to attach deeply to someone else.

By sixteen years old, I instinctively found baggy pants and loose-fitting shirts that made me look like I didn't care about being attractive at all. I did care, but I was more aware of my body than I wanted to be.

I hadn't met a boy I wanted to open my mind or heart to yet, and that had to dominate over any outward attraction. There was such pressure on people to pair up. I preferred the atmosphere of my youth group, where we could just be a friend group, play silly games, and talk about things that mattered. I had fun going with groups where we paired off with prom dates and I would enjoy the dance floor with male friends, but I never let anything move out of the friend zone.

During this season, our family decided to switch churches. Despite shifts in my family's church affiliation, Steve, Steph, and I decided to keep going to our youth group. It was home for us. Steph and I lived for weekends and youth outings. My brother and our friend Allan started leading Christian Music Only (CMO) dances. We loved our peer group in Erie Presbytery Youth Committee that met for retreats, dances, theme nights, and sporting events.

During this time, my faith in God's goodness, knowledge, and care was deepening. Psalm 139 became a bedrock chapter explaining our identity as God's purposeful creation, knitting us together in our mothers' wombs. Seeing each person as a creative masterpiece helped make me more willing to reach out and push past my natural reserve. I was also becoming more comfortable articulating my faith and trying to share thoughts in creative ways.

After listening to a speaker at our new church talk about God's unconditional love—the word in Greek was *"agape"*—I decided to put my thoughts into a song to sing while doing dishes with my brother and sister. They both have amazing voices and an instinctive ability to harmonize. The song had a playful tune and a strong rhythm pattern. When I recorded it much later, I prefaced it this way: "Love means such a variety of things ... We love friends, ice cream, storybook romances ... but Christ's unselfish desire for what is good and true and perfect for us, regardless of our response to Him, inspired in me an excitement about unconditional 'agape' love. I wrote the song in 1987."

AGAPE LOVE

So many misconceptions
Of what true love might be.
Fluttery hearts and cupids,
That's not the kind of love for me

CHORUS:
Agape love, agape love,
Given for you and me.
Agape love, agape love
By God's grace, it's free.

People are wandering round and round,
They search for things that satisfy.
But without Christ's love in their lives,
They're just living a lie.

People try to substitute
By filling desires of flesh.
But only the Spirit of God can fill
The desire of our hearts to experience

> CHORUS:
> Agape love, agape love,
> Given for you and me.
> Agape love, agape love
> By God's grace, it's free.
>
> The Lord is my Shepherd; I shall not want
> Anything else but Him,
> For in His love, I've found new life,
> And that is why I sing,
>
> CHORUS:
> Agape love, agape love,
> Given for you and me.
> Agape love, agape love
> By God's grace, it's free.

When I shared it with my youth group, they were encouraging and started to sing along. I felt safest with and closest to the girls in my youth group. We could talk about almost anything together, and we grew used to discussing deeper topics. I especially loved when we prayed for each other and talked about how to apply faith to life's challenges. But there was still a guardedness I couldn't shake that made me appear stronger than I felt and unable to express deep needs.

This show of strength often made for some unbalanced friendships with people who were drawn to my ideal convictions and displays of faith. I had a few younger friends that I met at youth retreats who would call regularly to talk about their struggles. I learned to quiet my own needs to counsel and care for them.

One younger girl regularly had seizures that affected her life every day, and she would pour out her frustration and hurt over long phone conversations. I spent most bedtimes searching scriptures for words of wisdom and comfort to store up for myself and others. I would leave these phone conversations feeling drained but happy. I liked that God could pour comfort and care through me, and it quieted my sense of inadequacy and shame. By living as my ideal self, I could feel worthwhile and ignore the pain and needs of my wounded heart. I was actively trying to tune it out by diverting energy and inner resources to others. Faith quieted fear.

Spiritual life became a form of escape as well as a firm foundation. I preferred to live in the realm of abstract thought over practical self-care. Faith created a refuge for my mind and soul. I regularly tuned into the music of creation. It seemed to vibrate with hope. I longed for what was good and lovely. I loved to linger and gaze at the colours of a sunset to feel what the word "glory" meant. I would find myself caught up in moments of divine clarity or flashes of insight that were helpful to me. Ordinary days could be infused with a sense of God's nearness.

I created a vast, spacious, ideal world that I could crawl into and draw solace from for myself and others. I regularly withdrew to this holy space, a quiet inner sanctuary that I tended to and processed in the privacy of my journal and in quiet moments with God.

CHAPTER 13

WEIGHTED

> The damage of past abuse is such that its effects
> are not just felt in some corner of their lives. But
> the effects are really felt in every area of life.
>
> —Dan Allender

At the age of sixteen, it seemed like the most natural thing in the world to apply to be on staff at camp. My natural gravity towards empathy, worship, and faith, alongside my desire to care well for children, made camp the perfect setting to allow my inner world to find a home. Every day I spent at camp put a song in my heart and a spring in my step.

Staff training was full of meaningful conversations about faith and how to live it out together as a community. We also exercised our creativity every day in planning games and activities, and taking on characters in imaginative playscapes. I loved all of it.

Alongside the joy of purposeful work and community, there was also space for honest reflection. We were encouraged to bring our true needs to God. Songs expressed emotions that I normally tuned out. My heart was finding safety to feel again.

By the end of staff training, the pull towards honesty made me aware of how my heart was weighted with my secret shame. I longed to lay the burden of the secret down—to stop hiding and explore this inner terrain with someone I trusted.

In one of our training sessions on boundaries, I learned that my experience was considered a form of abuse. I'd been molested. I also learned that everyone has a responsibility to report evidence of abuse or neglect. We were taught that a child under sixteen cannot be promised confidentiality. Any disclosure meant a report must be made to higher authorities—the Children's Aid Society. I also understood that if the victim was over sixteen years of age, he or she could decide to maintain control of the information and a report didn't have to be made. It was this understanding that made me feel I could break my silence. Since I was sixteen, the power of my secret might be less heavy if I could talk about it confidentially without fear of the consequences that had always kept me silent. I felt that talking about it might help me move on.

My employer, the camp director, was a wiser, older type that I felt sure would know how to help. As a male, maybe he could even help me discern whether I had done something to invite such attention or whether all males had self-control issues that I should guard against. The comments from the back of the bus made me wonder whether all guys were just wired that way.

At camp, the guys were better. They liked to take part in discussions of faith and generosity, compassion, and community. But even they could whistle or comment when the girls came out in their swimsuits. I felt more comfortable wearing a long T-shirt over my swimsuit at the lake.

As Staff Training Week was ending, I felt that this was the last chance to focus on my needs before work took over. Once the campers were on site, I would be working with children who would need all my attention. I finally worked up the courage to ask the director (I'll call him Jim*) to speak with me privately. We picked a space in view of others but far enough away to talk without being overheard.

Jim observed that I seemed distant, as though my thoughts were far away.

That felt like an accurate observation, since what I wanted to talk about had been shoved far from my conscious thoughts to keep it from infecting my days. I began to talk. The words felt heavy on my lips, as though they were weighted with the pain they carried. I didn't expect to cry. I so rarely did. But as I talked, the words seemed to wear tears as they poured out of my deep ache. I started sharing slowly, but gradually I sped up my story as if to get the hard parts over with quickly. I concluded with "Don't worry, I've forgiven him. I am better now. It doesn't affect me any more."

Beneath the words, Jim sensed my unspoken question and after a pause said with confidence, "It wasn't your fault, you know. What happened to you—it wasn't your fault!"

I didn't know I needed to hear that, but it did seem to open a gate where my emotions had been held, hostage. My body began to shake with sobs that I didn't know existed anywhere inside. Their intensity scared me.

Jim let me lean into his shoulder with a side hug that made me feel protected and safe.

I no longer felt alone in the pain. The chasm of silence had been breached; someone had finally entered the emptiness and brought comfort and help there.

Jim asked me more questions to assess whether this man was a predatory risk. In the 1980s, there was less clarity around sexual harassment and abuse policies. He trusted my judgement on the situation; it had been three years since the last offence, and his apology seemed to end the behaviour. He agreed that I should have the choice to keep the information quiet.

The truth still felt like a bomb that could do damage if it were made public, but it didn't feel so heavy after being able to talk about it privately. A pressure valve had been opened to release some of the strain. Jim prayed for me, and I felt a measure of relief to have an ally.

Shortly after my first attempt to talk about trauma, I met a girl a few years younger who had also been abused. I wanted so badly to ease her pain and help in some way. So I moved from finding a voice to explore my woundedness to trying to help heal someone else's. My role as counsellor, comforter, and healer quickly edited my own experiences down to things that might be useful or helpful to someone else. I focused on the resolved spiritual lessons that I had culled from my past. I knew that bitterness and unforgiveness only further wound the abused heart. But I knew so little, really.

At sixteen, I had barely begun to sort out my own messy places. Yet I felt compelled to try to use my Band-Aids to patch up another wounded heart. The one thing I could offer with confidence was prayer. My trust in God was a root system and anchor I could share. There was room to cling there together!

While I was at staff training for the first time, Steph was having a different adventure. She attended a leadership development camp that year. I had a day off when her camp ended. So I travelled three hours north with her dad to pick her up. The car ride felt a little long and awkward, but I was glad to see the camp where Steph was going to do some summer placements.

The site was just two buildings in an open field. But the people were obviously deeply connected as they said their goodbyes.

There were two guy leaders and three male campers. The five guys formed a group together and called themselves the Tent Boys. I was impressed by their creativity and humour as they sang harmonies to an old LifeSavers commercial: "Tweet, tweet, twiddle, twiddle, there's only one candy with a hole in the middle."[3] They changed the words to "there's only one religion with Christ in the middle." I remember thinking that the blond one was good-looking. I hadn't often been attracted to any guys who shared my faith.

On the drive home, I heard all about the three guys, the leaders, and most of the girls—though their names became a jumble of stories and generalized perceptions.

After spending the day catching up, Steph and I had laundry and packing to do to prepare for our first week as camp counsellors at two different camps. We hugged hard and prayed for each other before we parted for our next adventures. We were both excited and full of joy at the thought!

My first week as a camp counsellor finally arrived! I prepared first-day games and programming to help my cabin of girls meet each other and to have as little lag time as possible. Keeping everyone busy together with fun activities was key to helping them feel like they belonged in this new place. It calmed any homesick feelings before they grew. Before the campers arrived, I rehearsed questions that I could ask them as we walked down to the cabin to choose a bunk and set up their space. My shyness with strangers didn't matter. I had a role to play and would give it all I had to make camp safe and fun.

My first experience of counselling children at the camp was everything I had imagined it would be and more. Six bunks in my cabin were filled with young seven-year-old girls full of exuberance, personality, and fun. Because they were so much younger, I felt like a mother hen directing my flock from breakfast to bedtime.

I appreciated knowing the daily schedule, so I put one on the wall of the cabin so we could anticipate each piece of the day and prepare together. Swimsuits and sunscreen were put on before the rest hour ended so that we were ready for swim time. Silly hats and funny accents were ready to go for the movie star meal. A skit was practised and ready to share at the campfire. I loved my job of leading young campers through memorable, rich experiences where everyone mattered.

I also loved the tender moments when a homesick camper would share about her favourite parts of home and camp and trust me to take care of her needs for the week. I loved to reflect with them on God's ability to be present everywhere at once. God was with our families even while walking with us through our days.

I relished being surrounded by nature and calling attention to its beauty. I would point out the sunset and say "I spy! Look at God's amazing artistry in blending purple and red. I would never have thought to put those colours together! Let's soak it in, girls!" Wonder was the place where our spiritual life connected to the tangible world we lived in. Gratitude fuelled our souls each night as we would share something we were thankful for. Our hearts expanded as we thanked God for each other and the special memories we were making. I loved living out my ideals every day—starting and ending each day with a song in my heart, and often on my lips.

Unfortunately, even this ideal summer could be smeared with brokenness.

It all started with an injury. I fell while running down some stairs on my weekend off. Something wrenched deep in my low back as the wind was knocked out of me. Sharp pain rose in waves as I lay still while people around me asked whether I was okay. A friend walked me back up to where we had left the cars. My back throbbed.

I hated feeling weak, asking for help, and being needy. I tried to brush off the injury. But by dinner, I could hardly move. I spoke with my parents about the injury. I decided to get it checked out.

I was ushered into a medical office, where a physician noted a significant amount of swelling and bruising. He said he didn't expect lasting damage, but I might need Advil for the pain as it healed. Once the bruising went down, he suggested regular massages for a time to keep the muscles from creating scar tissue.

So began regular massage sessions with a non-registered health professional.

His professional-sounding chatter and
helpful therapeutic technique
disarmed the red flags I felt around him.
I was mocked for modesty and instructed to undress:
"Your shirt and bra are in the way."
Blurred lines:
Professionalism as he gave me privacy to follow instructions.
But he scoffed at me for my discomfort with nakedness:
"You haven't got anything I haven't seen before."

Then came the body comments.
"Many men prefer small-chested women"
my shape was critiqued as if I were an object
made for the pleasure of another.

He used his position of power to prey on my insecurity
He was older and flaunted his experience.
He held a position of authority: he decided my treatment.

"Why do I feel alarmed at his comments and attention?"
I dismissed my intuition:
"I'm just being silly and uptight. He's a professional"

Then he clearly crossed the line.

His hands moved to my bare chest
telling me how the massage feels great here too.
I was shocked as he suggested I remove my
pants for a full-body massage.

Panic. Clarity. Danger. Shame. Fear. Self-doubt.
I was alone, far from help, in a closed room.
I tried not to increase my vulnerability as I refused further treatment.

        I said no as I moved away. He left the room.

      While dressing, I resolved to never come back here.
                I would live with back pain.
             The treatment was too costly.
          I couldn't tell anyone. I felt ashamed.
                        Again.

From that moment, my summer became edited. I stuffed the hurtful memories down and focused even more diligently on the pure, good parts of life.

At camp, I told redemptive stories, shared profound quotes that were meaningful to me, and sang in gratitude and worship. The beautiful parts of my inner world found a receptive peer group. The children looked to me for help and strength, and borrowed my vibrant joy and faith. My back injury had healed enough to carry on.

Locking the shame and wounded parts away made life good. Forgetting my trauma made it disappear for a time.

But it resurfaced.

There was an end-of-summer sexual allegation from another patient towards my massage therapist. People were divided about believing it. I learned about the case as it was being discussed by my staff. I was hit hard by shame.

                    My silence protected a predator!
                        Bile rose in my throat.
                      Everyone looked at me.
                        Did I know anything?
               I couldn't tell them what I knew.
I couldn't confess my failure in front of the whole staff.
My brother, friends, and my employer all looked at me.
              They respected me, trusted me.

> I couldn't afford to lose that—
> to admit that I wasn't as clever as everyone thought.
>
> I shook my head and looked down;
> I felt sick with fear and shame.
> I told myself, "I am powerless, stupid, and weak."
> I believed that message for a long time.

The only time I questioned my decision to shut down the hurtful memories was when I realized I had failed another victim by not strengthening her report. My shame and self-contempt deepened. I had let a predator walk away. He won. But to change my answer would make me unreliable. I had no way to prove anything; it was his word against mine.

I knew then that my strength was only a show. I knew how weak I really was.

CHAPTER 14

PEDESTAL PEGGY

God is our refuge and strength,
An ever-present help in trouble.
Therefore. we will not fear, though the earth give way
And the mountains fall into the heart of the sea,
Though its waters roar and foam
and the mountains quake with their surging.

—Psalm 46:1–3, NIV

When I saw Steph again, I didn't mention my experience with the massage practitioner. It didn't fit with the life I was carving out for myself. I wanted to match Steph's exuberance and share the joy of our camp summers lived separately but with so many lovely similarities!

The community Steph found at camp was so good for her! I could see the maturation that happened in my friend through her summer away. And Steph was always generous with her experiences, so they had a way of widening my world as well.

At summer's end, Steph asked me to help her host a leadership camp reunion at her house, and I was introduced to her new friends. I remembered Lance from the Tent Boys. He stood out to me this time, not just because of his blond good looks but also because of the way he treated people. He was kind and mature, with a faith that propelled him to lead others with humour and sincerity.

He was one of the few who sought me out amidst the inside jokes that the group shared from camp. Steph tried to include me in the fun with brief explanations, but it was always funnier for those who had shared those memories. Lance pulled me aside and thanked me for the reflection I led. He mentioned that many teens aren't comfortable leading faith conversations with peers. As we talked, I sensed that Lance could become a valued friend.

We had a campfire in the backyard, and the whole atmosphere was like all the best parts of camp brought home to Osborne Corners. We celebrated a unity of spirit as we sang in the firelight.

And just like that, summer was over for another year.

Fall routines resumed in a predictable pattern of high school, church, and youth group events. Steph and I grew in leadership alongside our peers as we joined in hosting retreats, events, and creative projects.

Our youth group was a self-motivated, vibrant group of youth with an adult leader who encouraged us to act on our promising ideas. So that year, the girls in our group decided to join forces to write a play! In our story, the protagonist had to choose between a boyfriend she cared for but who didn't value or share her faith and her personal growth as a Christian. The heroine of the play chose to pursue faith in God over a boy she found attractive because he led her away from her inner convictions.

The play was a great success. The group writing pulled the girls of the group together. We leaned into one another's strengths with dance, choreography, singing, writing, and acting. It was a purposeful way to spend youth group evenings. The experience grew us personally and as a community. And we laughed—a lot—as we created characters with outrageous names, such as Monique Alexandra Francesca DuBois. I loved how creativity brought our group together and then allowed us to share something meaningful with our community!

My acting spilled over into my daily attempts to live out my ideals. Camp had fuelled my sense of who I wanted to be as a leader, a friend, and a loving person—my ideal self. Though I truly felt compassion for others, my heart remained strangely detached. I decided to be strong and brave—to not let myself need anything from another person. So I put on confidence, lived out my convictions, and actively rejected my fears and self-doubt.

Fear would surface from my subconscious at night. I still regularly had dreams about a threatening shadow that I would hide from. As the figure loomed closer, I could never cry out for help. My voice wouldn't work. The shadow would creep closer until I forced myself awake—physically shaking and heart pounding, with prayers on my lips. Fortunately, my automatic response to fear or need was to pray. The name of Jesus would immediately calm me, and songs of God's goodness filled my memory with imagery that could anchor my heart. I trusted that I was never alone—that God would never leave me or forget me.

I found comfort in knowing that nothing was hidden from God's caring gaze. I trusted that Jesus was able to see me and that he understood me better than I did myself. In my journal, I would ask God why I felt so splintered and adrift whenever I stopped being busy. It was the only time I let myself be still enough to hear the hurt inside. I had to believe that Jesus was big enough to lean on, to take care of me, and to listen to my cries when I couldn't cry out to anyone else. I would feel sheltered and surrounded by a peace that I couldn't explain. A warmth would pour over me, and I would feel comforted. My faith was more real to me than surface chatter and everyday high school happenings.

I was still close to my family. My conversations with my parents were full of the normal things teen girls share with trusted adults, but the relationship was also full of half-truths and dodges to protect my family from the secret of abuse. My woundedness was distanced from their comfort, guidance, and care. They didn't know it existed, and so the secret held us apart.

My parents were my greatest cheerleaders, but without acknowledging my whole self, I could never receive the affirmation they gave for my stellar performances in school, church, and life. Those words recognized the shiny outward projection that I worked hard to maintain, but they never reached the "real me" underneath.

Inside, I questioned and blamed myself mercilessly. My inner critic was harsh and punishing. It was a voice that kept me from the feeling of being cherished and loved. Such value was reserved for those who were as good as I tried to make everyone believe I was. My shameful experiences condemned me.

Generally, people believed in my exterior ideal self. I was seen as a successful and promising student, a kind friend, and a model Christian. They didn't see that I lived on an island no one visited.

I tried occasionally to invite a good friend to see my inner turmoil. I would withdraw from a social setting where everyone was having a good time to sit alone in the shadows, where my heart felt a kinship. When a friend noticed me missing—Steph usually did—she would coax me to return to the party to be happy and have fun with everyone. I would usually follow the friend back to the dance floor and try to shed my heaviness, but I couldn't help but feel that a part of me remained always in the cloakroom shadows.

Throughout my teen years, I regularly had dark moods that left me feeling alone, empty, and full of shame. But over time, I began to question whether closing myself off was my only option. I thought maybe it was time to explore my inner world with a friend.

Steph was a wonderful companion, and I decided to share these dark places of my secret world with her. Steph was kind and sympathetic, but neither of us knew how to respond to my big reveal.

We were just sixteen-year-olds sharing school days and youth events together. I told her my secret pain as we took a walk around the block at lunchtime. She did her best to cheer me up. She reminded me of all the great things in my life; my family and home life were wonderful, and the church was so good to me. The hurt I experienced was a few years in the past now. She encouraged me to leave it behind.

I also learned that what I experienced was common.

On a camping trip with five girls, I found we all had stories of feeling unsafe, used, cheapened, or taken advantage of. We felt closer because of our common pain, but none of us knew what to do with it. We didn't want to let it colour our lives.

I tried to dismiss the impact of past events and chose a strong veneer. I tried to minimize the pain, and I felt guilty if sadness or grief came to the surface. It made me feel as if my faith was weak if I couldn't forgive and forget. And my faith was the anchor that held me together.

I became more determined to move on and forget about the hurt inside. I had already decided to forgive my abusers. I was able to see good in my former caregiver, but anytime I was around this man, I had a radar that never turned off. I was hypervigilant, and anything he said or did was weighted with a layer of distrust.

When I had spells of sadness, my inner critic scolded me for dwelling on the negatives. I coached myself to look on the bright side. My faith community taught us to count it all joy when we endured trials of many kinds; to choose thankfulness and to let things go. I heard a lot of advice that I desperately tried to use as my code of conduct. I was thankful for my great family, beautiful memories built from family vacations, church experiences, and awesome friends.

So I let gratitude dictate the script I operated from. I lived the "perfect life" narrative and wrote my wounded self out of it. That part had no home.

I learned to live with pain. I didn't connect the physical pain of neck stiffness and debilitating headaches with my emotional detachment. I regularly dismissed my feelings and tried to manage any negative emotions with logic and denial. Why did something that happened long ago matter? My negative emotions and body clues were tiny protests that I shut down before they reached my consciousness.

I tried once more to tell my secret shame to a guy that I trusted. He was older, and I thought he might be strong enough to know how to care without hurting me further. Maybe he could even answer some of my questions. He was driving me home from a youth event, and we had an uninterrupted hour.

When I spoke up and shared my secret, he looked upset. I wasn't sure if he was disgusted or sympathetic. It was a long car ride, and things went silent. His distance was interpreted by my sensitive heart. What is there to say after a story like mine? He withdrew to his own thoughts, and so did I.

His silence and emotional distance confirmed what I already assumed. I was asking too much. I was too much. My shame was magnified as I felt that my stain was compounded by my inability to get past it.

Shame would always set me apart.

I felt repulsive. I felt cheapened in his eyes and felt that my bruises must be my fault. No good young man could help me or would be interested in a life with me—not if they knew. I had been a "plaything." How could I ever be respected and treated as an equal—a partner?

Though he remained a friend, even danced with me and teased me at social functions, we never talked about what I shared, and I never brought it up again.

My wounded self retreated deeper into the safety of anonymity—a no-name existence under the flawless surface I strove to preserve. I stopped inviting anyone to acknowledge my inner turmoil. The weeds that choked me were invisible.

I earned top grades at school, won leadership positions at church, and was a trusted guide and mentor at camp. A friend gave me the nickname "Peggy Pedestal" to capture how he felt that my peers all looked up to me. I smiled when he said it. But I laughed sadly to myself as I pictured a trophy to admire, glittering for all to see, but with a lead weight inside.

CHAPTER 15

THE HELPER

All I must do is die to me.
That is the way You make me free
I would give all my dreams
I'd give everything
Just to have you living in me

—Kathy Troccoli, "All I Must Do"

Steph, my brother, and I had a great summer at camp in 1986, and we were hired to return in 1987. These became important summers of growing confidence. I learned more about what my gifts were and practised using them effectively to lead and care for others. We had no one who played a portable instrument on staff, so my singing voice was often called on to start group songs when we had sessions outside or met around the campfire. I loved to make up actions to songs and use crazy voices for improvised characters and for telling stories. I soaked up the experience of living in a community where everyone felt valued, and we learned to lean into one another's strengths. People learned to count on me to follow through with excellence on anything they asked of me.

But sometimes I was puzzled by my emotions.

I would put my cabin of young girls to bed with stories and quiet songs until I heard deep even breathing around the room. Most nights I laid my head down and fell asleep quickly. But sometimes I had a restlessness that would surface in the quiet dark.

I remember, one night in 1986, moving quietly outside and sitting away from the porch light against a stump and crying under the night sky. My director was walking the site before bed and found me there. I couldn't explain why I was crying. She was good to me and prayed for me but thought I was overtired and needed sleep. But moments like this were prodding me to listen to my heart. I felt a deep sort of sad tiredness. I was glad God knew me and saw my broken places when I couldn't face them yet.

Because my faith had become such a deep, complex root system, I was often asked to share scriptures, thoughts, and encouragement. I mined my reflections for things that I could share. I chose resolved lessons of life that might be helpful for someone else. I found my sweet spot as I put experiences and thoughts into words. I was a natural storyteller and teacher.

Helping others became a deeper life purpose that continued in other parts of life after camp. I loved to share encouragement and inspiring thoughts as I prayed for friends that leaned on me. Without being aware of it, my interactions with others gradually became dictated by what I could offer. I grew out of touch with ways that I needed to lean back on friends. Many of my relationships stayed a little removed from my vulnerable thoughts and feelings. I gained esteem from being the strong one who could "help."

The damaging part of having to be strong was that I very seldom let down my guard. I had no off button. At home, camp, church, and school, I heard needs and rose to comfort or help. Empathy and faith came naturally to me, and I liked using these abilities to serve others.

Selflessness was encouraged. I didn't recognize how I stretched it too far by denying that I had any limits or personal needs. My stem of significance was being supported by weeds that placed my value in accomplishments, perfection, and the need to feel needed. I bought into a martyr syndrome that put everyone else's needs before my own even when I had nothing to give. I put up barriers in my relationships that kept me distanced. I refused to be vulnerable because I was afraid of what I didn't understand in myself.

The spring before I turned eighteen, I attended a camping weekend with a large group of youth from around the province. I enjoyed the playful and serious moments. But there was a guy I'll call Edward* who stood out from the rest. Edward was enthusiastic and had a charisma that drew people to him. When we sang around the campfire, he complimented me on my "beautiful voice" and sang exuberantly beside me. He noticed me shivering as the sun went down and wrapped his blanket around the two of us. I felt cared for. We connected in a way that was new and magnetic.

When the programming ended for the day, Edward invited me to join a small group of youth who were going to read scripture together and pray for a while before bed. We started reading aloud portions from Psalms and the Gospels. Edward was a dynamic reader and quickly grasped the emotion of a passage and applied the directives to his own life and heart. It seemed as natural as breathing for him to recognize his shortcomings and confess them, or to pray with a sense of wonder and gratitude. I participated enthusiastically. I loved to read aloud and share my inner faith world with others.

I was encouraged by such a vibrant leader among my peers. As the evening went on, Edward kept grinning widely in my direction and voicing his approval. He spent more and more attention on me. I blossomed under his attentive gaze. The group was gradually losing interest in this spiritual exercise, but Edward and I only grew more fuelled by it. Finally, we all drifted off to our tents for bedtime, but

Edward singled me out to say how happy he was that I had joined them and how he looked forward to connecting over breakfast.

For the rest of the weekend, Edward was never far away. He would find reasons to lean down and whisper something in my ear, to be my partner in a game, or to sit beside me while the speaker gave a talk. Because I had heard the sincerity of his prayers and his love for the elevated thoughts found in the Bible, I began to relax with him as I seldom did around guys my age. He was kind and thoughtful, and quick to notice the needs around him and jump up to meet them. Overall, Edward made a deep impression on me.

What I felt stirring towards Edward was not something I wanted to bring up with my girlfriends. They would tease and make more of it than existed at the moment. But if he stayed in touch after the weekend was over, I decided, maybe I would let myself speculate.

Edward called me a few times to get together for a hike or an ice cream. As the school year was winding down, he invited me to see the conservation area where he would spend the summer. He told me funny stories from his experiences with children the summer before. He was most enthusiastic about helping open the door of hope and faith to the young boys in his groups. Edward and I had so much in common.

As I packed for my third summer at camp in 1987, I felt like a veteran counsellor.

Edward wrote each week that summer without fail. I always wrote back, sharing a poetic thought, a flash of insight, or a funny anecdote from my days counselling young girls. I found my thoughts drifting increasingly to what I might tell Edward the next time I wrote or saw him. He was beginning to be a main character in my inner world. I was concerned that I might become too attached to someone who was just a friend. He had the potential to be a distraction.

Late in August, as the evenings grew cooler and staff came to morning devotions with a blanket wrapped around them, I got a beautiful card from Edward explaining that he had a three-day break coming up and would come to visit me. His visit aligned with my time off. My pulse raced when I anticipated seeing him again. I tried to downplay my emotional response and reproached myself for reading too much into his attention. We were just friends, after all.

As Family Camp ended, we had a speaker explain the significance of fasting as a way to connect with God's guidance and direction. I had always trusted that God knew what was best for me, but I was never sure when my own mind was asserting my desires and will over God's designs. I wanted so badly for my life to matter. I wanted to be swept up in a vision more beautiful than I could imagine or plan.

So, one lunch hour, I decided to miss lunch to have time to pray and be still to listen. I also had a feeling that I had better give to God my feelings for Edward and ask for direction about that relationship. I'd learned a scripture verse: "'For I know the plans I have for you,' declares the LORD, 'plans to prosper you and not to harm you, plans to give you hope and a future. You will seek me and find me when you seek me with all your heart.'" (Jeremiah 29:11, 13, NIV).

So I was determined to seek hard. I yielded my plans, my hopes, my dreams, and my heart, praying that my life would be God's to lead, shape, and guide. I felt refreshed and peaceful when I joined the afternoon activities with no hunger pangs from my missed lunch.

A few days later, when Edward met me and a few friends at a beach, my joy was an honest offering of friendship between kindred spirits. Edward displayed good empathy when he joined me in looking for ways to serve and care for my friends. What stood out were his kindness and outgoing joyful care. He also continued to pay close attention to me, anticipating my needs and listening closely to my thoughts. He entered every moment fully. Everything about him drew me out.

My reserved nature had never found such resonance in another human being. He was so outgoing and friendly that it was easy to follow his lead in meeting new people—something I had always had to work myself up for. I soaked in the feeling of connection to another soul. I was glad he would be visiting the area for two whole days. As he headed to his accommodation for the night, he made a point of calling back to me, "Goodnight, Peg! See you in the morning!" I definitely felt special. Maybe this was God's way of showing love to me. "Thank you, God," I whispered as I waved back. It took me a long time to drift off to sleep that night, but my dreams were sweet.

CHAPTER 16

FUTURE DREAMS

> You have searched me, Lord,
> and you know me.
> You know when I sit and when I rise;
> you perceive my thoughts from afar.
> Such knowledge is too wonderful for me,
> too lofty for me to attain.
>
> —Psalm 139:1, 2, 6, NIV

Edward arranged to meet me at a place where I volunteered to lead a children's programme. I'd agreed to lead the three-year-old group for half a day. That morning, we were drawing pictures of people and things that God made unique and special.

"Did God make Mommy?" asked Tommy*.

"Definitely!" I replied as I helped him find another crayon for Mommy's brown hair.

"Did God make fish? Cause I have a goldfish that I really like!" Samantha* gushed.

"Let's find a crayon for your goldfish ... What colour suits him best?" I asked as I held up two likely colours.

Samantha pointed to the orange. "That one is just right."

Julian* started to squirm, and I recognized the signs of a looming bathroom trip. I was just about to suggest the whole group take a trip down the hall to the restroom when I noticed Edward at the door, watching me with an amused smile on his face. I was surprised he had decided to come. His eyes were gentle and kind as he offered to help. I asked him if he would keep colouring with the group while I ran Julian to the bathroom. Our eyes and smiles communicated our mutual enjoyment and approval.

When I was done for the day, Edward invited me to go to the beach for the afternoon. As Edward and I hiked through the trees, we fell in stride easily but were surprised when we reached the shore. We were alone on our own private section of the beach. We admired together the perfection of the day—the blue sky that was highlighted by the puffy whiteness of the clouds. We voiced a sense of wonder and gratitude at the beauty before us. We played at the water's edge for a bit and compared stories and perceptions about the children we had spent the morning with and then widened the conversation to sharing parts of our summer that hadn't fit into our brief letters.

Edward spoke of how much my letters had encouraged and inspired him. I echoed his thoughts as I reflected on how I had gained strength and faith from his ongoing communication.

We lapsed into a comfortable silence as we stood gazing over the water together. He moved behind me and wrapped his arms around me. I relaxed into his backward hug. Edward said softly, almost in a whisper: "Someday ... I want to marry someone like you."

I felt my whole self warm to his words. My heart resonated with this friend who had become so dear in such a short span of time. I turned to look at him.

Edward looked lit up from the inside even as the sun shone on his face. His eyes were tender and seemed to gently support and hold me. He spoke again: "No ... I said that wrong. Someday I want to marry you, Peggy."

It was as if the heavens opened to smile on us. My relinquishing of the gift of this future dream was somehow being given back to me. Was this God's favour? Was God guiding me to this friend to be a partner in my life? He was someone who already showed that he admired and cared for me in so many gestures, words, letters, and in the way he resonated with my ministry heart.

I didn't say anything; I just leaned back into his arms as we gazed at the sky together, picturing a glorious future. As he stood behind me, he whispered that he had always dreamed of dating someone he cherished by saving the first kiss for their wedding day at the altar. That impressed me. I loved his emphasis on growing together in faith, maturity, and friendship before fanning the physical attraction that was already clear in the magnetism between us. We stood frozen in time for a few minutes before I realized that responsibilities beckoned and it was time to get back.

Edward held my hand and grandly swept a place for me to sit on a log as he played the role of a chivalrous knight. He offered to wash the sand off my feet before we put on our sandals for the hike back to the parking area.

He grabbed a sand bucket and filled it with water from the lake, not seeming to mind the dousing waves that soaked his rolled-up pant cuffs. He took my feet one at a time in his large, warm hands and gently massaged them while carefully removing the sand from between my toes. He then dried my feet with his towel—an intimate gesture promising care and humble attempts to meet my needs in life. In that moment, my heart was his. I was emotionally committed without speaking a word about it. When he left the next morning, it was with a new understanding between us. My mind glowed with possibilities.

My relationship with Edward continued to be a source of support and inspiration during the final weeks at camp. After a clean-up of the site and a debrief celebration, I was free to visit Edward where he worked.

Edward gave me the grand tour. As we walked around hand in hand, each location sparked new memories and exchanges. It felt as though our minds and hearts were so in sync that we would never run out of things to share and explore together. The day was perfect, the crispness of August warming to bright summer temperatures by noon. I was glad for the layers I could shed as the day warmed. Oddly, I never felt like lowering the layers that covered my secret broken places. I was growing in emotional attachment with Edward but didn't yet feel the time was right to share anything but the ideal parts of myself. It was our ideals and dreams that most connected us. We were both natural dreamers.

Edward started to confide that he had been taking medication for some time, but he had felt God's healing that summer and so had stopped taking it. I trusted Edward and the God who had led us together, and so I had no premonition of any bumps on the path ahead.

CHAPTER 17

CHOOSING PEACE

> Loss of a sense of self: Sexually abused persons often seem like strangers to their own soul and history. Many times, the chronic patterns of lying or deceit common to abused persons arise because of a forsaken history that forces them to concoct a past and a present that has no connection to their abused soul. The consequence is not only a loss of the past but also a loss of the ability to judge the present.
>
> —Dan Allender, *The Wounded Heart*

Grade 13 was shaping up to be a very different year for me. My spare thoughts were happily occupied with dreaming of a bright future. I had started knitting a scarf for Edward to find a place to unleash the stitches of brightness that were growing in me. I could picture spending the rest of my life with him. Around him, I felt attractive and at home; it seemed that my beautiful imaginary world was becoming real.

My classmates shared most courses that year, and we helped one another study at lunch in the hall set aside for seniors. My school friends had matured a lot, and I felt comfortable with most of them. My summers at camp also made me more self-confident and relaxed in my abilities.

Then something happened to shatter my complacency and make me question my dreams.

I was used to Edward calling a few times a week around nine o'clock as I was winding down for bed. We would talk, often for an hour, up until my brother's prearranged nightly check-in with his girlfriend.

One night as we were talking, Edward said he felt God was wanting to show us both something. He began to talk as though he were God's mouthpiece, reciting scriptures about God's knowledge and care for me. He got specific about affirming my gifts, and my heart, and he showed insight that seemed divine. The affirmation made tears stream down my face as it began to chip away at the shame root that was so much a part of how I perceived myself. God's love began to break through a little more, like a shaft of light.

Edward talked about being a truth teller that helped break down walls while I was a soothing presence to comfort and heal afterward. We made a great team, he thought.

Then Edward said that he thought God was calling us to go to Bible college in the United States, and that there would be plane tickets waiting for us at the Toronto airport if we had the faith to go.

This would be a crazy change of plans for me. I had read stories where God had led and provided in just such a way. Would God want to move in my life like that? I wanted to be open to God's direction. I decided to put my trust in God to confirm this idea through my parents' support. This became my test of discernment, like the Bible story of Gideon's fleece (Judges 6:36–40). If my parents felt good about me going to Bible college, I would take a step forward. But if they felt a caution against it, I wouldn't go.

The next day after school, I sat outside on my front porch steps to pray and to be free from distractions. Then I noticed something odd.

I heard the first plane fly over our property in a detached manner. But when ten flew over in the next few minutes, it began to grab my attention. By the end of the hour, almost one hundred planes had flown over my home. Could this have been God telling me that the tickets for my journey of faith were indeed waiting for me at the airport? The excitement began to build as I pictured myself as part of God's story—learning to be a world-changing, light-bearing follower. Was God turning my world upside down to bring about new growth, sweeping me up in a vision far greater than I could imagine? Was Edward right about God's plans for me?

I decided to test it out with my parents. That night after supper, I asked to speak with my folks alone. We settled into the living room, where the early fall sun still streamed through the large window. I began to feel nervous, but determined, as I tried to find a way to share my growing wonderings.

I had already made a list of the pros and cons of leaving. The biggest pro was my desire to do what God wanted me to do with my life. As I began to talk, I felt my mom tense. The idea of leaving high school before I finished my grade 13 year seemed outrageous. My mom was an educator, and school always came first. I assured my parents that I would listen to their counsel and had placed myself under their authority. But I wanted them to seek God about it and not just give an automatic answer based on their own thoughts and emotions. I asked that they take the next few days to think and pray about it. Then I said goodnight and headed off to bed.

Edward came down the next day for a weekend visit. He picked me up from my house after dinner to drive to a youth gathering. Suddenly he said that he felt as though God was guiding him to stop at the restaurant coming up on our left.

I found this a little odd but waited to see what Edward would do. He saw a group of guys sitting at a booth. I knew them from school as the wild party grads from the grade ahead of me. I stayed in the car while Edward strode purposefully into the restaurant to talk to them. Edward may have felt led by God, but I just felt uncomfortable. I had to fight the urge to sink low enough that the dashboard would hide me from anyone that might recognize me.

I didn't know what was being said, but I could see Edward's arms waving excitedly and the faces of the guys looking closed and amused. I was guessing that if Edward was trying to share his faith, the guys weren't wanting what he was selling. After about five minutes, Edward came back to the car elated and confident that he had accomplished God's mission for him there.

Somehow, I didn't feel as if I were in the presence of a hero from my fantasies, but rather a stranger that made me feel uncomfortable.

We were back on the road for only a moment before Edward announced again that he felt God leading him to turn left, and then right, and then he came to a stop in front of a house that had the porch light on. Again, Edward was certain that he was to speak with someone here. Moments later, a car pulled into the driveway and Edward took that as a sign that these were the people he was being sent to talk with. I again refused to get out of the car, and I even tried to persuade Edward not to intrude on people's privacy. But Edward was on a mission.

I knew God could set up divine appointments, but wouldn't the hearers be expecting, or at least open to, the encounter?

Again I watched while Edward approached the couple with enthusiasm. Whatever was being said, the body language of the couple quickly registered discomfort and then alarm. They finally asked Edward to leave their property or they would call the police. Edward called out a blessing for the couple as they hurried into the house before he came back to the car.

By now I was feeling upset.

In contrast, Edward was so excited he was finding it hard to contain his enthusiasm. He was almost vibrating with energy as he talked loudly and swiftly while in constant motion. I questioned Edward in the car to gain some understanding of the conversation I'd only observed. I wondered at the tone Edward used as he quickly shut my questions down and remained confident in God's leading.

When we pulled into the parking lot, Edward turned to me and said, "If you are not for me, you stand against me." Then he strode off alone into the trees nearby.

His wording was so similar to the New Testament: "If God is for us, who can be against us" (Romans 8:31, NIV). I couldn't help feeling that Edward equated agreeing with him with standing with God.

I was shaken. I headed towards the youth gathering and tried to make sense of what I'd seen and heard. Why would something led by God be uncomfortable and threatening? My pictures of Jesus were life-giving and beautiful. My experiences of correction and divine help were filled with a quiet conviction of the heart in an approach and timing that opened rather than closed an ongoing spiritual conversation. But I couldn't talk to Edward about my impressions and reservations. Instead I prayed for us both and was determined to clear the air with him and make things comfortable again.

***

When the programme finished for the evening, I asked Edward if we could speak privately somewhere. Edward drove me to a park where we could walk. I apologized for questioning him earlier. I felt perhaps I had misunderstood what I saw, and I reaffirmed my confidence in him.

Edward hugged me and thanked me for my gracious, kind heart. He danced with me under the stars for a moment. Then he surprised me by crossing a line he had declared that beautiful day on the beach—he kissed me. I was relieved to be at peace with Edward again and felt committed to our future, so I relaxed into his kiss. His hug became more exploring, and his kiss deepened in intensity. I had never experienced the rush of sensations that coursed through me. I felt loved and desired, but also disappointed and confused. Another of my ideals was being stripped away. I began to wonder whether my expectations of Edward were realistic. Maybe guys were wired differently. The weeds of identity as a peacemaker and a pleaser grew alongside my deep convictions and ideals. This physical encounter made me at war with myself. In my mind, I was already damaged goods. So my past experiences became the line I drew for physical closeness. I felt that was the best I could do to keep peace and be true to my convictions. And I consoled myself that this was the man that I would someday marry.

Edward drove me back to my parents' house, where he was spending the night. I moved into hostess mode, playing house. I found him a snack, a towel, and a washcloth as I made sure his bed was made and ready. He was exuberant and happy and found delight in the small ways I tried to please him.

We said goodnight and headed to our separate rooms for the night.

Somehow, the evening had lost its charm for me. As I talked to God about it that night, I wondered whether God was trying to show me the hard parts of marrying a young man with mood swings. I didn't question my commitment to him. The physical connection we had built this evening only heightened my sense of loyalty. And my fasting time in the summer was a sign I linked in my mind as an open door to this relationship, so I would give it my best to make it work.

I hoped our day together tomorrow would heighten my confidence that all was well and that this decision would lead me to a beautiful future.

CHAPTER 18

LOYALTY

> "For I know the plans I have for you," declares the Lord, "plans to prosper you and not to harm you, plans to give you hope and a future."
>
> —Jeremiah 29:11, NIV

The next morning, Edward joined my family at the breakfast table in high spirits. He was charming and polite to my parents and treated my family with warmth beyond the newness of their relationship. I admired the ease of Edward's manner. He never seemed intimidated in relating to people. He was always confident and expected people to like him. He approached everyone as a potential friend. I was so much more likely to hold back and see whether there was a space for me—a warm look, an invitation. I never assumed I would be welcomed by others.

Again I played the hostess, picturing that this might someday be my home, my husband. I wanted everything to match my ideals, which had been derived from my favourite family sitcoms. My future dreams included a husband who loved God and me. I someday wanted children that I could pour into with love and understanding. I also longed for the day when I would no longer be dominated by guilt and shame; I wanted to be free to love and be loved.

By lunchtime, though, cracks were beginning to show in the reality of a day with Edward. He had wandered into the woods for a walk alone that morning while I was showering. When I met him outside, he had something fluffy on his face. When I brushed it off, he explained that he had felt assured by the scripture where Paul is bitten by a poisonous snake and yet lives that God would protect him from harm no matter what he put in his mouth. What he meant was that he had been sampling weeds to see whether they would make him feel sick—and because he wasn't harmed, he was sure that God was protecting him.

This was an odd test in my mind. Why would anyone need to see whether he or she would get sick from eating weeds while taking a walk through the woods? And how did that equate with God's protection?

I decided to move the conversation to safer ground. We discussed the beauty of the day and decided to read some psalms of thanks aloud. I also ventured to show Edward a few of the poems and songs I had written over the past few years. He was full of admiration and sincere affection. He kept wanting to kiss me. I was responsive yet tried to keep us moving towards sharing thoughts and insights instead of physical connection, especially with my family present in the rooms all around us.

At lunchtime, another odd incident occurred. Edward was pouring water for everyone around the table when inspiration seemed to strike. As he filled the last glass, he began quoting from the Bible about his cup running over, and then he let the water flow over the brim of the cup and into a growing puddle all over the table. My mom quickly righted the pitcher and removed it from his hands, then grabbed a cloth to clean up.

There was an awkward look passed between my mother and

me, but Edward seemed oblivious and unconcerned—even jubilant. After lunch, Edward and I were talking on the lawn, sitting side by side. I stood to pull Edward up so we could go to visit a friend for the afternoon. When I reached down to help him up, Edward suddenly pulled me down on top of him and kissed me deeply and passionately. As soon as he released me, I rolled away from him and stood. As my eyes floated towards the back door, I saw my mom standing there looking shocked and concerned. I went to speak to her.

Mom mentioned that she saw the kiss and thought it was inappropriate. I explained that Edward caught me off guard and pulled me down. I knew the discernment I had asked my parents to give about going with Edward to Bible College was tipping quickly towards the 'no' side. I suddenly realized that I was okay with that. It wasn't really my dream. I just wanted to follow where God would lead, but I was enjoying my last year at high school. I didn't welcome upheaval. And having Edward as my only known companion was suddenly less appealing than it had been.

The rest of the day followed without alarming incidents, and Edward again turned in for the night.

The next day, Edward again was exuberant and a little over the top. My mom had arranged for the minister to come over to talk some sense into me. While we were seated in the living room, Edward came out in a towel, wet from his shower, and tried to share with my family some new theological insight he'd gained. I guess he was too excited about his thought to bother putting on clothing. I was embarrassed by his nakedness and agreed with my mother that he was exhibiting concerning behaviour and might need a doctor's attention. The minister listened to Edward while coaxing him to go and get dressed. Then he began reminding me that God's Spirit brings order, not chaos. Edward's behaviour certainly reminded me more of a whirlwind than a peaceful, safe place. When the minister and my mom talked to Edward about his illness, he remained adamant that he'd been healed and no longer needed medication.

As the afternoon progressed, Edward became more and more agitated. When Edward and I came back from a walk, my mom had contacted Edward's parents with her concerns.

It wasn't long before Edward's parents arrived to escort Edward to the hospital. Edward kept insisting nothing was wrong and pleaded with me to believe in him. Tears quietly rolled down my cheeks as he grabbed my hand like a lifeline. My heart felt as if it were breaking, but I knew I had to let him go to get the help he needed.

I promised to visit soon and assured him that we could still talk on the phone whenever he liked. His parents escorted Edward to the car and helped him into the backseat. He didn't resist, but he looked defeated, like a martyr—misunderstood and dejected.

I saw his posture of defeat and resolved to stick by him in this rough patch. His behaviour made more sense as I had the manic side of his illness explained to me.

I would hold on to what I knew of him before this weekend. That was the true Edward. This was an illness affecting his judgement. I would be steadfast and remind him of the best in him. I caught a glimpse of how I could be important to his recovery. My imagination painted visions of how I could pray for him, sing to him, be a steady presence to care, listen, and help restore the young man I had grown to care for. This was just a bump in the road. My future with God and Edward could still be bright.

CHAPTER 19

CONNECTED TO A WHIRLWIND

Be still, and know that I am God.

—Psalm 46:10, NIV

Life settled into predictable, safe routines of school, homework, youth group, Sunday services, regular phone chats with Steph, family dinners, and piano lessons. I had gratefully let go of any thought of leaving high school early to attend Bible College.

I was still knitting a scarf for Edward, which kept him in my thoughts and prayers. He called once or twice a week, but I no longer felt fuelled by our conversations. His monologs about the Bible became convoluted paths of confusion. Sadly, his strange interpretations were beginning to colour my reading times. God had always been my refuge, but now one of my ways of listening for God's loving voice in the Bible had become filled with static and chaos. I could no longer read with the trusting simplicity that had previously characterized my quiet times. Edward's odd twists of interpretation kept ringing in my head. I finally stopped reading the Bible and gravitated to reading simple stories of faith from Spire Christian Comics—Archie, Betty, and Veronica talking about God's love and restoration. I needed theology at its simplest just then.

I went to visit Edward at the hospital where he was being treated, with a desire to help. I had to be buzzed into his ward and sign in. The tight security took me by surprise. I'd never been to this part of the hospital before. As I walked towards his room, there were patients on the floor pacing and staring blankly, and I picked up a feeling of heaviness and despair. I felt uncomfortable by myself but persisted in my search for Edward.

Edward lit up when he saw me. He wanted to introduce me to some of his friends. My heart warmed at his enthusiastic response to my visit. As we walked to the common room, Edward never stopped talking. He was full of stories of God using him to be a light to people on his floor. He played the saviour role in every tale. The staff made him take his medication, though he still wasn't convinced he needed it.

I never tried to contradict him or upset him, but I began to feel divided in myself. My thoughts and perceptions weren't matching with Edward's, but I dared not voice them. I wanted to bring stability and peace, not conflict and agitation.

There was a piano in the common room. This was something familiar and safe. I gravitated to the keyboard and began to play and sing a worship song I had memorized in my piano lessons so I could play it in a church service that fall. Edward was delighted, and some of the other residents seemed cheered by the music. They urged me to play another song, and even a third, before I had to admit that they had exhausted my repertoire of memorized pieces.

Edward was restless and wanted to go outside for a walk around the property. He urged me to sign him out. I found it strange to think that I would be seen as responsible for Edward if I signed the clipboard. He had always taken the lead in our relationship. But I felt a walk outside might do us both some good. It was a crisp autumn day, and the fresh air was full of the scent of leaves.

The walk was a good idea, it seemed. Edward was full of energy and took a short run ahead of me and then urged me to catch up. Within ten minutes, we were both out of breath and out of sight of the building that enforced Edward's confinement. Edward was impulsive, and I was still getting used to his sudden changes in mood and direction.

There were some woods on the grounds, and he led me into them. Then, suddenly, he grabbed me in a tight embrace and kissed me deeply. I was already out of breath, then I felt conflicted. I loved this young man, didn't I? I thought God had opened the door to our relationship, right? Why did I want to pull away from his physical intensity? In my mind, this wasn't romance; it was just a passion that I had already been burned by before. How had I got here again—to a place where physical closeness felt forced, making me detach emotionally? What was wrong with me that I couldn't keep from being in these situations? Each encounter made me feel as if I lost a little more of my self-respect—another piece of me gone— my innocence, my idealism. I felt dirty and cheap. Yet I had never learned to have my own voice at these times. It was as if I became frozen. I had nourished the weeds that trained me to avoid conflict and to please people. Dissociation allowed me to retain my elevated ideals as a refuge. But I didn't know how to navigate this sexually charged space. I reminded him that I wanted to wait until we were married. Again I tried to please Edward without crossing the line defined by my past abuse, and then I moved us back to public spaces. I kept the visit short after we signed back onto the floor.

I consoled myself on the drive home that nothing had happened to me that hadn't happened before. At least I was dating this young man. I supposed I was still dating him, anyhow. I certainly felt committed, and we had never broken up. But this was hardly what I had imagined dating my future husband would feel like.

Things will get better once his medication kicks in, right? I wondered. It could take a few months to see if he was receiving the proper dosage, and a few months more to measure any changes.

Yet no matter what my mind used to console me, guilt and shame screamed louder.

"How can you lead others when you can't even lead yourself? You speak of God's love, but you know God must be disappointed in you! Where are your ideals now? Your fantasy world is just that—a figment of your imagination! You aren't worthy of God's best. Strive, give, care ... but you'll always be dirty and small in your secret self."

One more heavy secret. The silence of it rang loudly in my ears!

CHAPTER 20

GIVE YOURSELF AWAY

> Boundaries define us. They define what is me and what is not me. A boundary shows me where I end and someone else begins, leading me to a sense of ownership. Knowing what I am to own and take responsibility for gives me freedom. If I know where my yard begins and ends, I am free to do with it what I like. Taking responsibility for my life opens up many different options. However, if I do not "own" my life, my choices and options become very limited.
>
> —Dr. Henry Cloud and Dr. John Townsend, *Boundaries*

By December, the scarf for Edward was complete. I felt hopeful as I looked at this labour of love—every stitch filled with prayers and dreams for a bright future.

Even better, Edward was released from the hospital and living back at his parents' house. I couldn't wait to see whether we could recover the relational connection and ideal space we had shared before Edward's episode. He was better now. We could begin to build again.

I had plans to drive to his parents' house to deliver my knitted gift and go out for a dinner date at a restaurant of Edward's choice. As I pulled up to the house, I took a last look at my reflection in the mirror, tucked in a stray curl, and smiled at the bright, hopeful look in my eyes. I grabbed the carefully wrapped package and the poetic card I had poured my heart into and stepped lightly from the car. I was a little nervous as I rang the doorbell. Would his parents answer? What would I say to them? We had met only briefly that day when they came to take their son to the hospital—not the ideal way to meet the parents!

I was relieved when Edward opened the door wide, and he quickly buried my head in his chest with his exuberant hug. He had missed me and couldn't wait to spend time together!

As we sat in the living room, Edward mentioned that his parents were out for the evening. I shyly offered my artistic creation to Edward for him to open. I hoped he liked it and understood that it wasn't just a scarf, but a labour of love and steadfast hope. He quickly tore away the paper and lifted the lid of the box. When he heard that I had made it for him throughout the months of his recovery, his eyes lit up and he proudly put on my offering. It suited him perfectly in colour and style.

He slung his arm over my shoulders and pulled me in tight for a side hug. When he saw the card that had dropped to the floor, he bent to pick it up and apologized for his clumsiness in not opening it first. He made me feel like a rock star the way he exclaimed over my poetic efforts. Edward's gift to me was a carved Christmas ornament with the word "JOY" in the centre of it, along with a white dove and musical notes. He scratched my name into the edge, saying that the symbols reminded him of me. I felt affirmed as I understood joy as my heart language.

Then Edward leaned back on the couch with me tucked beside him and began to talk about events I had missed in his life and asked good questions to draw me out. I began to relax and enjoy the conversation, and I found myself sharing things I didn't normally talk about—ideas about faith, and concern for friends I cared about. Edward let me talk of things that burdened my heart, then he grabbed hold of my hand and prayed with me to share the load.

By the time we left for the restaurant, I was feeling alive and confident. When he had asked me where I felt like eating, I'd said I'd leave it up to him. I knew that no matter where we went, I would order chicken fingers and fries. It was inexpensive and predictable. I wasn't adventurous with my food. Decision-making was generally hard for me, so I preferred to defer, when I could, to someone else, or to fall back on a fail-safe choice that required little thought. What does the stomach matter to a heart that is full to the brim with hope and faith?

I clearly undervalued my body's needs.

Edward directed me to our destination. Conversation flowed along easily, though Edward's perceptions rang falsely to my ears sometimes. He still seemed to have a bit of an inflated saviour complex. I found it hard to relate to some of his interpretations of scripture, but I was afraid to disagree, as I felt it might trigger a negative response. The evening was largely pleasant for me, and I didn't want to spoil it. Edward was encouraging and laughed at my attempts at humour. I didn't think of myself as a funny person, so I was pleased when Edward understood my playful moments.

After dinner, we decided to take a short walk before heading back to Edward's parents. The brisk evening made our cheeks rosy, and we huddled close together against the cold. Edward kept trying to kiss me. Though I wasn't comfortable with such public displays of affection, I went along with his lead. I obeyed the strong impulse to never create unpleasantness between us.

Back at his parents', Edward became physical quickly, and I

scrambled to remind him of our talk about waiting for marriage. I tried to please him and my sense of rightness at the same time. I felt a wave of shame surface again—felt my cheeks flush and my throat constrict. This wasn't how I wanted this evening to end! I had to leave.

After promises that we would talk soon and set another date, I began the drive back to my parents. I found myself teary and sad as I drove in the silence of the night.

In my journal that night I wrote,

> Dear God, I've failed You again! I only want to do what's right. I keep making a mess of things—I'm sorry for being a disappointment. God, is it wrong to feel so distraught—does that disappoint You, too? Am I being selfish? I know what is right, so I struggle against myself. Am I just a stone pillar on the outside, as inside I crumble? I need You, God—I know you love unconditionally, but I can't seem to take that in—all I feel is disappointment mixed with the duty to care well for the partner I've been given. I wonder whether my heart will ever feel free.

CHAPTER 21

A BEGINNING AND AN END

> And I'm so glad, though it hurts to know I'm leaving
> Everything I ever thought that I would be
> Once I held it in my hand
> It was a kingdom made of sand
> But now you've blown it all away
> I can't believe that I can say that I'm glad
>
> —Amy Grant, Chris Christian, and
> Brown Bannister, "So Glad"

Though Edward was home from the hospital, our relationship never regained the comfort and connection that had characterized it in the beginning. We spoke regularly on the phone, but I didn't often make time for visits.

I was hired to work at camp for the upcoming season. But just before staff training weekend, Edward ended up back in the hospital. And by the time I returned from summer camp ready for my first year of university, Edward had left the country to attend a Bible college in the States. Edward drifted to the back burner of my thoughts and attention. Though we had never defined a breakup, it was clear that we were no longer acting like a couple.

I was moving on.

After a great summer at a new camp with a role tailored to my gifts, I was ready for the challenge of moving to a new city for school.

That fall, I moved into the residence on a full scholarship at Wilfrid Laurier University. My life moved into an exciting new time of meeting the twenty-eight girls on my floor. I decided from the beginning to intentionally live beyond my natural reserve. I pushed myself to be friendly, initiate conversations, and encourage those around me instead of withdrawing into insecurity.

I was nervous about living among girls from such varied backgrounds and value systems. I was thankful for my roommate, Leah, whom I knew from high school; we had shared youth and camp experiences over the years. Leah and I prayed that there would be at least one kindred spirit among our floormates. I hoped to find a friend or two who could share deeper conversations and connections. Being mutually encouraged by one another's faith (a notion I had learned from Romans 1:12) was something I held on to as I kept my eyes and heart open.

Frosh week quickly highlighted a few girls who shared my values. I found we were syncopating the pep rally cheers to leave out the swear words. There were also alternative activities run by the campus Christian groups during the nights when beer parties were on the schedule. A hike organized by Laurier Christian, fellowship executive to Elora Gorge, cemented some new friendships. I was thrilled to see several girls from my floor there!

The Christian girls on my floor started to meet regularly and look out for each other. When there were floor parties, everyone was expected to attend. One floor would invite another over for games and then a dance party where, inevitably, there would be a keg brought out to share. My new friends and I would take part enthusiastically in the ice-breaker games, and when the dance party started, we would have a can of pop and dance to a few songs. If a boy tried to pair off with one of us, the others would ask with a glance whether there was a need for backup. If the look said, "please help," the others would join the pair and form a dance circle.

We decided before the party that we would cut out once the drinking started in earnest. After we felt we had stayed long enough to honour our hosts, we'd head to my room for tea. So began a regular ritual of connecting, praying for each other, and laughing over a small pot of tea. I would pull out my guitar and songbook from camp and lead a time of sharing, reflection, and worship. Our prayers matched our desire to care well for the girls on our floor and the fellow students in our classes, as well as each other.

I decided that I would keep an open-door policy in residence. I voiced to this small circle of friends my ideal of welcoming people who came to my door as a gift from God. I would make time for them, trusting that God would help me manage my classwork around these divine appointments.

Living in Waterloo opened so many new opportunities. As I was settling in, I got a call from Steph's friend. I worked on staff with Lance when he came on-site as a program leader for youth camp during the summer. I had often heard him speak to groups, and I admired his fun, caring leadership style. Lance called to see whether I would be interested in leading a small group for some of the high school students who had been at camp with us. This was a group of campers who wanted to stay connected and keep exploring their faith and putting down roots that would nourish and ground them. In fact, the group would be called Roots.

I felt honoured to be invited to lead and embraced the role as a gift to my growth. Team leadership always stretched me. Preparing to teach and share kept me searching for creative ways to articulate my journey with God. I didn't know the other two guys I'd be leading with, but I trusted Lance's judgement. Lance offered to drive me to each meeting to make it possible for me to lead, since the group would meet on the other side of town. Lance also mentioned other leadership opportunities with camp people—monthly worship services, monthly study groups for those who wanted to dig deeper, and, of course, the planning meetings to prepare. I loved this new community Lance opened to me. I found it fuelling and hope-inspiring to see such a committed group of peers that set aside time to mentor youth.

I was soon swept up in a world of meaningful service, stimulating faith conversations, and growing friendships with people that inspired and nourished my soul both on and off campus. I was amazed at how quickly this new city felt like home. My heart was putting down new roots.

On campus, the Christian group—Laurier Christian Fellowship (LCF)—supplied friendships that went beyond the surface chatter that I often found draining. I loved that anywhere I went on campus, I would find faces I recognized and connections that I valued. Some of my camp friends also came to LCF, which brought a welcome sense of cohesion to the various communities where I felt at home. The campus group was always looking for ways to serve the crowds of students at the university. This resonated deeply with my desire for purpose and meaning.

My classwork was interesting and stimulating. It was great to be with others who enjoyed learning! I was happy to live this shared life with floormates, classmates, small groups, large groups, and planning teams. But it was sometimes hard to have no space to just let down my guard and to stop feeling that I had to perform and be "on" for others. I didn't have a private room. My roommate was great, but I could never really be alone unless I went to a cubicle in the library and tried to block out all the other cubicles around me.

Sometimes at night, I would face the wall and cry silently … and wonder why I was crying. Life was full of meaning, purpose, opportunity, and great people. Though my days were satisfying and full, I wondered why sometimes my soul felt ragged and worn and neglected. I felt disconnected from myself and depleted.

I would just assume I needed sleep and would rehearse in my mind what I would say if someone who cared asked how I was. I'd say something honest, but not too vulnerable. I didn't know how to explain the crying episodes or sadness that still loomed under the surface sometimes. How could I share something I couldn't even begin to unpack? It was easier to tell someone about physical symptoms. It was honest to say that I had a headache or needed more sleep, because that was always true.

I still hated feeling weak or needy. It was easier to be the strong one. Words could be constructed to hide behind, as well as to reveal. I was best at wearing strength on the outside and tucking away the parts that confused me or that I considered unhelpful.

One evening, I shared a thought with our small group floor Bible study that had stuck with me from a sermon. The distinction had been made between happiness and joy. Happiness depends on circumstances and life events and so can be fleeting. Joy, however, is a deeper reality based on God's goodness and care and can become an unshakeable reality to anchor us. I resonated with this observation. Joy was my native response to wholehearted worship, meaningful conversation, and transcendent beauty. I felt most alive when I felt joyful.

The girls and I suggested we be accountability allies to help remind each other to embrace joy. We called it a "joy check." It started as a fun reminder but gradually started to wear on me, as I wasn't always ready to think "joy" when in the middle of an essay or reading for a class. Joy could be tapped into as I reflected on beautiful things, but I didn't know what to do when I was numb or felt sad. I was confused by the evidence of trauma that would intrude sometimes in my reactions to life.

The chipper greeting from my doorway—"Joy check!"—felt like

one more place where I couldn't measure up to my ideals. I tried to shake the judgement my conscience served up, but it was a relentless tyrant. I was so easily disappointed in myself. I wasn't sure how to displace this perfectionistic streak that made grace hard to grasp.

I was getting ready for my first-semester university finals when I heard from Edward. He called to say he was home for Christmas break and wondered whether he could see me.

I was surprised to hear from him. My heart skipped a beat, and I wondered at the connection I still felt for this guy who had dropped out of my life for months. I had seen him as my tragic first love. I had given so much to making my relationship with Edward work, but I felt it only exposed something broken in me that I didn't understand. Reflecting on it only reinforced my feeling of shame; I wasn't sure whether I would ever find a healthy soul mate.

And then Edward was back.

What did it mean? Was I still to honour the signs I interpreted as meaning that God wanted me to be with Edward? After all that happened to sour my memories of the times we shared, would I be called to open that door again? Did I have a choice? Oddly, I didn't even ask that question.

I told him that he could come. I met him at the bus station, and he lit up when he saw me, as he always did. I had butterflies in my stomach, but I stepped into his embrace. He was wearing the scarf I had made. I was surrounded by it and by the memory of all the care and love that went into each stitch as I had pictured a happy future with him. He smelled good and seemed steady as he talked of Bible college and all he was learning. He filled the silences on the bus ride to my dorm. I didn't say much. I focussed on listening and making the empathic sounds that came naturally to me. My heart was beating a little too fast, and I was taking calming breaths while smiling and responding robotically. I wasn't sure what I felt or thought. Everything was happening as if I were observing it from a distance and trying to discern what I witnessed. I didn't want to ride the highs and lows of Edward's mood swings again. I was listening but wary.

Maybe it was this detachment that made the whole visit seem like a dream sequence. The part that stood out from all Edward said was his announcement that we should officially let each other go. He wasn't seeing anyone else yet, but he wanted to end things clearly between us so we didn't hold each other back.

Something inside me felt released, like a bird that was suddenly given the chance to fly from the cage. I was able to enjoy Edward as a friend now that nothing more was expected of me. I wasn't inclined to extend the visit. We had dinner at a nearby student hangout and then he walked away with a smile and a wave.

It was really over. My tragic romance concluded with a lighter heart than I felt it should warrant. Shouldn't I feel depressed? I couldn't explain how, but by cutting the emotional tie, the tragedy seemed much lighter to bear.

I made a new resolve not to trust signs to discern God's plans for me; I would look for the fruits of God's Spirit instead: love, joy, peace, patience, kindness, goodness, faithfulness, gentleness, and self-control. [4] Especially self-control!

CHAPTER 22

ATTEMPTS TO LOVE

> Rejoice with those who rejoice; mourn with those who mourn. Live in harmony with one another. Do not be proud, but be willing to associate with people of low position. Do not be conceited. Do not repay anyone evil for evil. Be careful to do what is right in the eyes of everyone. If it is possible, as far as it depends on you, live at peace with everyone.
>
> Romans 12:15–18, NIV

Another person was becoming a steady presence in my life. I enjoyed my weekly car rides with Lance. He was sensitive and kind, had great insights, and could follow my thoughts about classes and theology. He even understood my humour and laughed at some of the funny anecdotes that arose from my living with twenty-eight other girls in residence. Lance was often leading events where he asked me to help. Soon I was making phone calls, mailing invitations, and stretching to do things that were out of my comfort zone because Lance asked me to.

I loved the creativity of planning ministry events for camp youth. I sang on worship teams, helped lead small group discussions, shaped skits, and taught in tandem with a gifted group of leaders. And always among the group was Lance; he was thoughtful, funny, likeable—and dating a girl I admired who was attending Bible school in England that year. I felt lucky to call him "friend." Lance often called to check on details of ministry, but one time he said something that made me feel inexplicably happy. It was just a little statement, but such things can make lasting impressions.

"Hi, Peggy. I was calling to see if you needed a ride to Roots this week … not that I need a reason to call you."

That was it: "… not that I need a reason to call you." It repeated itself in my mind, making my heart swell with joy. I was thankful that he saw me as more than a willing worker. I was beginning to count him as a friend and was glad he felt the same way. Unexpectedly, I had begun to pray for a life partner, and a certain image filled my mind—someone like Lance.

Meanwhile, on my floor, I was enjoying the company of the girls. They would drop in and talk about anything. I loved our community!

As I respected and cared for them, the girls were also kind and protective. One day, Angelo walked into the common area lounge where I was reading. Angelo had a reputation as a player. He had already dated a few of my floormates and had a big presence in any crowd. Angelo slung his arm around my shoulders and turned on the charm. At that moment, one of my floormates who came from my high school, Patricia, came into the lounge and looked straight at Angelo, and said, "No. Not Peg. She isn't like that. You leave her alone, Angelo." And he did.

Another day, I was off to mail a stack of letters to youth involved in one of the discipleship groups when I bumped into another floormate. Diane commented on how many friends I must have to have so much mail to send. I laughed and explained what the mailing was for. Diane, in her typically exuberant way, exclaimed, "God must really like you!"

My most natural response was, "God really likes you, too, Diane!"

But she was trying to say something that required her special emphasis. "But Peg, you do so many kind things; God must *reeeally* like you."

Her approval touched me. I was glad to get to know such lovely people from such varied backgrounds. Knowing I had the favour and care of my floormates whether they shared my faith or not, made a deep impression. I was more determined than ever to serve them well. I loved that the small group that met to sing and pray in my room each week had grown to include people of different denominations. The caring atmosphere that was permeating the dormitory was beautiful to me. I loved how we looked out for each other.

There were bumpy patches that came from living so closely together. Like the time I came back from class and my roommate was fuming because I had locked the door on the way out. I didn't know that she was just down the hall in the lounge and hadn't taken her key with her.

I wilted quickly under criticism, and any mistake I made weighed heavily on my heart. It took a while to shake off the bitter taste of letting someone down or failing in any way. Condemnation seemed to confirm my harsh self-contempt. It lingered over me like a cloud.

I knew God was love, but somehow the shame that lay buried under the surface was triggered by any false move I made. Any evidence that I was wrong or disliked seemed to confirm my inner critic's belief that I was a disappointment. My heart would plead with God not to give up on me—that I would try harder, love better.

I could see God's love for others so easily but had a hard time trusting that love for myself. I was so aware of my flaws and weaknesses. Shame twisted and tormented me. My journal was the place where this pain was poured. I didn't know where else to process it.

> Dear God,
>
> I've failed you again. I want to love you above all. Search me—do I disappoint You? I know the answer ...
>
> God, is it wrong to feel so distraught? Why can't I just be free? I feel like I'm too much—too serious, too intense, too undisciplined, yet too dutiful ... committed but not free to fully love. I can't be useful to You until I know what's wrong inside and lay it down. I want to give all that I am to You, and yet I seem to be dancing like a marionette while demands pull the strings. Sometimes I feel less real, less human than a robot, and yet my human frailties are so real.
>
> I long to spend quiet moments like this with You. It's so hard to understand what I feel; it seems much deeper than words or feelings. How can anyone understand me when I don't understand myself!? Does everyone feel tormented by inadequacy and by fights with their pride? I feel a sense of duty to give yet don't know if I can accomplish a task without failure.
>
> Lord, I long to find Your unconditional love that understands and can help me to know what to pray, how to find answers, how to listen, how to freely give, freely serve, and freely love. Not out of duty

but moved by something more lasting and real. I'm sorry, Lord—I ramble …

I just need to forget about me and praise You, for You alone are true and good. Thank you for knowing me, for calling me your child. I was made to bring You delight. That is my desire: soften my heart, strengthen my faith, and help me to be selfless without denying "me." I don't know how, and guilt strikes either way. I love you, Father … I like calling You that. I feel like a child now. I'd love to crawl up into your lap and sit with You—to enjoy Your closeness. I feel so small, yet so full of yearning. It's good to have Your understanding and know that You are good. Draw me to higher places beyond myself.

My journal entries reveal the disconnect I lived with. I felt out of control of my choices and emotions, and often unable to achieve the goals I set for myself to be a good student while caring well for others. I had learned to be strong for others to lean on but hadn't developed the strength of will to tackle my own goals. I also found it hard to talk with anyone about it or reach out for help. The only way I knew was to shut down emotionally and focus on the needs in front of me. I gained a sense of value from being needed, without any awareness that I was nourishing weeds of pleasing and perfectionism while ignoring the natural, healthy growth of my true personhood.

In university, I continued to field regular calls from younger teens or peers in crisis. I constantly mined my own experiences and knowledge for helpful wisdom to share with my friends and tried to make myself available as often or as much as they needed. I found it hard to know how to end a phone call without hurting someone's feelings. I would often just stay on the line until the other person was talked out.

I valued these interactions, but there was a personal cost. After a few years, I began to hate the phone. I could lose hours as I engaged in small talk to put a friend at ease so he or she would open up about what was really on his or her mind. My schoolwork had to be crammed into late-night writing sessions, and my readings had to wait until urgency pushed them to the top of my list for an assignment or test. I maintained an A- in my classes, but that wasn't enough to keep my scholarship. The free education lasted only for my first year, and then I failed to keep it by three tenths of a grade point. A little more focus on school would have paid off.

Pleasing was an unconscious self-protective strategy that felt like love. I was learning how to open my heart to a wide variety of people and perspectives while staying true to my moral compass and deeply rooted faith. I was learning to love people, but I kept them at a distance, too. By divorcing my actions and knowledge from self-understanding and personal growth, I wasn't creating mutual relationships very often. My closest circle were asking questions and praying for me in a way that was penetrating my armour, but I wasn't ready to remove it.

Dissociation was a way to keep moving forward. I wasn't ready to probe and explore the terrain of my wounded heart. Tucking that away until the timing was right to open past trauma to the light of honest exploration was a survival tactic that worked—mostly. When I look back, I see God's protection and care in the dissociation. I needed to wait for a deep sense of connection and safety to do the hard work of healing. Meanwhile, it was my health that was showing signs of disease. The distress registering in my emotions and physical symptoms held wisdom for me, but I wasn't ready to listen to and unravel their messages yet.

CHAPTER 23

A GLIMPSE OF LIGHT

> The LORD your God is with you;
> He is mighty to save.
> He will take great delight in you.
> He will quiet you with His love;
> He will rejoice over you with singing.
>
> —Zephaniah 3:17, Paraphrase

It was a cold night in February when Lance and I had arranged a planning meeting to prepare for our monthly youth gathering. It was easiest for me to meet on campus, so Lance came over to my dorm to work. We were studying a minor prophet that I had learned about from a compelling professor in my Old Testament class. Hosea was a prophet who followed God's call to marry a prostitute. Just as God loved Israel even when the nation was faithless, Hosea was called to love a wayward woman named Gomer. The climax of the story came when Gomer ran away from her loving husband to return to her life of brokenness. She ended up for sale on the slave block, to pay off her debts. Hosea bought her back to prove his faithful, unconditional love for her.

Lance and I were immersed in the story and were discussing lessons about God's love for humanity regardless of our response or behaviour. I understood Gomer's sense of unworthiness that caused her to run from a love she didn't deserve. The hopeful message penetrated past the shame I wrapped my heart in. It felt safe exploring this terrain with Lance beside me, digging for truths that would encourage young people who looked to us for leadership. We were both inspired by our study.

Suddenly the lights went out in my dorm room. There was a dim glow from the windows that showed a storm brewing outside. It looked like sleet was bouncing off the glass. My eyes gradually adjusted to the dark, and I made my way to the door to see whether there was light in any other room. All that was visible were the exit signs that glowed softly in the hallway to break up the deepest dark.

Lance and I decided we would finish planning somewhere off campus where the power was still working. As we packed up our papers and headed for the door, Lance asked whether there was somewhere in the building where he could use a bathroom. As it was a girls' residence, there was only one public facility near the front doors. I led Lance to the door of the washroom and waited just outside on the steps.

Fifteen minutes passed, and I hadn't heard anything from behind the door. I wondered whether there was anything wrong. After another few minutes slowly stretched by, I decided to go to the door, open it a crack, and call.

"Lance, is everything okay?"

"I'm having trouble finding the door. It's so dark in here. I've been feeling my way around the walls. Could you open the door a little wider and keep talking so I can find you?"

I had never seen Lance vulnerable before. It was endearing.

"Of course! The door is this way. I'll hold my hand just inside so I can lead you out."

When Lance's hand found mine, a jolt of electric attraction surprised me. I led him around the door and abruptly let go.

Lance never seemed awkward or at a loss for words. He explained that after he found the sink to wash his hands, he became disoriented and couldn't remember which direction the door was in. He didn't seem embarrassed by his confusion but just laughed it away. He suggested we make our way to his car to finish the study at a nearby Tim Hortons.

When we reached the car, there was a layer of ice on the windshield. Lance was undeterred. He just calmly chipped it away and climbed into the driver's seat. He didn't seem daunted by the bad weather, and somehow, I didn't feel concerned about driving with him in the storm. He manoeuvred expertly out of the parking lot and onto the almost empty road. He drove slowly and carefully but found that the roads were quite slippery. He was driving down a small incline when the car slowly skidded sideways. Rather than panicking, Lance just kept his foot off the pedals and gently steered so that the car landed in an empty driveway. The car had turned a full 360 degrees, but somehow, with Lance at the wheel, it wasn't scary. He eased the car back onto the road and drove us the few blocks to the Tim Hortons. The weather was still cold and wet, so we huddled into our winter jackets with the hoods up and moved quickly to get inside, where the light and warmth beckoned.

We easily resumed our place in the Bible story and divided up leadership responsibilities for the upcoming event. I would write a monolog from Gomer's point of view after she had been bought back by a husband she had betrayed. To be met with love when she knew she didn't deserve another chance was the connecting point for all humanity. Kindness instead of judgement. Acceptance instead of scorn. A love powerful enough to transform shame into belonging and to make vulnerability safe and free. I was inspired by the content we had explored together. Lance would create the handout and study portion for the night, and we would both work with teammates to lead small group discussions and prayer.

By the time we finalized the plans, the storm had stopped. The sun was setting on the horizon, and Lance dropped me off at my dorm, where the power was back on. We shared one more laugh about the misadventures of the evening. Rather than feeling like something traumatic, the storm felt like the backdrop for a story of connection, humour, meaning, and friendship. My heart felt fulfilled and light as I headed back to my room for the night.

CHAPTER 24

❧

INHALE TO EXHALE

I have made you and I will carry you;
I will sustain you and I will rescue you.

—Isaiah 46:4, NIV

My natural introversion didn't have anything to do with how I lived. I was determined to be what I wanted to be. I didn't worry too much about personality traits or personal limits. I was always able to perform as needed. That was enough. I ignored signs of wear and tear on my emotions and body.

At camp the next summer, my fellow assistant director, Pat, became like another big brother. He worked hard but knew how to make it fun. He was so good with people! I often marvelled at his ability to connect with kids, staff, and adults from any background. I was glad to be able to ride on his outgoing personality when approaching the new school groups that filled the spring site. He would make me the star of a campfire story or "the wise, knowing one" in a magical trick. He brought out confidence in me.

Pat was also good at conserving energy through the summer by respecting downtime and programming it into both our days. We worked hard from early-morning devotions until the camp curfew at 11:00 p.m. But during our rest hour, he insisted that tasks could wait. He invited me to chill to Christian music we both liked as we claimed different couches across the room from each other to rest.

He also encouraged my love of music. During our time off, I practised guitar with Pat, which prepared me to lead with him during camp worship. We sang harmonies well together, which was my favourite way to be playful.

On days off, he would suggest we paddle around the lake away from the business and the noise of the active site. We would paddle out to a quiet, deep part of the lake. He would bring his fishing tackle, and I would gently shift the canoe to wherever he thought the fish might be biting. We could talk or just sit and enjoy companionable silence. I always felt refreshed by the quiet beauty. Any waterfront had a soothing effect on me.

I was learning from him about healthy rhythms of work and play—activity and rest: extroverted, high-energy leadership, and introverted quiet and stillness.

I was learning that I had to breathe in or fuel myself to breathe out in giving service. It's crazy to imagine that for years I had felt lazy for my need to inhale as I focussed on efforts to serve and exhale! That summer was the beginning of my learning how to practise rudimentary self-care.

When Lance showed up on-site to lead a youth camp, Pat and Lance joked easily and worked well together. They both knew how to bring out the best in me, put me at ease, and make me laugh. I was always amazed that they made me their equal, since I often felt in awe of their confidence and giftedness.

I often saw Lance as we led camp groups together. He was becoming one of my favourite people. He was unfailingly kind and valued the ways I could give. He asked great questions to draw me out of my natural reserve. I didn't always have an answer to how I was feeling, since my inner world surfaced only in quiet and reflection. By this time, I had almost buried my preference for solitude behind the roles I played: hostess, facilitator, leader, worship leader, friend, and counsellor. I didn't know yet my unique needs as an introvert.

In the middle of youth camp, Lance got some bad news. One of our kitchen staff had borrowed his car for a trip into town for a food item needed for dinner. The police arrived on site to speak to Lance. His car had been rolled upside down in a ditch beside the twisty gravel road. The driver wasn't hurt, fortunately. But apparently our staff member had failed to mention that he didn't have a licence when he asked to borrow the car. Another complication came from the absence of car ownership papers. They were not in the glove compartment. The car belonged to Lance's parents—who were on vacation in Japan. What a mess!

I had missed the craziness on-site because I was down at the archery area, leading a group. But I was quickly filled in when I came back to the dining hall. As a director, I had to sort out how to handle the issue with our staff member who had borrowed the car.

Later, Lance sought me out to debrief the event after programming for the day was done. I loved that Lance looked to me as a friend for sympathy and connection. He leaned on me for comfort. The shoulder where he leaned his head remained touched with a warmth that glowed on in my memory as I headed to the staff lodge for bed.

CHAPTER 25

LEARNED HELPLESSNESS

> Learned helplessness: the person has been taught that nothing he or she can do will make a difference, that they can do nothing right, that others know better than they do, and that they have little or no power and control over either their own lives or external events. The term was coined by Martin Seligman.
>
> —Steve Hein

In September, I was put in a small group with some new people. One of these was Markus,* who was in Waterloo for a semester. He was quiet and mainly kept to himself.

It was a priority for me to include everyone in the group and create community moments together. At Thanksgiving, a friend and I bought a turkey and followed the cooking instructions to share a meal with our group. We laughed when neither of us knew what the instructions were talking about when it said to remove the giblets before cooking. "What's a giblet?" We gradually figured it out amidst much self-deprecating humour and laughter. In the end, we were proud of our accomplishment in creating a taste of home life while we were all away from home.

Camp leadership had taught me to be friendly and draw out those on the sidelines of any social circle. So when Markus* invited me to have dinner at a restaurant with him, I gave an automatic acceptance. Another time, he asked me to play Scrabble and have coffee at a nearby coffee house he liked. I sensed he was a little lonely, and so I tried to bridge the gap he must be feeling. I often went out with various friends and didn't think of these outings as dates. Our interactions increased in familiarity and friendship. I was pleased that Markus was spending more time with the group instead of opting out.

I regularly used shoulder massages as a way to care for friends. This was normal in our camp world and was a way I enjoyed serving others. Markus often asked for one when we were together.

One night, we were left alone after the group dispersed. Markus invited me to rest my head on his lap while he gave me a head massage and talked. He knew of my frequent headaches, and so I felt the care and thoughtfulness of his attention. I had never seen him as anything other than a friend. So when he leaned down and kissed me, I was surprised. I realized I had allowed myself to drift along with a current of friendship to some sort of grey zone where, clearly, he interpreted our growing closeness as much more than I'd realized. Fortunately one of my housemates came to walk me home at that moment, and our attention was shifted. I took the chance to escape the confusing dynamic.

I wasn't sure what to do about the awkwardness I suddenly felt with Markus. I decided to wait and see whether it would resolve without drawing attention to it. He was here for only another month and a half before Christmas break. Surely he would sense that a relationship was not sensible.

A few days later, Markus told me he wanted to show me something. I followed him to a room I'd never been to before.

He shut the door behind me. Before I had time to register what was happening, he started to kiss me and push me down onto a couch. I was scared. He was twice my size and strength. He didn't seem to pick up the subtle hints that I didn't choose this. I realized too late my mistake in not talking to him about the surprise kiss. His hands were groping. He was hurting me. I was scrambling to think of a way to please him and get away safely without being pushed beyond the boundaries of my past experiences. Why did I feel so powerless?

Then I heard a friend's voice calling my name. It lifted me out of my state of frozen shock. I pushed Markus away and scrambled to my feet, rearranging my clothing. "I have to go!" was all that came out of my mouth. I dashed out the door just as my friend was heading down the hall to look for me. I headed towards him as he asked whether I would sing with him at our LCF meeting that day. He'd brought along his guitar to fit in an impromptu practice.

I told him that I would love to sing but needed the bathroom first. I took some deep breaths to calm my racing heart. I felt the familiar shame wash over me. I did what I could to recover myself so I could join my friend and head over to the class where we held our LCF meetings.

The irony of the song we sang together, "Quiet Love," was not lost on me. As I sang the words about God's love—"a love that listens to the cries that no one hears"—I felt my heart squeeze back tears that I never allowed myself to feel or shed.[5]

Fragmenting myself was necessary for survival. It was as if I had a switch I could flick to turn my feelings off. I was becoming quite good at living out of my ideal self while relegating pain to the outskirts of my consciousness.

Later that night, I knew I had to communicate with Markus. What I had intended as kindness and friendship, he had interpreted as intimacy. He did not share my faith or understand my heart. Our conversations felt shallow to me, and I had never intended to be close to him. I wrote him a letter. I took ownership for sending him encouraging messages when I had never seen any possibility of a close connection. I was clear about not wanting to date him, and I asked that he not tempt me in an area I considered myself weak in. I thought I had made myself clear and there would never be more to worry about with Markus.

I was wrong.

My letter was flawed because it trusted him to lead the relationship. I reinforced a helpless posture. I don't think Markus had dating on his mind. I had little knowledge of how to hold appropriate boundaries to protect myself and honour my convictions. I also didn't value myself enough to have any expectation that I should be treated well. Shame still made me feel cheap and unworthy.

One night I was away with a group when I was awakened from a sound sleep by the door cracking open and a hand clamping over my mouth to keep me from making a sound. Markus climbed under my covers and was clearly not leaving until he was satisfied. I swallowed back my fear and confusion and got to work on pleasing him to get him to leave me alone. He didn't hurt me this time, but I felt defeated and shaken by his visit in the dark.

I found it hard to turn down a sense of hypervigilance for weeks after that. I had a new awareness that there were no locks on my bedroom door. I had never thought about that before. I didn't tell anyone about my struggles. I was so embarrassed by my inadequacy and powerlessness.

What kind of leader was I?

I talked for hours on the phone with youth and peers to coach them through life's twists and turns, leaning on scriptures I had internalized and used to help myself.

But my duality seemed to mock me. How could I hold such high ideals when my reality was so messy and broken? I didn't know how to process what was going on inside, so I stuffed it down deep, where it couldn't interfere with my days. There were only a few weeks left before I could move home and drive in just for exam days. Then, after Christmas, Markus would be far away, giving me all the space I craved to feel safe again.

On his last night in Waterloo, I attended an event where I knew I would see Markus. I felt a dangerous connection to him. I wanted to make things right between us before he left. Then I could say goodbye for good. Yet I knew any contact was risky. He tried to get me alone with him, but I ended the conversation and left. Afterwards, I was the only one left in my student home that night, and I had a powerful urgency to not stay there alone. I decided to head home even though it was late by the time I finished my cleaning chores.

It was an icy night. I took the back roads to avoid traffic, but my car skidded off the road on a curvy hill before it nestled safely under a guard rail. After a bit of a hike, I was deeply grateful for a middle-aged couple who let me borrow a phone in the wee hours of the morning. They were kind enough to call the police and stay with me until my parents arrived. Having a car accident that night still seemed safer to me than staying in a house alone when Markus knew where I lived.

My mom asked me on the way home why I had decided to drive on such a stormy night instead of sleeping in Waterloo until it cleared. I just told her that I couldn't wait any longer to get home for Christmas. I was used to half-truths and dodges.

How could my mom understand my sense of powerlessness with Markus without understanding the context of childhood sexual abuse? I couldn't explain why I felt powerless. I didn't know how to talk about any of it. I wanted to protect those I loved and my reputation. I remained detached from my wounding experiences and pushed them down out of my consciousness.

What I find remarkable when I look back are the well-timed visits, interruptions, and unlooked-for help that emerged when I felt powerless. Though hypervigilance and self-protection were ingrained in me, they hadn't kept me safe. Yet, time after time, a friend would show up or I would find a good Samaritan to help me. There was such evidence of God's caring presence even in the hostile world I encountered.

I resonated with Gerard Manley Hopkins's poem "God's Grandeur" as we studied it in my English class. I felt both the bent earth and the hovering presence of the Spirit's bright wings.

> The world is charged with the grandeur of God.
> It will flame out, like shining from shook foil;
> It gathers to a greatness, like the ooze of oil
> Crushed. Why do men then now not reck his rod?
> Generations have trod, have trod, have trod;
> And all is seared with trade; bleared, smeared with toil;
> And wears man's smudge and shares man's smell: the soil
> Is bare now, nor can foot feel, being shod.
>
> And for all this, nature is never spent;
> There lives the dearest freshness deep down things;
> And though the last lights off the black West went
> Oh, morning, at the brown brink eastward, springs —
> Because the Holy Ghost over the bent
> World broods with warm breast and with ah! bright wings. [6]

CHAPTER 26

❖

RELATIONSHIPS

And we know that in all things God works for the good of those who love him, who have been called according to his purpose.

—Romans 8:28, NIV

One of the most beautiful parts of my life continued to be time with my sister. I loved when she came for a weekend visit! Hosting her in my space felt special. I loved doing things with just the two of us there. One Saturday evening, we walked down to Reuben and Wong's, a restaurant I used to go to with my floormates in my first year. We ordered a brownie ice cream sundae and could eat only half of it before we were stuffed. It came in a large salad bowl, with five different kinds of ice cream scooped over a brownie with warm fudge sauce and whipped cream! It was so good! Kathy and I laughed and groaned about having to roll our way back to my place.

Kathy had just started high school, and I wanted to hear all about it. We never had difficulty talking about anything and everything.

Maybe because I always felt a little protective of her, she made me feel strong and daring.

Kathy had a knack for unlocking my fun side. We went back to my room and put on chin-a-grin shows for each other. We would draw eyes on our chins and go upside down on the bed and cover our noses and eyes. Then we would sing a song or recite a poem, looking ridiculous. We loved to perform and make each other smile. But we could get serious, too. I loved hearing about her friendships, commitments, and whatever she was thinking about.

She and I both struggled with overcommitment and boundaries. Thinking through these hard growth areas was good for us. I was learning by watching how my healthier friends navigated their time, relationships, and energy with intentionality. As sisters, we did our best to help each other.

Of course, we also talked about guys! Kath and I talked about the qualities we wanted in a marriage partner someday. I was glad she had a few close girlfriends at school who helped her discourage unwanted attention.

Long after our weekend of fun was over and Kathy was back at home, I continued to think about and pray for a healthy partner. I kept picturing someone remarkably like Lance.

Lance was so dependable, safe, steady, and peaceful to be with. He had a self-confidence that allowed him to steer his life rather than be driven by it. I admired him.

Through a period when I felt unsafe alone in my bedroom, Lance's voice as he visited a housemate would draw me downstairs in my flannel pyjamas to be near him—even if I just intended to sit on the sidelines of the conversation and listen.

The funny thing about Lance was that he never left me on the sidelines. He would always find ways to include me and was so authentic himself that I would admit things to him that I would usually withhold in conversation. He always expressed interest in anything I had to say. And I loved listening to him talk. His thoughts coincided with my own on so many topics, yet his ideas grew me, too. I always felt cared for when Lance was around.

When the second semester started that year, I was a little surprised that Lance sought me out at one of the events we hosted together. He suggested we get together sometime that week.

I was a little confused. There wasn't a planning meeting or structured event to work on together. *Could this be a date?* I knew he had ended a two-year relationship with his girlfriend Carol* that fall. I thought maybe he needed a friend to talk to. I was pleased that he sought me out and was happy to meet with him.

He picked me up after dinner one night that week. We drove to a nearby Tim Hortons. It seemed to be our default meeting place.

As I had suspected, he began talking about his past relationship and why it had ended. I felt honoured that he chose to confide in me as a friend. He retraced the journey of his connection with Carol and their gradual growth apart. Lance spoke of the distance between their priorities and vision for the future.

I felt sad when I realized how the relationship had wounded them both. I liked Carol and had gone out with her several times with a group of friends the previous semester. She was fun and playful, and I enjoyed her company. It became clear, though, that a poor alignment of needs and priorities had left them both trying to patch up a gap in their connection in ways that only further distanced them. I listened carefully, affirming the good intentions and efforts I saw on both sides. But it was clear that Lance just wanted to heal and move on.

Lance told me that there was one more important thing to say. But he had to excuse himself for a bathroom break first.

When he returned, he said something like, "Ideally, I wanted to wait for a quiet moonlit beach to say this. But circumstances are not allowing this conversation to wait … I have feelings for you, Peg. I have for a while, but it has been growing so gradually I can hardly say when it began. The trouble is, Carol picked up on it at our 'welcome back' party when she returned from England. She thought that I acted differently around you. Carol confronted me at the end of the party by asking me if I had feelings for you. I hesitated in answering ... which is in itself an answer. I had to say yes, but then I assured her that I had never acted on it and that I would work on making the feelings go away now that she was home. The feelings never did go away, but only grew stronger whenever we were together."

Lance was quick to add, "I'm not looking for a response from you right now. All of this was just necessary for you to know. Just because I have feelings for you doesn't mean I expect anything from you. Although obviously it would be great to know what you think. But please don't feel pressured to say or do anything, okay?"

I was in shock at the turn in the conversation. My emotions soared as I realized that the guy I most admired liked me and had developed feelings for me—persistent ones—over time. *He liked me!* My inner self wanted to get up and twirl with joy.

I also found it honouring and endearing how vulnerable he'd been, and yet he didn't pressure me to respond or try to please him. He didn't expect anything from me; he just freely exposed his heart in a sincere display of unconditional care!

Then my empathy for Carol kicked in, and I felt awful to realize that I had been a source of pain to a friend. I had flashbacks in my head of the last few times we'd seen each other and was reminded of a slight cooling in our friendship. I was puzzled by it. Now it all became clear.

There was more.

Lance said that Carol wanted to meet with me, presumably to find out what my intentions were.

All these emotions were too much to process in the few seconds it took for them to flash through my mind and heart.

I then clicked back to the present. I suddenly realized that Lance had just been extremely vulnerable, with no assurance from me that

I saw his declaration in a positive light. I had left him hanging while I processed everything.

I stammered out, "Lance, I respect and admire you. I have a lot of questions about my future to figure out. But I have liked you for a long time too."

The look of relief on Lance's face made my admission worth it. We decided to go back to my room to have a little more privacy to talk.

I told Lance that my summer plans were to go on a mission trip to Eastern Canada with Mennonite Central Committee–Youth Mission Canada. I would be spending the summer away. I also shared that I had questions about my future. I didn't know where I was headed. Would God call me to missions in another country or to serve here in Canada? Was I meant to marry, or would singleness make me more fit to serve wherever God led? And most of all, I wanted God's best for my life. Were Lance and I God's best for each other? Or would caring mean releasing him to be with the person who would be a better partner for him?

The shame root rose in me with this thought.

Why would God choose me to be a worthy partner for someone like Lance? He was thoughtful, bright, kind, entertaining, had a pure heart, was good-looking, and was a brilliant leader. He could choose anyone! I could never be his equal.

What was I thinking? I couldn't let myself dream of a future with Lance. How could Lance ever care for me if he knew more about my weak and shameful past? I was dirty—used and cheapened—and he only knew me by the honourable roles I played. There were so many secrets. I couldn't let these feelings go anywhere until he knew who I really was—the whole picture.

Lance had his own thoughts. He shared a scripture he had found particularly meaningful right now—Psalm 27. He read it to me, and I felt my confusion and burden lift as he read,

> "The Lord is my light and my salvation—
> whom shall I fear?
> The Lord is the stronghold of my life—
> of whom shall I be afraid?
> I remain confident of this:
> I will see the goodness of the Lord
> in the land of the living.
> Wait for the Lord;
> be strong and take heart
> and wait for the Lord."[7]

The promise that we would see God's goodness calmed me. I could trust God to work out the messiness as we waited for the right time to discuss our relationship again.

We mutually decided not to act on our feelings. Lance felt he still needed time to heal, and I had so many unanswered questions as I prepared for my mission trip.

Lance and I committed to praying as we waited on God's guidance. We wrote out our prayer focuses. Then we joined hands and prayed together for each other—for God's goodness to be shown in the days ahead in our lives and in Carol's, and for God's wisdom, kindness, truth, and grace to fill my conversation ahead with Lance's former girlfriend.

I was nervous about meeting with Carol, but if she wanted to talk with me, I knew it was the right thing to do. I took courage from the promise that I would see God's goodness here and now, in the land of the living, this side of heaven. I would put my desires aside and care well for my friend who was hurting. That was just how it had to be. I would "Be careful to do what is right in the eyes of everyone. If it is possible, as far as it depends on you, live at peace with everyone" (Romans 12:18 NIV).

As we talked, Lance and I discovered that we were both looking forward to a cottage getaway at the same time and place.

My roommate had invited me to a weekend away at the end of the semester. Her brother had invited Lance. Unknowingly, we had been invited to the same cottage weekend!

We both felt that it would be wounding to Carol and a betrayal of our commitment to wait and not act on our feelings if we went on a vacation to the same cottage together. I was disappointed, but it seemed like giving up my holiday was the right thing to do. I told him to go and enjoy the restful break.

Neither of these hard things could feel too bleak, because Lance liked me! (I was squealing inside, yet a picture of composure outside.)

After Lance left, my joy was quickly tempered by logical objections, such as, *But does he know me?* I knew there would need to be further conversations with him—ones that might reveal a person he couldn't care for: the fearful, shameful me that lurked under the surface, whom I worked so hard to hide. Were my wounds too deep to ever find forgiveness and healing? Could Lance care for me in my weaknesses alongside what he knew of my strengths?

Well, I was certainly not going to let myself get too emotionally attached to the idea of a relationship that might never be. I felt that when I shared what I had done in the past, he would probably run. I certainly wouldn't blame him. I thought it best to put all my cards on the table, and then we would see.

Those were questions I had to shelve for now. It was exam time, and I had a hard conversation ahead of me.

CHAPTER 27

AN AWKWARD CONVERSATION

Faithful One, so unchanging
Ageless one, You're my rock of peace
Lord of all I depend on You …

You are my rock in times of trouble
You lift me up when I fall down.
All through the storm, Your love is
The anchor, my hope is in You alone.

—Brian Doerksen, "Faithful One"

A few days later, I found myself in my upstairs room after dinner with Carol. The conversation was a bit surreal, like something from a movie. The version of the relationship sounded so different as described by my friend. She described Lance as preoccupied with doing too much ministry and said he didn't know what he wanted, he was undependable, and he didn't know how to love.

But she wanted to work it out. They had made a commitment. The relationship wasn't over, as long as I stayed out of it. And she asked what my intentions were.

I was working hard to process everything coming at me, sifting these new images being shared through the filter of what I knew of Lance. I made it clear that I wanted to apologize for any pain I had caused my friend unknowingly. I was sorry that I was perceived as a threat. I would never have intentionally done anything to hurt her.

Then I told her that I intended to keep focussing on personal growth. I needed clarity about God's plans for my life. I had lots of questions without clear answers. I was preparing to go on a summer mission trip. That would be my focus for the present time. I didn't know whether God was calling me to a life of international missions or a life here in Canada. I didn't know whether I was called to be single or to marry one day. I only wanted God's best for each of us and would pray daily that God would lead and direct.

For now, I could assure her that Lance and I were committed to taking time to pray, seek answers, and wait. We were friends—that was all.

"Do you have feelings for Lance?" she asked.

I didn't know how to answer that. I could only assure her that I cared for Lance as a friend and certainly respected and admired him but had no intention of pursuing anything more with him. (In my head I added, "yet!")

After an awkward silence, she got up to leave.

I walked her to the door.

When I returned to my room, I took a deep breath to try to relieve the tension I felt. The strained conversation pricked at my insecurities. I felt that Lance's admiration and respect weren't real, since they were based on my outward persona—the person I projected to hide behind. He saw only my ideals—the strength I wore like armour to cover my brokenness.

I felt raw, soul-weary, and ready for a good cry.

But there was no time to feel. I had studying to do. I'd had years of practice at shutting down feelings. But I also had years of faith built into me. I was so glad that God knew all of me and that my roots were deep enough to sustain me when doubt and fear felt overwhelming. I would need all the years of faith-building to trust God to work out my future.

CHAPTER 28

WAITING

> Trust in the Lord with all your heart
> and lean not on your own understanding;
> in all your ways submit to him,
> and he will make your paths straight.
>
> —Proverbs 3:5–6, NIV

While this meeting was going on, I didn't know that Lance was struggling with his own inner turmoil. He wrote for hours.

He wrote one letter to Carol reaffirming his resolve that their breakup was best for both of them. He voiced his hopes for healing and the restoration of peace between them, even as he assured her that they couldn't go back to dating.

He wrote another long, honest letter to me to reveal his relational shortcomings as he anticipated what might come up in our future conversations. He didn't hold back in describing his failures and feelings while also capturing a sense of expectancy and hope in God's ability to heal and bring life and peace to all of us.

His letter was waiting for me the next day. As I read it, my heart was moved by his vulnerability, honesty, and clear ownership of where things were at while he maintained clarity about God's forgiveness and strength.

> I hated having to lay all that on you last Saturday night. But it was necessary. Thank you for being so understanding and supportive. I felt at peace that night.
>
> Peg, last Saturday, all I told you is that I had feelings for you. To elaborate further, I see Christ so clearly in you and am attracted in a big way to who you are. I love to be with you and long to be closer friends with you and know more of you. In the past year and a half, I have imagined many times what it would be like to be in a close relationship with you and I really believe we could be a strong unit. I know that there is a part of you that no one can touch, and I know there is a part of me deep within that is the same.
>
> I know it would be foolish to begin a relationship right now or within a few weeks or months. I want any relationship I have, to be God-directed.
>
> Peg, as much as I know all of this, I have had a rough time dealing with strong feelings for you. Now, why do I tell you all this, eh?
>
> Peg, I don't know how you feel about me. Some things you said last Saturday seemed to indicate that you may have some similar feelings. I'm not

sure. But you don't even have to feel like you have to tell me now that I've told you. And also, this romantic talk about a relationship between you and me makes many assumptions - like you feel the same, God directs and leads it, we build a stronger friendship, we get to know each other better, we're compatible in that sort of relationship, we share the same desires and goals, etc. I don't want you to feel that because I've said these things that I'm pushing you into something. As I said, healing and restoration must happen and there would need to be a very significant period of trust, communication, and friendship building. Who knows how long the process described in my last sentence might take? Months? Years? ... Peg, I tell you this cause I need you to know how I feel. You may feel very differently, and I am prepared for that. As well as waiting, I'm seeking to put my full hope in God for the future.

So, so far, I guess I've said that my feelings for you are very strong, but I know that a close relationship with you shouldn't be pursued now but only in God's time and in the proper development of friendship. Fine, right? Well, I have a few problems left.

First of all, I am beside myself to know how to relate to you in the meantime. Do I ignore you? Do we continue as we have in the past while, seeing each other here and there and enjoying brief encounters with each other? Can we become better friends now? Can we intentionally spend time together to just enjoy being together?

We've already decided that going to the same cottage on holiday is not a good idea. What about the youth retreat coming up? I was considering asking you to work with me, but then thought 'oh, that'll seem like I'm pushing her towards a dating relationship.' Could you tell me how you feel about these situations?

Lance confessed his failures and knew that Carol's perspective of the relationship was different from how he saw it. He wanted a chance to talk about how our conversation had gone.

So, Peg, there is my heart in five double-sided handwritten pages. All this stuff was racing thru my mind, and I knew that tomorrow night it would just leak out all over the place and not be very coherent. So, here it all is, on paper so that you can put it all in perspective and figure out how I'm feeling.

Again, Peg, between last Saturday and today I have dumped so much on you. I want to say again that you need not feel obliged to say: "Oh, this is how I feel about you, Lance …" or stuff like that.

Well, then again, that probably would be helpful.

Yeah, that would! But you don't have to!

What I'm tryin' to say is that I don't want you to feel like I'm leading you into some sort of way you have to respond. Last Saturday everything I said was necessary for you to know. So, we need God's abundant mercy to be lavished on us to sort through all this stuff. Again, I turn to Psalm 27, and I pray that for both of us God may be our:

LIGHT
SALVATION
STRONGHOLD
DWELLING PLACE
BEAUTY
SAFETY
SHELTER
ROCK
SONG
JOY

"I AM CONFIDENT OF THIS: I WILL SEE THE GOODNESS OF THE LORD IN THE LAND OF THE LIVING. WAIT FOR THE LORD. BE STRONG, TAKE HEART, AND WAIT FOR THE LORD." Psalm 27

See ya, Peg,
Love Lance.

After reading his letter, my mind and emotions were too worked up to settle on homework. I did what I usually do when I need to sort out my feelings: I poured out my heart as a prayer in my journal. I won't write the full entry here for you, as you might find it tedious. Just be assured it was heartfelt and extensive. I certainly was not inclined to think less of the young man who spent time sharing his heart in such a letter.

Lord, Lance touched a place in my heart that I didn't know existed; it has caused me to hope again. Lord, I feel so unworthy of such pure, tender love. Help me to deal with these feelings of guilt, fear, and inadequacy; help me to experience Your love. Guard me from myself—my own feelings and dreams … Teach me to trust and hope in You alone! I want You to always have first place in my life.

Help Lance and I to follow Your path—to build a stronger friendship and to commit one another to You. Bring healing and restoration as only You can! Give us a unified sense of how to relate to one another so that neither of us feels uncomfortable … Guide our time together publicly—our roles at the youth retreat are clear; help us to reflect Your goodness and light to those we work with and care for.

Help Carol find peace, healing, and forgiveness—may she find room in her heart to receive Lance as brother and friend … and more, only if that is Your best for them. If You desire to restore their relationship, give that desire and feeling to Lance and help me to stay out of the way. This one's hard, Lord. [I had a choked-up feeling in my throat as I wrote that line.]

Keep me joyful in hope, patient in affliction, faithful in prayer (Romans 12). May my love spring from a pure heart, sincere faith, and a clear conscience (1 Timothy 1:5).

Help us all to let go of the hurts of the past. You are my hiding place.

"Hiding place" was right—only God knew the burdens my heart wore. Though it was a stressful time of year already with final exams to finish, I knew I had to have an honest conversation with Lance soon.

It would have to happen tomorrow night. I was nervous about it. I didn't want to lose his respect and friendship. I was certain that I could never be God's best for Lance, since he had no idea about my shadows—the secrets I never shared. I was convinced that I had to be as completely honest as he had been. I needed to know his response before I let hope and love grow too big inside.

CHAPTER 29

SO VULNERABLE

> There is no fear in love. But perfect love drives out fear, because fear has to do with punishment. The one who fears is not made perfect in love.
> We love because he first loved us.
>
> —1 John 4:18-19, NIV

The letter Lance wrote gave us a way to begin. Lance picked me up from my rented room, and we sat on the couch in his parents' basement with only the silence of the empty house as a backdrop for our heightened emotions and desire for full disclosure. Lance seemed anxious to hear my response to the previous week's conversations.

I assured him that my respect and care for him were only heightened by getting a glimpse of his heart and struggles. I had always looked up to Lance, and his honesty and vulnerability only made him more relatable. I still found it hard to believe that he could have feelings for me.

We got to the part of the letter where Lance wrote a confession of his failure. I couldn't hold back any longer.

It was time to open up my places of shame and failure to him.

I couldn't look at his face as I broke my long silence about my caregiver's wandering hands, the masseuse's predatory behaviour, Edward's pressure to get physical, and Markus's forceful escalation of our friendship. I accepted ownership of not saying no to Edward and sending the wrong signals to Markus. It still baffled me that Markus would have misunderstood my note waving him off. I told him that I was not interested in a relationship. I didn't understand how things got so messed up. Was there something wrong with me? Did I attract trouble? Did I wear a big sign on my back saying "victim"? I tried so hard to project strength, confidence, and control, but that message didn't get to the people I most needed protection from. My armour only made it harder for healthy people to get close to me. I buried my needs so deeply that it appeared I needed no one. But my armour didn't keep me from being hurt again and again.

Lance let me talk, interrupting only to ask for clarification or to express anger. He was angry at those who would hurt me—not disgusted by me.

How was that possible?

I had never allowed myself to feel anything but shame and self-condemnation. Yet here was my friend, offering a fiercely protective, loving impulse that broke my composure.

I couldn't pretend I wasn't hurt, confused, and ashamed any more. Lance's anger opened up a new door for me; for the first time, I acknowledged that I could be angry that these things had happened to me!

I had always accepted blame. It had never occurred to me to feel angry.

I had thought of anger as an ungodly response. I felt I had no right to nurse negative feelings. I had been taught to love and forgive others, which made it necessary to disconnect from sadness, fear, anger, and doubt. But Lance's anger felt caring and right! It opened my wounds to a shaft of cleansing light. It meant that what had happened to me was wrong and damaging.

We talked all night.

I was trying to make it clear that he shouldn't mix himself up with my murky past. I was convinced that my experiences must be a result of being sexually awakened when I was just eleven. I thought I must be sending out some kind of signal that I was broken or easy. I certainly felt full of self-loathing, powerlessness, fear, and shame. I was surely, in my estimation, not a fit companion for Lance's ministry goals. I felt my stain would colour anyone I was with.

Lance cut in on this self-talk.

He reminded me of my pure heart. His empathy and conviction about the beauty he saw in me began to open a door that had always kept my true self locked away and alone. For the first time since I first told an adult about the abuse in my past, I felt as if love were reaching deep enough to enfold me. I felt surrounded by it, and instead of dimming that brightness with my failures, the light covered my stains and left me feeling cared for and understood—not condemned. I felt seen and known and sheltered. I felt a love that protects.

Lance had offered comfort in a way that broke through to my weary, battered heart. He helped me to begin the process of trying to understand myself and gather back the broken parts that had always been locked away, pushed down, ignored, and rejected.

Lance saw all of me: the ideals I lived and the shadows that loomed over me in my nightmares. Somehow, he still cared. He wasn't repulsed. My shame didn't cause him to run from me. His feelings for me hadn't changed. In fact, we naturally drew closer.

After tears, hugs, and heartfelt conversation, Lance suggested we pray together. Those prayers were a joint alignment with goodness, life, peace, strength, and help. Lance understood my needs and joined me there.

Even more, he saw us as equals, both of us reaching out to God's restoration and care. He gave me dignity and respect—things I hadn't been able to accept for a long time. When others gave me compliments or tried to build me up, it often bounced off because they were only complimenting my armour. Lance's friendship, offered in the backdrop of the dark shadows of my memories, made a deep and lasting impression. I could be loved just as I was. He recognized the beautiful bud of my character even when I was wrapped in weeds that were draining me.

We were just putting on our shoes for Lance to drive me home when his parents were getting up for the day. His dad came down the stairs in his pyjamas as Lance said, "Dad, I want you to meet my friend, Peggy."

I could see the question in his dad's eyes. "Is this someone significant?" My heart automatically answered, "No. Not likely."

Lance explained that we'd been talking all night and that he was just going to drive me home. We exchanged polite greetings. That was enough, for now.

I was struck by how Lance's parents implicitly trusted him. I was grateful that there were no more questions. I felt so drained. It felt as if a deep wound had been exposed and probed to allow some of the poison out. I needed some recovery time and sleep before I'd be ready to carry on an ordinary conversation with anyone.

CHAPTER 30

❖

HEARD

Amazing Grace! How sweet the sound.

—John Newton

Hi Peg!

Have you caught up on your sleep yet? You looked alert on Sunday night anyway.

Peg, Saturday night was really meaningful for me. The time we spent together was so peaceful and trusting and intimate and God-centered and holy. As I woke the next day (or same day) and went about the day and thru today and in prayer, I have felt confident about what and where my relationship with God needs to be in the next while. I have not felt uncertainty about where you and I stand together also. This is good! So, I just wanted to tell you how meaningful the sharing we experienced was. I desire to bring it all to God regularly (and, of course, not to anyone else) and thru

God be able to forgive your Caregiver, Edward, the massage guy, and Markus as you have. This is hard! Ever since you've told me, regular rushes of anger against each of these people have occurred. Peg, I care for you so deeply and can't fathom how someone could hurt you like that. Yet, I must surrender my anger to God and seek the gracious forgiveness of Jesus to reign in me and saturate my attitudes.

Peg, I also pain a lot thinking about you having to go thru all this. The thought of each situation puts an ache in my stomach. Peg, your love is so big for everyone but you. I am praying earnestly that God would heal this part of you. It need not ever happen again, Peggy! God can and will prevent this! Peg, these things didn't happen 'cause you brought it on, or you are at fault. You shouldn't feel shameful or guilty. With God, there is forgiveness WHOLE and COMPLETE! God is so thrilled about you. You are His treasure. You are the apple of His eye. He has knit you together to be a unique and wonderful child, Peg. He has worked good out of all situations in your life and formed amazing gifts in you that are amazing blessings for your friends, those you minister to (who are your friends), kids at camp, students at school, me, etc., etc., etc.

Peg, but I hope that the pain and memories are not haunting you. I am praying that they won't. If you need someone to talk to more about this, I am here.

It's opened my eyes a lot to you in realizing that you have been dealing with this over the past few months. It has helped remind me that anyone I know could be dealing with intense pain and I may not know therefore I need to have the compassion and sensitivity of Christ with all people at all times.

So, Peg, thanks. Your friendship has been a support and inspiration for me over the past year and a half. We are closer friends now and will be able to be more supportive and inspiring to each other in the future. I haven't shared as much of myself as I did with you for quite some time. It was very healing and wholesome for me, and I really do trust you.

I look forward to the weeks and months ahead. There is so much to do right now. Camp stuff has to start. Please pray for me to focus on God and serve Him well.

Also, since Saturday it has been hard to know that you and I can't continue to be as close as we would like. I can accept this. But, as I told you, the feelings can be, WOW, strong. As we wrote, please pray for my surrendering feelings and dreams to God.

Thanks, Peg! May God's grace be real in your life today and this week!

Love,
Lance

I was deeply touched by this letter and promptly replied:

Lance!

Thank you for your letter, your support, your friendship, and for seeing the best in me while helping me in my struggle against the worst in me! Thank you for sharing yourself with me—for trusting me enough to share with me your heart and for the courage and strength to be vulnerable.

Thank you for caring enough to share this burden. Continue to pray for healing, Lance, and I will pray for God's mercy and forgiveness to reign in both of our hearts. I can't find words to express how much your support means to me. You have helped me to see God's love again. I am so repulsed by my actions that I didn't feel as though love could reach me. I certainly didn't expect such a loving response. I didn't know what to expect. Saturday was so beautiful for me, Lance! I was so blessed through our time of sharing; it was a cleansing time for me—so godly, with a level of trust and intimacy I've never experienced before! God is so good.

Today I've felt new hope and joy, as I am confident that God has both the desire and ability to transform all our mistakes into something good. May God sustain you; may He be your refuge and strength (Psalm 46, Zephaniah 3:17, Philippians 4:4–9).

You are a blessing to me! (Isaiah 32:17)

Love, Peg!

CHAPTER 31

❧

PROCESSING

Jesus said, "Everyone who drinks this water will get thirsty again and again. Anyone who drinks the water I give will never thirst—not ever. The water I give will be an artesian spring within, gushing fountains of endless life."

—John 4:14, MSG

Though I sent Lance an upbeat note, I had a lot of processing to do. Why was it that Lance's anger moved and touched me deeply?

When others heard my story of childhood sexual abuse, they brushed it off, minimized, redirected, grew silent and distant, changed the subject, or expected me to be able to help others with my experience.

Rarely had I given my sadness space to feel the pain of it—to acknowledge the losses that happened when my caregiver broke trust, abused me, and normalized it. The secrecy then cut me off from the help of my parents and church community to process or heal from the experience. Years of silence and pretending left me out of touch with my fragmented soul. I had a hard time trusting my own judgement, since I clearly was not good at avoiding dangerous guys. Shame cut me off from seeing the gift in my budding womanhood. Being female felt like a curse. My development got frozen at a time when my identity was just forming.

The Christian community I was in was such a strength but was also full of messages that got twisted because of my woundedness. When I heard the call to "die to me," I thought that meant turning off my personality, preferences, choices, and feelings to serve whatever need was most urgent or dominant. I didn't realize yet the freedom of asking God to connect me to my truest self—the version of me that God envisioned when I was "knit together in my mother's womb" (Psalm 139:13 *Zondervan NIV Study Bible* [NIVSB]). I also didn't understand that discerning where and how to care was a big part of living out our unique offerings to the world. By striving to generate a life of sacrifice built on my ideals, I was heading to burnout.

Abuse marked me with a deep sense that I didn't matter. I lost sight of myself. Being used implicitly carries the message that "What you are thinking and feeling doesn't matter. You don't matter." So, I assumed I didn't and shut down any protest that said otherwise. But triggers happen, and nightmares break in, and even things that are denied shape perceptions, relationships, and feelings.

I tried so hard to forget about the bad moments in my past because I wanted to focus on all of life's gifts. I wanted the trauma to just disappear. But buried feelings don't just die. Containment is helpful and necessary for all of us, but dissociation took it to an extreme that cut me off from my own needs. I had no idea how to digest and allow feelings to be explored and unpacked so they could be useful and released. I became highly sensitive to triggers, and my nervous system radar was set on high alert. Hypervigilance was normal. I was in a chronic stress mode that was wearing me out.

I was taught to forgive, but without recognizing the damage.

There was never any acknowledgment that what happened to me was a violation, a trauma, a deep wound. There was only that whispered apology on that dark day the abuse stopped when I was just thirteen. I began to understand that forgiveness happens in layers as new illumination comes. Forgiveness was the right path, but I only ever took the shortcut. I was so grateful for those whispers of understanding and warmth that often poured over me when I sought God alone in the woods or during times of worship.

In my culture, from the time I was a very young girl, I was taught that how I felt was secondary to pleasing the adults in my life. Give a kiss, laugh when they tickle you, sit on their knees, and let them have fun with you even when you are not having fun. I didn't know that I could say, "No, thank you" or "I need space, please."

The recurring act of molesting a young developing girl had taught me that I was an object and that pleasure was dirty and forced. That young adolescent version of me learned that my mind and soul could not be trusted to judge what was right, that I had no ownership over my body, that my "no" was never heard or respected—that I was powerless.

The later assaults taught me that if I wanted a need met, there could be a price. Do you want to be cared for and listened to? Do you want someone to massage your sore back? Do you want someone to hear the beautiful thoughts that shape themselves into poetry? Then you may open yourself to being violated again and again.

Rejecting the first trauma only served to minimize my experience and make its recurrence seem to be no big deal. It had already happened before; what was one more time? The weeds of shame became part of how I operated and saw myself.

The impulse for life, for connection to another, to be known and loved, and to let someone matter—to give and share my heart—sometimes led to healthy places, but sometimes it didn't. I began to hate any sense of need that could make me vulnerable. I tried to shut off my heart, but it was still beating, still wanting, left starving.

It was only as I grew into honest and vulnerable friendships that I found the beauty of mutual attachments.

Earlier, I thought that loving others meant sacrificing for them, listening, taking on their hurts and troubles, and trying to carry them. Selflessness had an elevated place in my thinking as I admired Jesus's care for others. But I lost sight of myself. I was a martyr to my vision of selfless care, but my understanding was finally being opened to another possibility. I had many friends that were different. They were great at serving others but gave from a place of self-worth and confidence that God could pour through their unique gifts and expressions. Their self-awareness and boundaries made them good at giving out of fullness and not taking responsibility to fix the lives of others. My friendships with them felt mutual.

Lance was one of these. He respected himself and chose to do things that were fuelling for him even as he drew out the best in others. Could someone so healthy be a good match for my messed-up soul? I was trying to prepare myself to let him go so that God's best could unfold for Lance. Because how could I possibly be God's best?

Yet Lance cared enough for me that he had regular rushes of anger towards those who hurt me.

Had I ever let myself be angry?

Not really. I made excuses for others and took the blame on myself over and over. I could only be angry at myself. My perceptions were shaped by weeds of self-contempt. I depended on perfection, achievements, success, and helping others to hold up my fragile sense of worth. I didn't know I was nourishing weeds that would also rob me of creativity, intuition, and joy. I was building an identity from performance instead of a sense of inherent value.

Lance's protective impulses were new territory. Maybe what happened to me was serious and wrong and deserved attention.

When I mentioned the abuse in my past to others, I talked about events as though they were resolved. I projected strength and invulnerability, and claimed a hollow victory. I propped up my armoured self and claimed healing that couldn't possibly begin to touch what I had never opened a door to—my wounded heart.

I was thankful for the vibrant friendships and caring help that was sprinkled throughout my life. I had an awareness that God saw me, knew me, and understood me. This knowledge of a Loving Presence with me moment by moment in my days was the steadying influence of my life. My faith formed a strong root system. God's goodness and light kept my wounds from choking me in despair. God truly was my refuge, comfort, hope, and strength. But now I felt God leading me to waken my true self again and to see the weeds as something I clung to in self-protection to cover my hurt and fear. I felt God's goodness beckoning me to choose life, yield to the work of removing the weeds, and bloom into the vision God had for me.

I was given an affirmation when my Bible study group at church gathered around to pray for me before I went off on my Canadian mission adventure. In their prayers, they called me God's "Bubbling Brook" who would carry the Spirit's joy and blessing to others throughout my life. The name resonated with my heart's deepest desires. I found it beautiful to picture myself as a joyful cascade of water rippling and dancing over rocks and around obstacles to bring refreshment and hope while being fuelled by God's vast waterfall of resources in the heights. My eyes misted over as I allowed myself to believe that God saw me that way. I wanted to live into that image! If only I could stop stumbling over my sense of shame and self-doubt to let God pour living water in and through me. I longed to be fully alive to the possibilities!

CHAPTER 32

A SPECIAL BIRTHDAY

*His divine power has given us everything we need
for a godly life through our knowledge of him who
called us by his own glory and goodness.*

—2 Peter 1:3, NIV

That spring, I worked for two months at an asparagus farm while I was preparing to be a team leader on my two-month mission trip. I enjoyed the camaraderie of our crew as we rode the five-seater picker down the rows to cut and organize the asparagus for sale at the market.

Before orientation week, all the youth mission participants were to read a book on intercession, prepare thoughtful reflections on life questions, make physical exercise part of daily rhythms, and raise the funds needed to go.

This became a healthy time for me as I focused on growth, faith development, and physical endurance. I had a workout album that Kathy and I would exercise with most days after work. Living back home created a great bonding time with my brother, sister, and parents! I loved having extra time to talk and hang out in the evenings and on weekends. We most often spent Saturday mornings lingering at the breakfast table, sharing thoughts and anecdotes from our weeks. Mom was still one of my closest friends. I enjoyed the more serious talks my brother, Steve, and I could have now that we had outgrown the competitive sibling stage. I loved being more available as a big sister to Kathy! She was such a gentle, lovely companion! I also enjoyed helping her with schoolwork. Showing her how to decode the beautiful imagery of poetry was especially satisfying.

After picking asparagus in the fields all day, sometimes I had evening events in Waterloo. The fields where I worked were halfway between Brantford and Kitchener, so Lance's house became the natural stopover to shower and get ready for the evening. Though we were committed to not dating, we were still able to spend time together talking, sharing life things, and continuing to serve together in youth ministry.

Lance was also committed to a rebuilding time in his life. We were often inspired and encouraged by one another as we each pursued restoration and wellness. Our interactions refreshed and fuelled us.

We would occasionally eat out together, and our conversation would be peppered with laughter and fun anecdotes. But we were also able to speak deeply about the terrain of the heart. Lance would always ask how I was doing and mean it. We were learning how to support and care for each other in our friendship. We found empathy and understanding as we shared meaningful discussions about faith, self-discovery, and the probing questions we were both drawn to ask.

Lance became my sounding board—the person I trusted most to ask me good questions and share wise insights while strengthening me to think and make good decisions. He believed in me and was inspired by me, without me having to perform or be perfect or play the role of "Peggy Pedestal." My fears, worries, and self-doubt were given space to process alongside my dreams and goals. The beautiful and weak were all heard and accepted.

Lance never fed my sense of shame, though he knew my failings better than anyone. He let me make sense of my vulnerability and my strengths. I felt so safe with him that I allowed myself to explore my emotional landscape and reconnect with my true self more regularly. I was so used to hiding that it took practice to let myself come out of numbness and listen to my feelings. But Lance asked insightful questions and was so honest himself that I felt as if I would be cheapening our friendship if I offered responses that were less than true.

Throughout university, I was exploring and owning my perspective instead of just offering what I thought others wanted to hear. Lance was building on that foundation by fostering a connection that comes from sharing all of who I was, not just the noble parts.

The time for my mission adventure was fast approaching. After we had been hanging out together one evening, I was in my car getting ready to pull away when Lance held my door open, leaned down, and whispered, "I love you," before he kissed me. He then shut the door and stepped back.

The possibilities of that kiss lingered for the hour's drive home and beyond. I wasn't sure why Lance would confuse our friendship just before I was to be away for two months. Yet the assurance that I was loved by the person I most admired and leaned into for support made me feel braver and safer as I prepared to step out into new experiences. I was determined to put no expectations on a future with Lance, but I was grateful for the ways he made me feel strong, capable, and whole—even while practising vulnerability.

My days were now coloured by preparations. I was so grateful for the people that responded to my mission support letter. Promises of prayer, cards of encouragement, and financial assistance poured in day after day. I had enough money to pay for the trip plus a little extra for school in the fall. My heart was buoyed by all the kind words and caring support. I liked the disciplined rhythms of exercise, quiet journaling, and praying for others that marked each day.

My time of departure was fast approaching.

I was going to celebrate my birthday far from everyone I knew and loved; I was hopeful that I would be with new friends I would make among my teammates. I knew myself well enough to know that I would naturally live in my role as team leader and keep my teammates at arm's length with my strong veneer. I hoped I could still connect honestly with someone through the summer months.

Lance wanted to set a date to celebrate my birthday with me before I left. He came to my house for the first time. He was so attentive to my family, and I realized I felt proud of him as I introduced him around. My brother already knew him from camp, and they reconnected with a warmth that made me glad! I loved watching his gentleness with my sister.

As he talked to my parents, he was unfailingly kind and asked good questions to draw my family members out. He was good at reading people and situations. I couldn't help but feel the contrast of having Edward over for dinner! Lance made others feel seen and heard as he uncovered their interests and listened attentively. He felt comfortable in his own skin and didn't try to impress. I realized how relaxed I felt around Lance. He brought out the best in me without making me feel like I had to be an extra sparkly version of myself. I liked who I was when I was around him.

We took a hike together, had dinner with my family, and then went to have some time to talk privately in the rec room basement. Lance's gift to me was two long letters to take with me on my travels to remind me of the person he knew and saw in me. He also wanted to affirm my identity as seen by the God who made and cherished me. I still struggled to feel God's love penetrating my numbness and shame.

He started to read to me: "I care deeply for you, Peg. I want you to grow into the fullness of life in Christ. As a gift (birthday, send off ...) I've written out some of the amazing facts about who you are in Christ! May your heart find joy in these amazing truths!"

Lance wrote out some Bible verses of God's knowledge and care on fancy paper. This is a glimpse of what he wrote:

> You are a beloved child of God ... part of God's family everywhere you go ... you stand in God's grace and pleasure, not judgment and fear ... God adopted you - it's not dependent on you ... you are a new person with fresh pages to write in front of you - not defined by the past ... God wants to help your soul find rest and peace ... You have full access to the resources of God's Spirit for life and godliness, power, and love ... God's resources can meet all your needs ... You have been given a way to see the world as God sees ... You are free ... You can overcome darkness ... In your weakness, God is strong ... You don't have to be more than you are made to be - a clay vessel containing a beautiful treasure ... As you share in another's suffering you share Christ who both suffered and comforts.
>
> Peg, I rejoice in who you are - that you are an incredible blessing - and pray that you find your identity rooted in God that is unshakeable!

As Lance read each scripture out loud, I felt some of the shame begin to move aside to make room for all I was trying to take in. Although my brain could hear these words as generally true, it was hard for me to receive them and let them penetrate my feelings toward myself.

I was so used to feeling that God must be disappointed in me because of the gap between my ideal and my struggling self. As a leftover from my superhero fascination, I had a hard time letting go of polarized thinking where people were all good or all bad; I didn't know how to accept myself as a mix of both.

I wanted to be all light. My heart cried for it. But my mind also remembered all my failings. What was it going to take for these truths to become real for me? I didn't know. But I would pack these words, cherish them, and bring them with me on my summer journey. I would read them through when I needed to be reminded that God was enough, that I was cherished, and that I wasn't alone in the dark any more. The Light of Life was here. Right here. At this moment, I could feel it!

When Lance finished reading, he prayed for my trip ahead. Then he said he had one more gift to share. The words he had shared so far were Bible verses for all humanity as God's image-bearers.

What he shared next was for me alone.

"Last time we were together, I told you I love you. I don't say that lightly. Before you go away, I want to take time to tell you what I mean by that."

For twenty minutes, Lance read all the qualities he saw and admired in me. Tears quietly rolled down my cheeks as Lance applauded my faith, my leadership, and the ways I treated others. He was trying to help me see myself through the eyes of unconditional love. I wasn't sure everything he said was true, but I so appreciated that he was trying to help me to see past the trauma that shaped my sense of worth. In his eyes, I saw myself as beautiful, admirable, trustworthy, and strong—even though I'd shared with him the fuller story of my brokenness.

Lance's gift was overwhelmingly perfect. Written and spoken words were my heart language. Lance was reaching me in a way that was most meaningful for me. Having this written down allowed me to carry these words to remind me that I had a dear friend who saw me, believed in me, and would be praying and cheering for my growth and protection through a summer of new experiences.

Then the letter got even more personal.

> Peg, I'm so glad I finally wrote all this down, 'cause since I've known you, I've often been so captivated by you and so often had trouble dealing with my feelings. I've never known anyone like you. I'm fascinated by you. I admire and respect you so much! I have felt drawn to you for so long!
>
> I've been writing all this about you and to you 'cause I'm trying to sort out my feelings for you. When we were together last, I told you that I love you. Yet, what does that really mean?
>
> Peg, we won't see each other for two months and we seem to be at the beginning of a close relationship. We still are uncertain as to what sort of relationship God desires for us ...
>
> So, to start, all the things I've written about you are things I value in people. I can't believe they are all in you! So, I guess I love who you are! I love who you are becoming!
>
> Then, I love to be with you. When we're together, I always feel like we function on the same channel. I grow in love for God and desire to live my best self through being with you! I learn from being with you! You bring out the best in me!
>
> When I said I love you, I meant that I'm drawn to you - to who you are, to be with you, to all of you!

So, my desire in being one who loves you is to not love what I get, but what I can give. I want to love your welfare, your interests, your needs, and your desires. I want you to know all God is about and all that God has for you! I want your deepest needs to be met!

Peg, I know that love isn't a feeling. Well, I do feel tons. My heartbeat increases every time I know I'm gonna see you or talk to you. I think of you a lot. Fine, but I don't want that to be what I mean when I say, "I love you."

God is love; I want to love you as God loves. His love is so much, but one of the most fundamental parts of it is unconditional acceptance. Peg, it was hard and deeply moving all at the same time to have you open up so much of your life to me - last time we were together and other times too. Peg, as much as I've written all these amazing things about you, you could feel that you have to live up to all of them at all times so that I'll keep loving you. Don't let this be so. When I find things I don't like about you (haven't found any yet, but I'm sure there'll be some) or know more of you in weakness, I want my love for you to be a constant - a decision, a God-inspired love.

I really felt a need to write all of this 'cause I told you that I love you. I love many people. But what I said to you was unique and I want you to know what I meant. What I've written shows some of what I meant, but it also shows that I'm still unsure of what it would really mean to love you.

It may be premature to talk so much about love. Again, I realize that after summer, I may need to love you by just being a supportive friend. Nevertheless, this letter is an attempt for me to tell you how I love you, now, June 27, 1990.

Peg, I do love you. I eagerly await what God has planned for you this summer! Thanks for being a dear friend! I will pray for you throughout the summer!

"May the God of hope fill you with all joy and peace as you trust in Him, so that you may overflow with hope by the power of the Holy Spirit." Romans 15:13

Love Always,
Lance

So often in the past, guys had replaced words with attempts to force closeness through physical contact. But Lance got it right. Words are my language.

I include portions of these letters to demonstrate how different this relationship was for me. I needed to understand fully what Lance meant when he said, "I love you!" or it would be a source of painful conjecture and insecure spirals. Love expressed in a quick phrase would have left me confused and wondering whether I could count on it or how to respond.

Lance's words taught my heart to hope that love could be what I imagined it to be: a steady mutual affection; a partnership springing out of deep, constant friendship and trust, and rooted in shared faith. Lance's offer of love left me free to try my wings and fly. It didn't constrain me or tie me into an unhealthy alliance. This love believed in me and encouraged me to discover and explore, with the knowledge that I had someone in my corner who would pray and care and communicate. He offered constant friendship with the hope of exploring whether we could become more.

I admit that I was a little overwhelmed by Lance's gift; the hour was late. But I wanted to assure him that I heard and appreciated his vulnerability and care, that I returned his desire to love him well, and that I would hold him in my heart wherever I travelled that summer.

We promised to write to each other. I made sure he had all the addresses I could be reached at during different points of the summer.

We ended the night of honest connection with a lingering hug and expressive kiss. Then Lance's car backed out of my laneway, leaving me with a heart full of joy, love, and dreams of a happy future. How could they help but be happy with Lance's letters of belief tucked gently under my pillow?

Family photo just after I was born

Stephen and I visit our grandparents

Young Peg

Dreams of a sister

Biking with Kathy at our new home

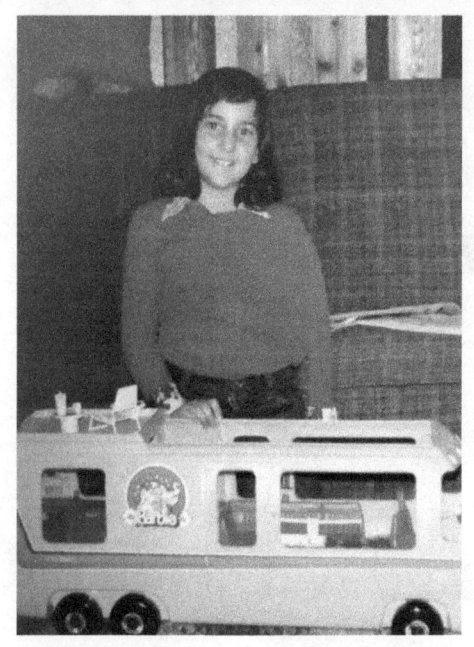

Barbie Motorhome and Broken Collarbone

Our last visit with Grandpa in hospital

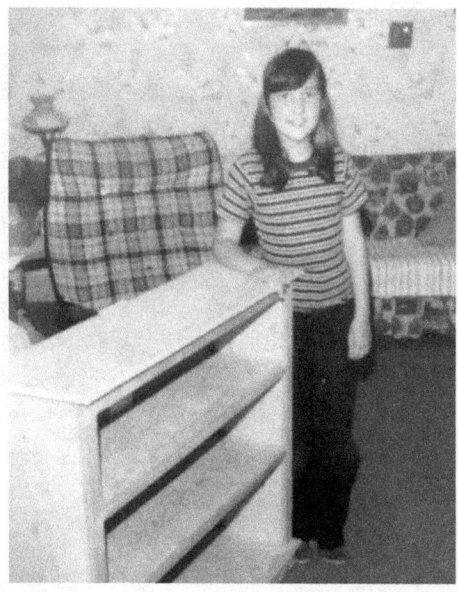

A special birthday gift made by Grandpa

My Grandparents in Peterboroough

Peg at camp

Youth group church play

Steph and I heading to prom

Then I met Lance

Dating

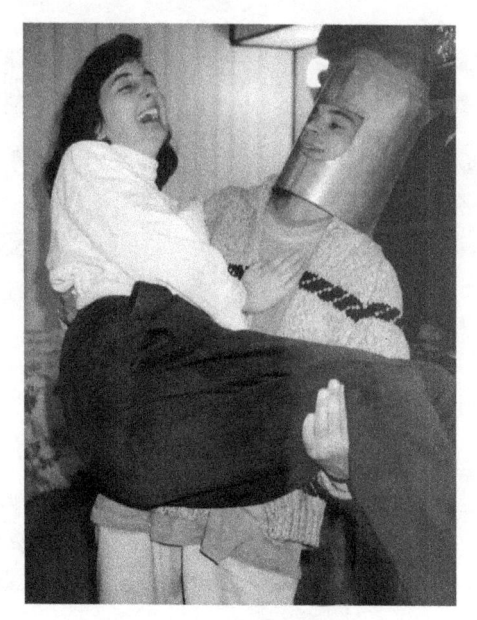

Lancelot

Engaged (photo credit: Gayle Harrison)

Wedding Day (photo credit: Gayle Harrison)

My Family (photo credit: Gayle Harrison)

Kindred Spirits and Bridesmaids
(photo credit: Gayle Harrison)

Groomsmen (photo credit: Gayle Harrison)

Merging families (photo credit: Gayle Harrison)

Wedding dance party
(photo credit: Gayle Harrison)

Recording Band: Peripheral Vision (photo credit: Gayle Harrison)

CHAPTER 33

CANADIAN ADVENTURE

For God has not given us a spirit of fear, but of power and of love and of a sound mind.

—2 Timothy 1:7, NKJV

The next day was full of the whirlwind of packing, last-minute errands, and then double-checking that everything was ready for my two-month adventure. My parents dropped me off at the orientation event full of good wishes and promises to pray for me.

The orientation prepared each team with skills we would need to serve the churches that were partnering with us. We divided up into daily workshops in small groups to prepare street dramas, a children's ministry leadership curriculum, clowning, and music so that each team was equipped to serve in our host communities.

We were met with a warm reception at our first placement. My fear of strangers was getting displaced by the kindness we encountered. Confidence, faith, and fear were still taking turns at the forefront of my mind. Confidence was a fragile thing.

I wrote to Lance about some of my experiences:

> I prayed for a bigger view of God. He is expanding my vision as I daily talk to people of Chinatown, the Markham area, and Toronto's downtown core. My fears are gradually being replaced by a deep love and burden for people and the loads they carry. As I was walking to put a wrapper in a nearby garbage can today, a homeless man asked me for spare change. I began to talk to him with two teammates at my side. We asked him a few questions and he seemed to be glad to talk. He began to tell us a bit of his story ...

Though my days were full of new people and experiences, Lance was never far from my thoughts. I collected postcards and took snapshots in my mind of beautiful, inspiring stories and anecdotes to share with him.

Our two weeks in Toronto were busy, crowded, stimulating, lovely, and full. Our mild-mannered teammate from the Prairies had to learn to be an aggressive city driver to drop us off and pick us up around Toronto each morning and night.

The big city was wide awake at all hours. Though I could appreciate the beauty in the bustle, I gravitated to quieter environments. I enjoyed moments off to the side, connecting in meaningful conversations.

After our two weeks spread around the Toronto area, the youth mission teams gathered back together to debrief and have a shared experience of praying on Yonge Street downtown. We broke into small groups to walk and pray. I stopped to listen to the angst and sadness of a street busker. I applauded his efforts at the end of the song and commented, "You sing with a lot of passion!" He thanked me and asked whether I was a musician too.

I mentioned my attempts at songwriting and my joy in singing. He asked me to sing him something. Wanting to infuse some hope into this corner of Yonge Street, I gathered a few of my teammates to join me in singing one of the songs we'd been taught at orientation: "Deep, deep whoa oh oh … deep down in my soul - well, I've got the joy … hope … peace of Jesus." We sang back and forth and moved to the rhythm we created as we sang. It was an unrehearsed moment of joy that we poured out as our offering to the street. A small crowd gathered and clapped along. I loved amplifying faith, hope, and joy in a way that resonated with the crowd. My spirit soared as I felt my gifts move in harmony with my teammates to allow the Spirit of joy to flow through us.

When we finished our song, the busker smiled wide and said, "You sing with a lot of passion too!"

I said that it was easy to be passionate about my faith when it brought me great comfort and joy. The rest of the group drifted to other conversations and receded into the background. The young man asked if he could show me something. He sat beside his open guitar case and pulled out a Bible.

"My grandmother gave me this before I left home. She was such a loving lady."

I sat beside him on the sidewalk and started asking questions about home, life, and family. The man shared freely his hopes and disappointments. I realized that his long hair, angst-filled song, and intimidating appearance hid a heart much like mine. I liked him. Before moving on down the street, I offered the best gift I knew to give as a way to care for him.

"Would you like me to pray for you?"

His yes was spoken quickly. I poured out my heart for God's goodness and direction, care, and peace to fill this man's life. When I finished, he had tears in his eyes and said he appreciated that I took the time to talk. He decided he would call his grandma that night. I was moved and grateful to be part of a God moment in someone's story. I touched his shoulder, stood up, and waved goodbye.

By the time all our teams met back at the park at the appointed hour, I felt differently about Yonge St. As an introvert, I'd been turned off by the sensory overload of downtown Toronto at night. But the conversations I had and the prayers I prayed had opened my heart to see people in all their colourful variety. I felt connected to people through our common search for a place of belonging and happiness. I opened my heart to listen and care.

The teams sat on the grass and talked about our experiences. Some were discouraged by the darkness they saw, others were moved by pain, and I shared my encounter of hope. We decided to spend time praying for the city of Toronto as we sat in the heart of it. In praying, we saw ourselves as partnering with what God wanted to do in this space and time in history. We'd been taught about the pattern of God choosing to work through people to accomplish good things. I felt full of the desire to care about what God cared for—to cooperate with the godly impulses of my heart. I was ready to be swept up in a bigger story. I was captivated by the vision of all humanity being restored to become all God created us to be and living in harmony with one another and all of creation.

It was in this state of mind that I began to be aware of a cry from behind me. A young girl was sobbing and crying out: "No, stop!"

Her cry for help seemed amplified over the backdrop of one hundred teammates' whispered prayers filling the quiet of the park at night.

The soft sobbing behind me turned to loud pleading as two male voices yelled at each other.

I felt compelled to move closer to the girl's cries, but I didn't feel it would be wise to wander off by myself in the dark. I tapped a few guys and girls nearby and motioned for them to come with me. I didn't want to do anything risky, just move into the sightline of the girl I heard as we prayed for her situation. I wanted the girl to know we were near if she needed help.

We moved to the top of the rise, where we had a good view of the praying teams and the disturbance below. Two guys were having a yelling match about stealing something. It seemed to be drug related. The girl collapsed on the ground nearby, pleading with them not to fight. One guy pulled a knife. At this point, a few of the guys I brought with me to pray ran back to the main group. I continued to pray for God to bring light and peace here. The girl had unconsciously moved closer to where I was standing with my friend. I wanted to reassure her with a caring presence. I knelt near her, touched her shoulder, and said, "You're not alone." I continued to silently pray. The girl seemed worried.

"You shouldn't be here!" the girl said. "It's dangerous."

"But you're here," I countered.

Before the conversation could go any further, I heard singing coming from over the rise of the hill. The girl looked up at me, confused by the sound.

Moments later, one hundred teammates came over the hill, singing with an acoustic guitar a worship song about the majestic love of Jesus.

The girl stood quickly and shouted, "No, you'll make things worse!"

The guys who'd been fighting went from circling and threatening each other to standing apart with looks of confusion on their faces. The guy with the knife was still waving his arm in a wide arc, but now his gesture was aimed at the group coming over the hill.

I wasn't sure what God would want me to do now, so I just kept praying for protection, peace, and light to pour into the place where I was standing. The girl ran over to the guy with no knife and held on to him, trying to convince him to leave. The singers made a large circle that filled the open grassy space and continued from one song to the next, ignoring the threatening gesture of the guy with the knife, who started to yell at us, "Get out of here! This is our turf!"

His anger and territorial stance seemed tiny and impotent in the face of God's joy and peace that filled the space. It was clear he didn't like to feel powerless, but he seemed unsure of his next move. The girl was relieved to have a distraction from the fight and just wanted to leave. She convinced the guys to exit with her; their quarrel was forgotten for the moment.

The mission group sat down on the grass in a big circle and continued to sing worship songs. Gradually, we noticed a small crowd gathering around us. We stopped singing and began talking with individuals in small clusters. It seemed that the area had so often been a scene of gang violence that the neighbourhood seldom enjoyed the beauty of the park. They were thankful for the presence of the team. A peaceful hush had fallen over the area, and everyone spoke in quiet tones, wanting to know more about these young people who brought fearless joy to their space. I was moved by what I saw and heard as I joined one of the little groups that formed naturally to talk and pray.

Later that night, back at the church that was hosting us, one of the leaders gave a stern rebuke to the group about taking matters into our own hands and reacting in fear instead of listening to the promptings of God.

I was surprised, stunned, and crushed by what I heard. Did the leaders blame me for moving closer to the girl in the park? Had I read the situation wrong? Was it not a godly prompting that I obeyed? I felt smothering self-doubt engulf me, stealing away the joy of the evening. Had I put people in danger by my actions? How could I be trusted to lead a team if I was mistaken about God's nudges and promptings?

My heart broke as the lecture washed over me and the familiar voice of shame and condemnation took hold. I had only wanted to do what was right—to please God. I was devastated and decided to go to one of the leaders and ask for prayer and clarity.

Gareth asked me what was wrong. Once I started to explain the promptings I felt and my actions in response, I began to sob out an apology for leading others into danger. I was in a full-blown shame storm. I didn't want to lead if I couldn't trust my judgement.

He quickly interjected. "Peg, it wasn't you that he was correcting. The beautiful ministry in that part of the park might have never occurred without your movement to care. There was a piece of the story you missed. While you were with the girl on the hill, the guys you had with you ran back to the group yelling that there was a knife fight going on and asking for volunteers to go and stop it. The leaders had to give an authoritative call for everyone to calm down, assess the situation, and decide together how to respond. It was the rash decision to jump in the middle of a knife fight that the leaders were speaking to."

Gareth's words brought reassurance to my heart, and he prayed for me for a renewed sense of peace and confidence. I went to the girls' sleeping area drained but relieved, ready for rest. As I lay in my sleeping bag on the church floor, my mind replayed the day's events. I wrote about my experience to my mom and dad, then Lance, and regained perspective and joy in the retelling. I ended my letter to Lance as follows:

> Just want you to know that things are going well here and that you are daily in my thoughts and prayers. As I read and reread your letter my heart is full of thanksgiving; I'm so excited about what God is doing in and through you. Lance, I've learned so much from working with you in the kinds of settings you're in now. Because of this, I am confident that God is encouraging and inspiring others through you! May God be your source of life and strength as you pour out so faithfully and naturally in your care for people. May you rest in God's quiet love today!
>
> Thank you so much for your special send-off / birthday gift; it has often spoken inspiration, hope, and light when I've most needed it! Every

time I read it through, I feel like you are right here standing with me, encouraging me to press on. You don't know what a blessing God has brought me through you!

Self-doubt could quickly paralyze me. I gathered to myself the reassurance of my leader, the friends and family that were praying for me, and Lance's birthday gift letter. I leaned into all the people that continued to believe in me when I found it hard to believe in myself. Little did I know how much my insecurity would be triggered by our next assignment.

CHAPTER 34

TRIGGERS

> Born lonely, we try to fit in, to be the kind of person that will cause others to like us. Craving and needing very much the affirmation of others, we compromise, put on any face, or many faces; we do even those things we do not like to do in order to fit in. We are bent toward the creature, attempting to find our identity in him. Slowly and compulsively the false self closes its hard, brittle shell around us, and our loneliness remains.
>
> —Leanne Payne

My team's next stop was in Niagara-on-the-Lake. The lush farming area full of fruit trees and wide-open spaces was such a contrast to downtown Toronto's concrete and crazy traffic. My team welcomed the colourful vineyards, forests, and fields of growing things.

The church greeted us with a hot meal and warm welcome before they escorted us to be billeted in local homes. Before we separated for the night, I wanted to meet with Dan and the minister to get a picture of what planning and programming were needed for the week ahead. Dan and I followed the minister to his office. As the discussion began, Dan took the lead. He had been the one making phone arrangements before we arrived. The conversation held a general picture of upcoming events, but I wanted a more detailed understanding to help the team prepare. As I began asking questions, the minister seemed annoyed by me. Then he cut in with a question that surprised and silenced me: "Who is leading this team, anyway?"

I was stunned and didn't know what to say. I wasn't sure what I had done wrong. Dan and I had been working together for three weeks now and were comfortable dividing up leadership responsibilities. I generally took care of the details of planning programmes, tracking expenses, and mentoring the girls while he mentored the boys and managed team billeting arrangements, communication with each church, and big-picture details.

I remained quiet while Dan stepped in with a few more questions, and then we headed with our teammates to the homes where we would be staying for the next week.

My interactions with the host minister didn't get better. Each time, I felt criticized, judged, and repeatedly silenced. He would openly rebuke me in front of my team. I shrank as I tried to quietly navigate my team through preparing and offering our gifts to serve the congregation without drawing too much attention to myself.

Each night, I shared a sleeping space with two awesome girls from my team. Usually, I enjoyed their company, but that week I felt repeatedly bruised and rumpled in spirit and at times didn't want the exertion of being with others. I felt increasingly tired and hurt, but I had learned to shut those feelings down to rise to meet the needs around me.

Each night, I would lie awake after the others fell asleep, and in the silence, I tried to figure out what I had done to receive such strong criticism from the minister we were working with. I was used to looking for my missteps and brokenness. I carried an inexplicable feeling that something was just wrong with me. Was I too domineering? Too outspoken? Too bossy? Too much? Too … something? I pulled out my journal:

> Dear Jesus,
>
> I need You … God, I feel like such a failure sometimes. I don't want Dan to feel intimidated or to hate working with me. I feel as though the minister sees me as a domineering leader pushing Dan into the background. I was asked to help lead the team, and I try to help by decreasing demands as Dan coordinates logistics. God, I'm frustrated; I don't know what to do. Perhaps I should remain silent unless asked to comment? I don't want to be in the way. It hurts to feel silenced.
>
> Lead me, dear Shepherd. I long to do only what is right. Any joy and blessing I felt last night were robbed by doubt about my part in putting it together. I feel like a failure.
>
> Help me to simply serve and give. I don't want control or power. I just want to serve with excellence and lead well. I need You. Let me hide in You.

I wasn't aware of my habit of looking to others to decide my worth. I felt safe and loved when people responded well to me. But the first hint of disapproval could send me on a spin that was hard to recover from.

At the end of the week, we were debriefing about our last large event. The minister was with us and started to criticize only the parts of the programme that I led. I felt crushed.

God,

Awaken my heart to know your love, for my heart is in shreds today. I feel so unlovable and like a complete failure in Your eyes, Lord. I feel like giving up, and yet I know that that would let fear and despair win. God, I cry out to you in distress—"Lead me to the rock that is higher than I!" (Psalm 61).

God, may I be as one of these little songbirds— able to sing throughout the dark nights and storms, flying above circumstances, held by Your powerful hand! Be strong in me; place Your hand in mine that I, too, may offer grace, compassion, patience, gentleness, and selfless love! Help me to remain true to You and not be distracted into the bondage of a critical spirit. Help me to always be thankful, full of hope and joy and faith!

Lord, I give You my hurt. Help me to return love in the face of discouragement. I can't prove myself. You are my Shepherd, Lord; help me to be blameless in the sight of others as far as it concerns me. I will leave the rest to You.

God, I can't even see any good in me anymore. I am completely shredded. Restore me, God; give me hope that You can use me and breathe life back into me. I feel I have nothing to give, but I will trust at all costs! Lead me, my King!

I prayed for the minister whose words hurt—that his ministry would be fruitful and that God would guide him with wisdom and love. I prayed that God would guard and purify my heart from pride, self-condemnation, hurt, bitterness, and fear. I prayed for my team leader, Dan, and for increased sensitivity and selflessness in my leadership with him.

And I ended with "Astound us, Lord! Help us believe for big things. Advance light and love in Canada!"

My time in Niagara was ending, but I would carry the sense of failure from this place like a weight for the rest of the summer. My confidence was shaken. I did my best to coach myself into a better mental space. Then I pulled out the well-worn sheets containing words of life from my friend, Lance, to gain the courage to carry on.

CHAPTER 35

❖

REGROUPING

For as long as I shall live
I will testify to love
I'll be a witness in the silences
When words are not enough
With every breath I take
I will give thanks to God above
For as long as I shall live
I will testify to love.

—Ralph Van Manen, Robert Riekerk, Paul Field,
Hendrik Henk Pool, "Testify to Love"

It was timely that all the teams were gathering for a midsummer retreat weekend before heading to our last assignment. We were travelling in a caravan to Gaspe Peninsula, a beautiful outcropping of land where the St. Lawrence River feeds into the Atlantic Ocean.

I had done what I could to pick myself up and raise my spirits after my confidence was so shaken. I wanted to be the kind of leader my team deserved and an assistant to Dan that would be a strength and help, never a burden. So the insecurity and shame pricked by the Niagara experience had to go underground for now. I relied on my ideal self to cover any woundedness or fear. I would be joyful, positive, helpful, and encouraging—all the things I valued so highly. I would wait to examine the complex emotions of my failings until I was with someone safe who knew me well—someone like Lance.

The retreat was a great break for my team. The days were marked by debriefing, worship, relaxing, camping in tents, and cooking over a fire. I was able to pray with a fellow team leader that I had worked with on the Laurier Christian Fellowship executive the year before. Anina was a good listener and related to the bumpy moments of learning to help lead a team. Our conversation touched an authentic place in me. As we prayed together, my heart found a measure of peace again.

The last day of our retreat blew in with a fierce storm. The Gaspe area juts out into the Atlantic Ocean and is known for its extreme weather. I was one of the lucky ones who stayed dry during a windy, heavy rainfall. Several of the tents were soaked through, and people's sleeping bags and possessions were floating in water. There was a common building where we could take shelter to dry out and share mealtimes.

Our leaders focussed our attention on the good fruit that came from our bad weather. They pointed out the gift of bringing all the teams together under one roof instead of being dispersed over the campground area in little tent clusters. We rejoiced together in great conversations, Bible study, worship, and laughter that was refreshing and unifying for all of us.

* * * *

My team had its last placement with a congregation in New Brunswick. Campbellton was a place where the 60 percent French-speaking population spoke quickly, but the pace of life was slow.

This location was such a contrast to Toronto's busy streets and aggressive driving. In Campbellton, drivers stopped to allow pedestrians to cross the road, and they might even roll down the window to talk for a minute before driving on. When shopping in the grocery store, our team learned to never be in a hurry. Inevitably, the person ahead of us would have an unrushed conversation with the cashier. People were valued here more than frenetic activity and hustle.

I was thrilled to see a fat envelope from Lance shortly after I arrived in Campbellton.

> Hi Peg!
>
> I'm home now. For so long I'd been wanting to write you, yet the possible time to sit and do so kept disintegrating, but you have been in my thoughts and prayers every day! I have longed to tell you so much. I've longed to hear what God has been doing in your life and outreach. It has been incredibly uplifting to read and re-read your letters. I find your love for God so inspiring, and God really used your letter to increase my faith. Also, the encouragement and love you expressed were so refreshing for me. I needed your letter! Thanks, Peg! Thanks, God!
>
> Peg, the prayers of you, me and so many others are being answered. The words themselves and the spirit behind your words in the letters show clearly the work of God in very tangible ways. I found my heart beating quite quickly most of the letter. I was able to taste most of the situations - the people, the events, the feelings that you've had, the tone of your experience so far, and the movements that God was

> directing in you and in the team. Thanks so much for taking the time to share with me tastes of your impressions, snapshots, and yourself!
>
> Knowing who you are and knowing the unique unity we have has been a source of support for me. God uses you to help guide me into His best that unfolds in my life. Thanks for being a bubbling brook in my life!! You are a joy, Peg!

Lance's letter was ten handwritten pages of news from home, glimpses into his heart and growth, camp happenings, and encouragement! It was a gift to soothe the sore parts of my heart and remind me of the experiences that had shaped me as a leader. It was an expression of timely care that fortified my service for those last two weeks!

My team was asked to host a vacation Bible school programme every morning. We created a relaxed camp-like atmosphere. I pulled out camp action songs to share with the kids. I loved hearing them belted out as the children dispersed down the streets.

Each day, our team met to pray, plan, and pull together events with people from the local church. We planned group-building games and performed our skits for a backyard barbecue where I was introduced to the fantastic taste of barbecued salmon. This coastal town knew how to cook fish!!

The congregation made us feel like family, and everywhere we went, we were met with generous care. People seemed eager to meet Canadians from across the country. With each beautiful encounter, my faith in a diverse community rose. And with each memory-making moment, my first impulse was to craft it into a story to share with Lance.

Hi again!

Lance, thanks just for being you! I delight in you, my friend!

Campbellton, New Brunswick, is a quaint little town surrounded by the Appalachian Mountains with a swift current river separating it from Quebec in the North. Serving God here has been so much fun! We are running a vacation Bible school as we prepare for a Saturday-night youth rally in the park, share at adult barbecues, develop relationships with the locals, and connect with needs through service projects. Next week we weed gardens for the food bank in town, paint a new church, and put up drywall in the church basement. Though this sounds busy, the pace in Campbellton rarely feels hectic; this small town moves like a tortoise. I love the relaxed flow of activity, yet I also sense a lot of apathy and boredom among young people. God has many fans here, though, and I am excited to connect with people where they are at.

How is your summer going? What kind of things are you learning? I pray that God is continuing to meet your needs. May He be a refuge and strength. Bask in the light of His love for you, dear friend … I love you, Lance; I hope it's all right to miss you, because I do, but I rejoice in God's unfolding plans for us, knowing that good is at work through our different ways of serving.

There is so much I want to tell you about. It's been a very different summer than I expected; it has served to awaken my heart to the fact that "home" is a "mission" for me. I guess I had always romanticized going away to serve in an unknown land. The cross-cultural experiences right here in Canada have been wonderful for me—Chinatown to French-speaking east coast, big city to small town—but all over, people are the same. And wherever we go, we meet brothers and sisters in faith and feel as one—immediate kindred spirits! There is also as much need in little Campbellton as there is in the big TO. The one big lesson for all of us, I think, is the power of prayer to move barriers and open hearts to love well. God has blessed us in so many ways; team relationships are deepening, and we are learning to serve amidst all kinds of interesting circumstances. I'm feeling pretty ready to come home now, and I'm excited about our trip to PEI on Friday! And then … home I come! It'll be good to see you and all my family back in Ontario—Yay!

Until then, may each day be a wonderful celebration of divine love! God is on the move!

Love always,
Peg!

My final week went smoothly with work projects, team camping, and Eastern Canadian hospitality events that kept the team well-fed and connected to a vibrant community.

Our team supplied volunteer labour to weed and remove pests from the local food bank gardens. To keep their produce organic, they had an unconventional way of ridding their plants of potato bugs. The man in charge gave out pairs of gloves and explained that when we saw the round red bugs all over a leaf, we simply had to clap our hands together around the leaf to squish the bugs, rub palms together to make sure they were dead, then move on to the next one. Gulp!

I lasted for about half a row. But when one clap of my hands caused a squirt of bug guts to hit me in the face, I was done. My whole body was covered in goosebumps, and I knew I'd hit the threshold of yuckiness that I could manage. I liked to think I would serve at any task, but squishing juicy potato bugs crossed the line for me. I relinquished my row to more able teammates and went to join the weeding crew. We worked hard in the warm August sun and were rewarded with healthy-looking fields, hearty thanks from the coordinator, and some ice cream!

After a farewell party from our hosts on our last day, we stuffed all our gear into the van and headed down the coast to meet the other teams for a wrap-up retreat in PEI. Our summer adventure was nearing an end. We celebrated lessons learned, meaningful moments, and our teamwork as we affirmed one another's contributions. It was the perfect way to finish off our experience. It had been a good summer, but I knew I hadn't allowed anyone to become close enough that we would stay in touch.

The trip home was slow and sleepy as we drove straight through from PEI to Toronto, where our Western Canadian friends caught flights. Those of us from Ontario caught different van rides and dispersed.

Before I knew it, I was home!

CHAPTER 36

HONEST REFLECTION

> It's a tyranny this hating to need,
> Starving for truth but crushing the plea
> Behind these walls, I built to survive
> I lost sight of me.
>
> —Peggy Wright, "Walls of the Heart"

I had just a week to rest up and prepare to move back to Laurier that fall. But after my first day home connecting with my brother, sister, and parents, and enjoying a long rest, my biggest desire was to drive up to camp to visit Lance and reconnect to our community at youth camp.

After greeting other Silver Lake Camp friends, I knew Lance well enough to know that his way to unwind when the programme was done for the day was to find a snack in the kitchen. I checked there first when I arrived on site and was rewarded with a huge smile and lingering hug. It was wonderful to be in the same space again.

The conversation rolled easily from topic to topic. I wanted to hear all about how things were going at camp, and he was just as eager to hear about my experiences. We eventually made our way to Vespers Point, where we could sit and talk more privately.

Lance was great at asking questions. Somehow I found myself confiding in Lance about the more confusing emotions and experiences of my summer. My loss of confidence and sense of inadequacy in Niagara, my victories plummeting under disappointment in myself as a team leader—all of it poured out under Lance's understanding, caring gaze. But rather than just sympathize, he was able to help me untangle my feelings to gain a better perspective as he reminded me that my worth was not tied up in whether people were pleased with me or not. He prayed for me, and I found a peace I had not been able to find on my own.

Lance instinctively knew what I needed and offered it freely without reserve. His authenticity in sharing highs and lows beckoned me to put my own thoughts and feelings into words that often revealed me to myself. Lance was a peaceful presence, offering me a solid place of safety to explore my truth and find rest.

Lance found me a place on-site to crash for the night and made sure my needs were met before heading off to his own bed. His support and thoughtfulness made me feel heard and cared for. I had rarely felt such a deep connection with a kindred spirit. I fell into a deeper sleep than I had found in a while. My heart was at peace after unburdening to such a trusted, helpful friend.

I reflected on my time with Lance in my journal when I returned home.

> God, I come to you as a child to a Father today!
>
> Thank you for Lance—his friendship, his life, his character! Thank you for teaching me through him. God, I sometimes feel like I have two left feet, or I've learned to depend on him too much.

Encourage him! Affirm him even now as he goes into his program meeting. Hold him and uphold him. Thank you for loving Lance when I'm not quite sure how.

Thank you for the time with Mom and Kathy today! Teach me how to love them more, too! Teach me to love as You do! Make me an encouragement, carrying water to parched places as Your bubbling brook. Thank you that You are the source of love.

I love you, God!

* * *

A week later, I was settled back in Waterloo in a small basement apartment with my good friend Carolyn. I was happy that it was just the two of us this year. We enjoyed setting up our home together and decorating the large bulletin board wall with encouraging quotes and pictures that made us smile. It was a much longer walk to school from Lonelm Court in Waterloo, but it was a space where I could be myself, unwind after busy days, or work hard on my essays and assignments, motivated by Carolyn's equal dedication and focus. Carolyn and I created healthy rhythms together as we made time for schoolwork, social connections, long walks, and the cooking of nutritious meals. She taught me the joy of putting fruit in my salad. Yum! We also laughed a lot. She was an awesome companion, and I enjoyed my third-year classwork in such an encouraging, stress-free environment.

Lance lived a twenty-minute car ride away but was nearby at the University of Waterloo daily. He arranged to meet with me shortly after I settled back in town.

We walked to a nearby park. I was walking quickly, as I did when I was rushing to classes. Lance took hold of my hand and slowed down our pace. He encouraged me to relax and enjoy being unhurried for a while. I could feel my adrenalin gear down in his peaceful presence.

Lance shared more stories from his summer about the young people he'd invested in mentoring. He also talked about silly moments and themed events he had created with his programme team. "People before programme" was a phrase Lance used when planning with teams so that they remembered to adjust their programme to meet the needs of the group they were leading. "If a plan isn't working to increase the value of the experience, then the plans have to flex for creativity to serve the group." He was such an inspiring, fun, gifted leader that I never tired of hearing him process his thoughts and experiences!

Lance was so easy to talk to. I was struck again by how great he was at asking questions and probing deeper for understanding. He also had great insights and wasn't afraid to challenge any thinking that he saw as illogical or unhealthy.

As we sat on a park bench, I leaned into Lance and let myself fully relax.

Lance turned me towards him so he could see my face as he asked an unexpected question: "Peg, do you need me?"

I didn't know what to say. I had always assumed that needing God was right but needing people was a mistake. I had always found needy people kind of draining. I didn't think I was supposed to let myself "need" anyone. Yet Lance was someone I definitely wanted in my life.

I talked in circles without saying anything concrete. "You're good for me. I love spending time with you. I really care for you …" I was running out of ways to say the same thing. I couldn't bring myself to answer his question directly.

I ran out of words and lapsed into silence. After the quiet stretched between us for a moment, Lance closed the conversation by adding, "I don't want to be a distraction. I just wanted to know if you need me the way I need you."

Oof! Those words pierced me like an arrow. They asked me to risk being vulnerable. They cut right through my pretence of strength, my self-protection, and my fear of facing my own needs in a relationship.

I didn't know what to say in response. We walked back to my place. I confessed to Lance that I still thought of myself as damaged from abuse but didn't understand its impact on my relationships yet.

Lance walked me home while we both kept the conversation light or lapsed into a companionable silence. I was still experimenting with this new level of honest confession but hardly knew my own thoughts well enough to put them into words.

After he left, I prayed and then sat down at my writing desk and began a letter to him. Writing has always been a tool to move from fuzzy thinking towards clarity for me.

>Lance!!
>
>You have touched my life so deeply! Your life has brought comfort, joy, beauty, peace, colour, and a depth of love and understanding that overwhelms me as I try to grasp it. One thing I know for certain: you are a blessing to me. I appreciate your ability to quiet my mind and heart in a way that restores my soul. You are not a distraction; my time with you only makes it easier to give again to others, to delight in people and share joy, to listen …

Around you my heart is surer; my steps are lighter, and my thoughts more creative. You are good for me. Thanks!

I guess what I'm trying to say is, okay, I need you. God knew I needed you!

And with that admission, our relationship had just solidified past the friend zone!

CHAPTER 37

DISMANTLING WALLS

Surrender your walls,
Step into the light
And live authentically.

—Peggy Wright, "Walls of the Heart"

That fall, I was surprised by how my conversations with Lance brought my emotions to the surface! I had never had someone in my life who was so committed to exploring the inner terrain of my thoughts and emotions.

I had always seen myself as a joyful, successful leader who occasionally had spells of self-doubt and insecurity. I couldn't explain the emptiness, loss of confidence, shame, and sadness that were sometimes triggered or surfaced when I stopped being busy.

Don't get me wrong; life was full of goodness. I enjoyed my classes, and Carolyn was the perfect complement to my daily rhythms as a housemate. We encouraged each other's faith, good work habits, social connections, and creative fun. We had both started significant dating relationships, so we had lots to talk about and share.

But during that wonderful year, allowing myself to need Lance, lean on him, and depend on him was harder than I thought it would be. It surprised me how often my exterior strength crumbled in the face of Lance's earnest emotional honesty. This level of intimacy was new territory for me. It felt like a betrayal to hide behind my self-protective walls with Lance. Yet he was unaware of how sensitive I could be.

Early in our relationship, Lance came over for the afternoon completely secure in relating to me as a strong, joyful companion. This gave him the confidence to share whatever he was thinking. We had just officially become a couple. Lance kissed me and sat close beside me on the couch to talk.

He casually mentioned that I had bad breath and that maybe I'd like to brush my teeth before we settled in.

I was mortified by his comment. We didn't see each other as often as I would have liked. I wasn't comfortable needing him or placing any demands on him. And now we finally had a date in person. I was thrilled that we were together in the same space! I wanted to feel attractive and enjoy our date, to relax and snuggle a little. But his comment pricked at my insecurities. I was hurt that he seemed to need me to change to enjoy time together. As I moved robotically to the bathroom to brush my teeth, I teared up with the feeling that I wasn't good enough. *How could I have ever thought I would be good enough?*

I was becoming convinced that dating was a bad idea. Vulnerability was too hard! Tears insisted on rushing to my eyes. I tried to hold them off because I felt like a baby and I didn't know how to explain my reaction. Once I calmed down, I checked to see that any trace of tears was gone from my face before returning to the couch with Lance. I didn't want my overreaction to spoil our time together.

I didn't give enough credit to Lance's perceptiveness. Before I walked away to the bathroom, he saw my face redden and felt the comfortable space change between us. When I returned and tried to talk, there was a quiver of my lip that gave me away.

He asked what I was thinking.

I hardly knew how to tell him that his honesty had hurt my feelings. I felt silly and childish. I had always buried hurts and hadn't learned to talk about them honestly. I was embarrassed by my overblown reaction.

But he was persistent and really wanted to know me. He wouldn't let it go. He revealed the truth when he guessed that his comment had been hurtful. The dam of my reserve burst as I started to cry.

He apologized and opened his arms to me as the tears came. I cried into his sweater. He admitted that he felt so close to me that he thought his honest perception would be appreciated. He assured me that he would never intentionally hurt me and was committed to learning how to love me well. He asked me whether I would stay open to him and not close him out.

I was learning that shame and withdrawal were my default. When I felt bad or silly, I assumed I was unlovable and hid my emotions. But that didn't make them diminish. I had a sensitive heart conditioned by self-contempt.

That year, Lance was teaching me to move towards relationship—not away—when feeling hurt, sad, confused, or full of shame. God was using our relationship to show me an unconditional love that invites connection as a way to heal.

I couldn't decide whether this level of emotional honesty and vulnerability with Lance was scary or freeing. It was too new a feeling to be sure. I was aware that this relationship touched me more deeply than any I had experienced before. I was embarrassed that I cried every time we were together in our first year of dating. Chronic hiding was hard to displace. I guess it was leaking out of my eyes.

He took the time to write to me after our date.

Hi Peg!!

I want to affirm my love for you in writing. Last night showed me how I can hurt you and can be insensitive to you. I realized that I can't promise that I won't hurt you again, because I am human … I am committed to persevering in my love for you. My goal is to love as God does - unconditionally, faithfully, and actively. Last night I relearned, too, that I must give myself fully to God before I can give out of fullness to you.

I delight in loving you. I am compelled to want to be there for you anytime you are overwhelmed, any essay, any time you learn something, any time you are feeling giddy and silly, anytime you are in need. My desire to show my love for you is very strong. Your infinite worth is fixed in the heavens and fixed in my heart.

I love you always, Peg!

Love,
Lance

Colossians 3:15—"Let the peace of Christ rule in your heart …

He was so steady and unconditional in offering grace, truth, compassion, and peace to me. Lance's love for me gave me a mirror to begin the process of restoring and healing the way I saw myself. His love was becoming an unwavering reality. He recognized my joy and my emotional range as the gift of a bubbling brook, and I was realizing that he was like calm waters that allowed my turbulence to find rest. I began to call him my "still waters."

One mindset loop I regularly found myself stuck in went something like this: "I feel ashamed of myself because I feel sad, mad, or doubtful. I have a deep faith in God; I'm supposed to be joyful and hopeful, so it's wrong to feel as I do, which makes me feel unlovable ... a disappointment. I feel ashamed of myself, which makes me sad ..." And around I'd go again!

I had never tried to put this spin into words. It was just a merry-go-round in my mind that was very familiar. People speak of forming mental ruts, and I had definitely formed a deep groove in this neurological pathway. I would find this rut anytime I failed at something; felt fragile, shamed, or criticized; or when the shadow memories of my past intruded.

It was embarrassing to admit this thought train to Lance, but though he seemed puzzled by it, he never changed how he saw me or felt about me.

I didn't understand this spin. It was so automatic. I thought it might have something to do with the deep trauma buried inside that got triggered. I knew that my identity formation became messed up. Being female had never been something for me to celebrate. Being emotional was not respected. I had learned to reject my desires and generally would defer and please others to keep the peace. I certainly never celebrated my feelings. School taught me to form rational arguments and logical conclusions, which made emotional responses suspect. I associated feelings with being broken or needy.

My head knew that God is love, but I didn't realize that when I shut out feelings, I was also cutting off a significant way that I am wired to connect and experience God and relationship. I understood and spoke eloquently to comfort and reassure others, but God's love couldn't reach my sense of self. Admitting fears and doubts would inevitably take me for a spin on the "shame wheel."

Lance's response to my spin began to cut through my sense of shame and self-rejection. He let me know that I was seen, known, and loved.

Instead of minimizing and devaluing my feelings, he helped me explore why I might be feeling the way I did. Why was I sad? Was I ignoring my own needs? Had a conversation with someone hurt me? Did an experience trigger a reaction to something from my past? Gradually I was learning that my feelings made sense. They often held pieces of wisdom for me to uncover. Together Lance and I probed the shadows that I ignored and hid from.

The first few times I cried, Lance wasn't sure how to respond. He wondered whether he was supposed to make me feel better—to fix it. That's generally what we do with problems; we problem-solve. But in time, we both learned to just give the emotion space in our healthy connection. Staying present was something I had never done before. Absence, both mental and emotional, was a self-protective mechanism that allowed me to function when I was victimized.

I always felt more whole after talking through and understanding my fears, insecurities, and reactions. It was validating. It was as if I got a piece of myself back.

Shortly after we started dating, as Lance began to understand the terrain of my stumbling thought patterns that led to a spin, he made scripture posters for me. He cut them out in cloud shapes, like thought bubbles, on pink and orange poster paper and gave them to me as a gift.

> Peggy,
>
> I love you. My love for you inspires me to protect and cherish and encourage you. This gift is from God and me for you—'cause we love you and believe in you!

"His word is a lamp unto your feet and a light unto your path." Psalm 119

Love,
Lance xoxo

Each poster had a scripture.

The first reminded me of God's protection and care: "Keep me as the apple of Your eye; hide me in the shadow of Your wings" (Psalm 17:8).

Another spoke about the steadiness of God's goodness and love: "Give thanks to the Lord Almighty, for the Lord is good; His love endures forever!" (Jeremiah 33:11).

One poster described God as my shelter: "The Lord will strengthen you and protect you from evil" (2 Thessalonians 3:3).

When I felt overwhelmed I could turn to these scriptures: "His divine power has given you everything you need for life and godliness through your knowledge of Him who called you by his own glory and goodness" (2 Peter 1:3) and "I cannot do it … but God will." (Genesis 41:16).

Our anchoring scripture was included: "I am still confident of this: I will see the goodness of the Lord in the land of the living. Wait for the Lord; be strong and take heart and wait for the Lord" (Psalm 27:13, 14).

When feelings of failure and defeat overwhelmed me, I could read, "His commands are not burdensome, for everyone born of God overcomes the world." (1 John 5:4).

Anxiety and fear could be entrusted to God's care and attention, "The Lord is near. Do not be anxious about anything, but in everything, by prayer and petition with thanksgiving present your requests to God and the peace of God will guard your heart and mind…" (Philippians 4:4–6).

A few posters reminded me that my perfectionism and harsh

inner critic didn't measure my value and worth: "There is no condemnation for those who are in Christ because through Christ Jesus the law of the Spirit of Life has set me free from the law of sin and death" (Romans 8:1–2) and "Let us fix our eyes on Jesus, the author, and perfecter of our faith" (Hebrews 12:2).

There was one to remind me that I was God's creative idea: "You created my inmost being. You knit me together in my mother's womb" (Psalm 139:13).

Finally, there was a scripture I could read when I got caught up in performing to be loved: "Be still and know that I am God" (Psalm 46:10).

I put these scriptures up around my room. These were truths to land on when my brain would spin—truths I could pray into. They helped ground me. I committed each one to memory over time.

Lance helped me to understand that I was seen, known, and loved by the one who made me, decided my value, and had plans to lead me into spacious places of freedom and hope.

CHAPTER 38

GROWING PAINS

> You can see me -
> And you believe.
> You think I have a future
> You call me to dream
> I don't know where it leads,
> I just know I have to try
> So, I'm pressing on here.
>
> —Peggy Wright, "Believe"

One source of tension that grew as I learned to rely on and be vulnerable with Lance was the limited amount of time we had together. I did get to see Lance as we led youth events and drove to retreats, but that was no longer enough for me. I needed time to take off the pressure to perform and just be with him.

In September 1990 I wrote this in my journal.

> I have many questions, God, about loving him …
> How can I need him without placing expectations

or demands on him? I find the phone so frustrating, yet to ask for more of his time seems as though I'm constricting him. He seems content because he's being fulfilled by just having support that he has lacked. I'm glad I can love him this way, yet I don't feel I'm being honest with myself or with him. It's easier to suppress doubts, desires, fears, and yet I know it could be so good to learn and pray together. I need that, but does Lance? I need to spend time with him regularly. Does he? Am I being selfish? Am I demanding? Should I just push this all aside as if I'm content? Help me to sort out how I feel. I don't know anything about these needs, these desires ... Are they normal? Are they healthy? What should I do with them?

I need you, God! Can I trust this kind of love?

Help me to find peace. Help me and Lance to support and love one another—or, if that is not your plan, don't allow us to commit that deeply.

If he doesn't need me, Lord, then I don't want to need him; don't allow doubts to fill me, God. I feel overwhelmed. I need to move past this; there is much to do today!

I give You Lance. Love him as only You can! Hold him today.

Be my refuge. I will hide in You! Lord, I hate needing anything from anyone. Yet I'm learning that I can't stand on my own. Can I trust others? I don't want to be demanding, yet I have needs that I'm afraid to let myself feel. They make me feel small and insignificant. Pressures to perform weigh on me. Everything looms so largely: responsibilities, needs of others. I cannot, but You can, God! I can trust You! I am not alone. Thank you for standing beside me.

Now, God, please help me to give, to encourage, to listen, to love. I need to call people. Make me strong. Why are my emotions so close to the surface today? I will rest in You!

Lance was great at being spontaneous and fun. One day he came to my door dressed up as Sir Lancelot and used a toothbrush in a mock battle with my roommate's boyfriend, Greg. He made me laugh as he literally swept me off my feet.

He would also drop by after playing floor hockey with the guys at a nearby church. But he was always exhausted by then and would often fall asleep when I gave him a back rub.

I felt as if I were competing with so many things in his life. I didn't want to just wait my turn to come to the top of the pile. The busyness went both ways, but somehow it made me feel vulnerable just to hear about what he was doing in the week, as I wondered where I fit in. We would be talking on the phone, and I would ask him what his schedule was like, and he would talk through his days without me seeing any empty spaces.

I didn't want to get in the way of things that Lance used to refuel, such as tennis with a friend, hockey with the guys, and time alone, but I also just needed to know that I was important enough to gain space on the calendar each week.

I don't remember how I brought this up. I always found it hard to feel needy. I had been learning that when I had sensitive things to talk through, it was best to write them down ahead of time and read them aloud with Lance for discussion. This is an excerpt from a letter I wrote after we talked through prioritizing our relationship.

> Lance,
>
> I love you and want you to feel secure in my love for you. There is nothing you could do that would be beyond this love. As we make mistakes, let them be building blocks in our relationship! I love to share anything I can with you, and at times it's hard to not have you enter more fully into my life and LCF events, but Lance, I love you more than I love the things you can do for me. Hearing your heart and knowing your love is steady helps me deal with the spaces when I can't see you. Know that I want to be your best cheerleader as you pursue the vision that God has for you. I want God's best for you - I always will! So, let us consider how we may "spur one another on toward love and good deeds"[Hebrews 10:24, NIVSB]. I love you. I admire and respect who you are and who you are becoming. I can always count on you to come with grace and listen well and want the best for me, too. May every day be a celebration of God's love working in and through us.
>
> Love,
> Your Peg.

I don't know how that conversation went, exactly, but I do know that this was a resolution, not the heightened feelings in the middle of it. My resentment that sports and time with other people were fitting into the calendar before scheduling time with me dissipated after I heard Lance's heart!

I was relieved, however, when we decided to plan ahead with Lance and Peg days. They went on the calendar first, and then other things got planned around them! This was the security I needed to know that our relationship was important to both of us. Without this time commitment, I couldn't grow beyond being independent and self-sufficient to a new place I had never been before—interdependent. To lean into another's strengths and our connection was a new experience. To deny my needs was so natural that I required a deep sense of safety to bring them honestly into our relationship. I hadn't yet learned that I had developed some unhealthy relationship patterns.

CHAPTER 39

STRIVING

The helper pattern: This is where we make other people's needs more important than our own. And an example might be, we get home from work, our body's telling us we're tired and we need to rest. We get a message from a friend and they're in need, and we prioritize their need as being more important than our own. And that's a consistent pattern of how we relate to people in the world.

—Alex Howard

When I was in a crowd of people, I had a radar for those who were feeling uncomfortable or shy. I calmed my self-consciousness by starting a conversation with someone to try to put him or her at ease. Having a role gave me comfort in a group, too. Fortunately, I met many people who were awesome and good for me, but I also tried to support people who were dealing with some serious, complex issues.

I had a few teen friends who had dark moods regularly. I felt such empathy for each of them and found joy in remembering together that God's love never abandons us or forgets our needs and feelings. I passed on comforting passages from scripture that had often spoken to my soul.

Sharing words of comfort and unconditional love was like giving myself and others an inspirational talk, but I didn't have the skills or knowledge to care well for myself as I gave to others. When my young friends called, I felt I had to listen as long as they wanted to talk no matter what I was working on when the phone rang. I would end up staying up late to finish an essay after spending more than an hour on the phone. I talked to many of them almost weekly for years. It just felt like the right thing to do. I loved my friends. I felt needed and valued when I was able to help.

I loved to be a person who cared for others. That wasn't the issue. But I would lose myself in caring. I didn't know how to listen to my needs in the mix. I was told that Christians put others before themselves, so I was determined to do that. But ignoring my physical well-being, my emotional needs, and my commitment to my schoolwork and responsibilities left me cutting corners. This kind of giving wasn't sustainable and put undue stress on my overall health. I couldn't figure out how to limit what I gave, since the needs around me were very real and felt urgent.

The truth is, I did relate to and feel deep love and compassion for the youth I talked to. I remember one "tough girl" who was really bugged by my seeking her out in a group and caring about her. She pushed hard to see whether I would stick around and still show her love. It was through our relationship that the truth that love is a choice and an action rooted deeply in me. One time she said to me, "I could beat you up, you know. Then you wouldn't love me!" I looked at the anger mixed with fear in her eyes and felt God's unconditional love well up in me for her. I replied, "Yes, you could beat me up! But you couldn't make me stop caring about you and loving the person I see inside." She just glared at me before walking away.

I was surprised at the depth and sincerity of love God put in my heart for my younger friends. They often challenged and inspired me through their deep questions. I was grateful for their searching because it deepened my faith. I wrote a song for them in 1991. It may have also been a song for the little girl in me.

A SONG FOR CINDY

You've been hurt too many times
The wounds are deep
Again, the scar is hit before it's healed
Inside this hardened shell
There waits a little girl
Longing to spread her wings

Cindy, don't turn back my love
For Cindy, my heart it bleeds with yours
I long so much to hold you
I want to lift you up
To the warmth and light above

Your sneakers scuff the floor
You've heard it all before
Words echo back, empty to your ears
"Why?" you cry so many times
"Does anybody hear?"

Cindy, don't turn back my love
For Cindy, my eyes are wet with tears
I long so much to hold you
I want to lift you up to the hands that bear your scars

> There you'll find true love
> Like you've never seen before
> It sweeps in waves to the shore
> Searching for each crack it longs to fill.
> That little girl will find true love
> Cindy.

I knew deep in my heart that love and hope were what we were all searching for. But life could be hard for so many of us. When conversations turned to talk of suicide, I didn't know of any support lines or places youth could turn in in 1990. So I would listen as they talked themselves empty of their anxiety, fear, depression, or hurt. I would try to anchor them with truths and encouragement about the potential and beauty I saw in them.

I didn't realize how I carried the weight of those calls in my body as I braced myself for the next crisis. This added to the tension I already carried as I tried to ignore my pain and respond to the pressures of my responsibilities. I had a few episodes where I woke up unable to turn my head to one side because of muscle tension. The doctor prescribed muscle relaxants, but no one taught me how to deal with the underlying issues. I had a stress response that was becoming my normal operating system to keep me prepared for danger. One way it showed up was in a helper pattern, where I tried to prepare for and fix the crises of others. I was pouring energy outward while ignoring the cries of my own heart and health.

My coaching was not well rooted in my own self-care. I needed to hear and receive the words I was giving away, but they seemed to roll off and never convince my interior world of a sense of safety and worth.

I defined myself so strongly as a helper that every visitor, every phone call, and every request for me to give or lead was a yes, unless it would double-book me. I wanted so much to love people well, and I was such a pleaser that I didn't want to let anyone down. To disappoint someone became the ultimate sin. But I didn't realize that I was letting myself down—that saying yes to everything meant I was automatically saying no to self-care, school, and some mutual friendships that got crowded out. I wasn't owning and making choices. I rerouted energy from nurturing my personal growth and identity formation to feeding the dysfunctional weeds of earning my worth as a helper and pleaser. I was getting depleted.

The drive that kept me from ownership of my direction and daily choices was part of the unexplored regions of my heart. I could dress it up in spiritual language to win admiration. I'd say that I trusted that "God wouldn't give me more than I could handle"—a popular truism at that time in my church circles. Somehow this absolved me by making it God's responsibility to keep me from feeling depleted, exhausted, and empty.

I would cry myself to sleep some nights from sheer exhaustion while also feeling guilty that I wasn't living up to what God wanted from me. Jesus said, "I come to bring life in abundance," and I would feel discouraged that my experience of serving God didn't line up.

My body started to show increasing wear and tear.

Sinus infections continued to plague my winters. I would get two or three each flu season. The only way I knew to treat a cold was with an over-the-counter decongestant and an antibiotic if the discharge got too thick to pass—which happened every time! So that meant two to three antibiotics each winter for years! I had a bad reaction to sulfa drugs, but the others seemed to clear the congestion. I had no idea I was creating a serious problem with my gut health. I didn't know that there was a better way to get to the root of these problems.[8]

Headaches were normal for me and were worse around my periods, which were so difficult to manage that I would miss a day of school each month. A girlfriend in my first-year university told me about naproxen for period pain. It allowed me to stop missing days, but it didn't make me feel any less moody and uncomfortable. This kind of medication put a burden on my cleansing organs.[9]

I had learned to become numb to headaches because they were too constant to acknowledge. When I mentioned them to my doctor, she said to try Advil instead of Tylenol if I wasn't getting relief.

I didn't like taking medications unless the pain got so bad that it interfered with my plans. I tried to limit myself to just a few times a month. I learned to push through the pain and tune it out. I wish I had known about dietary changes to reduce inflammation and all the natural remedies that work with our bodies to support balance and healing.[10]

Lance started to recognize when I had a headache before I did. He would ask whether my head was hurting, and I would take a minute to sink down into my body to let myself feel to confirm that I had a bad headache.

I started to get sick often. I seemed to catch anything that was going around.

My environmental allergies were getting worse. Every time I went home, my allergy to my dog was heightened. He was a non-shedding poodle, but my allergies didn't care. Now his dander could set me off. Anytime I changed to a new environment, my body would protest with itchy eyes, a watery nose, and postnasal drainage, making my throat irritated. I always carried antihistamines with me, since allergies also created asthma complications.

One day I was biking to Steph's house down the highway and my airways started to react and close off my oxygen supply. I hadn't thought to have my inhaler on me. All I could do was stop moving, get off my bike, and sit on the grass while I focussed on each inhalation. I counted each wheezy breath in and out to try to calm my pounding heart, and I prayed that I would be able to slowly walk home. After sitting for about twenty minutes, I slowly made my way back home to my inhaler and relief! That experience taught me to always have my asthma medication with me.

I didn't know why my symptoms were worsening. I didn't understand the downward spiral of the stress mode I lived in.

Somehow, I was still able to keep up with full-time school, Youth Eventz groups, youth worship services, Laurier Christian Fellowship executive, church commitments on weekends, and a regular stream of lunch dates, phone calls, and visits.

Amid demanding days, times with Lance became a needed refuge and respite. Lance didn't struggle with rest. He had a stillness inside that was medicine to quiet my drive to perform and my inner critic, who couldn't tolerate laziness. Productivity was a measuring stick I used to evaluate every moment of my days. Somehow my worth seemed to depend on it.

CHAPTER 40

FUTURE FEARS

Our sense of calling can get lost when we take on someone else's calling as our own.

—Meryl Herr

As I was growing in my relationship with Lance, I was also wondering about my future. After my summer travelling with our youth mission group and my experiences with our interdenominational ministry, my vision for my life work widened. Lance was really committed to youth in the United Church. But my family had just gone through a painful breakaway from the United Church. The clash between liberal and conservative poles in Brantford made my minister decide to lead the congregation independently of the structures that were pressuring him to compromise his convictions. I wasn't sure where my faith fit in.

I loved living my ideals without concern for denominational divides. I wanted to find what unified Christ's followers and pour my life into loving, positive movements of service, intercession, and care. I wasn't sure how I fit into Lance's world and sense of calling. I was just learning to explore the terrain of my own heart and mind, and I didn't want to get lost in deferring to others again.

On a long drive with Lance to Lowville, Ontario, I started to share my thoughts, questions, and concerns.

I remember saying something like "I feel that my interdenominational and cross-cultural experiences have broadened my understanding, and I am no longer sure I fit in the confines of one denomination. I know you are really committed to United Church youth. I support that, but I'm concerned that I will miss out on what God is growing in me. I don't want to lose my calling by disappearing behind yours ..."

Things got quiet while Lance digested all of this.

I was surprised by his response: "So you think we should split up?"

I didn't think that was what I was saying. My heart certainly didn't jibe with that comment! It jolted me from head to toe.

Unfortunately, we had just pulled into the parking lot, and we had to table this conversation for later. It was time to focus on collaborating with the local team to pull together skits, music, sharing, and prayer for a creative evening service in a few hours. We exchanged an apologetic look before we headed off in different directions. I worked with the music team while Lance led a group of youth in creating a thoughtful drama.

Leaving the conversation unresolved left me feeling off-balance. It was a good thing I knew how to practise containment and focus on the task at hand. The thought of breaking up left an ache in the pit of my stomach that lingered throughout the day.

Lance and I worked with the teens and adult volunteers all afternoon to prepare an energetic, creative Lowville youth service! This kind of experience with United Church youth felt inspiring and natural to me. It helped put my restless thoughts aside. Lance and I made a great team.

We were among the last to leave as we made sure clean-up happened thoroughly and that every person who wanted to connect with us had a chance.

It was late when we hopped into the car for the drive back to Waterloo. We were quiet at first until we reached the long stretch of the highway.

I can't remember which one of us brought up our earlier conversation. I know his suggestion that we split up shook me. I realized I hadn't even entertained that option. It was the safety of our partnership that allowed me to dream and connect to my inner world. I was wishing I could take back voicing my questions, fears, and doubts.

But the mood shifted as Lance said something profound that became etched in my mind and calmed my heart: "Peg, we can't ever know what the future holds, but we can look back and see the places we have travelled together. Do we see good fruit there? Do we see God at work to grow us into more of who we are meant to be? If so, then we can use those milestones to give us confidence as we look to the unknown ahead. We can rest assured that God will continue to bring good fruit through our relationship in the future."

Shortly after this conversation, I wrote this card:

> Lance,
>
> I was counting my blessings today and freshly acknowledged that ... you are a treasure! There's no one in the world like you, dear one!
>
> You bring form and life to faint dreams. You are a mover, a shaker—and yet your ability to make things happen is balanced by attention to detail, and your heart never forgets the presence of people who desire or need to be stretched, cared for, or

given an opportunity, and who need to know God's love!

You also have a wonderful inner life that I am just beginning to grasp. I love the sense of priority, order, and discipline that exists in your private world! Your life is truly "a pouring out." I admire and respect you vastly, Lance Wright! I love your warmth that includes everyone in a room, and your sincerity as you desire to be godly in relationships, ministry, and fulfilling responsibility. You are quick to recognize mistakes and always look for the first opportunity to make things right. Thanks for your honesty and integrity in our relationship, Lance!

I delight in you—all of you—and I am thrilled to be your partner in facing all that life brings! Let's walk together in the light of God's love, celebrating God's goodness in service to Him, our King!

My deepest love always,

Peg xoxo

"Though the mountains be shaken, and the hills be removed, yet my unfailing love for you will not be shaken nor my covenant of peace be removed" (Isaiah 54:10, NIV).

We didn't know what the future held for us, but we decided to continue to walk hand in hand to meet it. I found tremendous peace in that.

CHAPTER 41

THAWING

> Those who really love you are not fooled by mistakes you have made or dark images you hold about yourself. They remember your beauty when you feel ugly; your wholeness when you are broken; your innocence when you feel guilty; your purpose when you are confused.
>
> —Alan Cohen

Being emotionally vulnerable was tiring. It was hard work to stay present and in tune with my emotional world. It took energy to understand the currents that ran under the surface of my days.

So many feelings that had never interfered with life before now seemed to be pouring out of me every time I was in the safety of Lance's presence. It was like a thaw after a long time of numbing and containment. I was conscientious in following through with whatever people asked of me. But I often felt raw as I met the challenges of my days.

Containment had kept trauma from sitting on the surface of life. The damage would surface only occasionally in a stormy journal entry or tears on my pillow at night. But now I was hypersensitive to triggers of shame. I felt fragile.

I voiced my frustration about this to Lance. I asked him whether he regretted asking me whether I needed him. I felt as if I were more than he had bargained for. I felt like the needy one in our relationship. I preferred to be strong and confident. I felt like a burden that Lance was trying to help instead of an equal partner. Now it was me asking if Lance needed me.

His letter in response to that conversation was incredibly healing.

> Peg!!
>
> My thoughts are never far from you, so I want to share some with you!
>
> I love you for who you are, Peg! I find it hard to understand how you can not like yourself at times. The more I know of you the more I love You! Over the past six months, I have seen and been with you through intense struggles. I've shared with you that this has been hard for me. You share your life with me. I am amazed that you want to do this with me. My love is not turned away by these struggles but deepened. I want to fight for you against the shadows! You are my delight, my treasure, my partner!
>
> Please don't ever fear me turning away my love cause I've seen you in weakness. I love you, not just you when you're strong, but just you - and so long as you are you- which is always - I love you!

At times I wish I could in return bring to you similar struggles with similar emotions and intensity, but I don't have them.

I need you, the same as you need me but not always in the same way. I am a deep-rooted independent person who - up until the present anyway - has constant emotional stability. Very rarely will I bring to you tears from emotional turmoil raging within me. Yet I need you as my partner, I need you to know me, I need you to love me, I need you to support and encourage me, I need you to dream with me, I need you to know about my days, I need you to inspire me and focus me on God and I need you to help me seek God and pray and I need you to build a life together and I need you to care for me and I need you to make decisions with!

Peg, I love you and I need you!

Love,
Lance xoxoxoxo

Lance's love was transforming life for me. He was breaking through my self-protection and fear of vulnerability and rejection. It takes time to believe in your worth after feeling so cheapened by abuse, but I was starting to believe that Lance's love was a place of rest: safe and not dependent on my performance each day.

I was getting a glimpse of what it takes to heal a wounded heart.

CHAPTER 42

SUMMER IN THE CITY

Therefore, since we are surrounded by such a great cloud of witnesses, let us throw off everything that hinders and the sin that so easily entangles. And let us run with perseverance the race marked out for us, fixing our eyes on Jesus, the pioneer and perfecter of faith. For the joy set before him he endured the cross, scorning its shame, and sat down at the right hand of the throne of God. Consider him who endured such opposition from sinners, so that you will not grow weary and lose heart.

—Hebrews 12:1-3, NIV

As my third year of university ended, the Youth Eventz core team was planning a new way to care for youth that were no longer able to fit in a summer camp experience. The programme was called Summer in the City. Lance and I joined the team that would create these weekend experiences in each of the cities where there were already groups of teens involved in our Youth Eventz programmes.

Despite spending the summer doing what I loved with amazing colleagues, an unexplainable sense of weakness started to show up.

Waves of insecurity and self-doubt could creep in just before I was responsible to lead something, especially when speaking to the group in a session.

My notes were prepared, but I would doubt that I had anything to say that would be meaningful. I felt pressure to come through with something great; this was due to a perfectionist streak I had often used to motivate action but that also created subterranean anxiety. I was afraid that I would speak too long, that I wouldn't capture the interest of young people, that another leader would do a better job. I felt as if my value to the team had to be proven by my offerings. I regularly questioned my worth.

I would pull Lance aside to ask him to pray for me. He would allow me to talk and process my fears out loud. I remember many stormy, tearful conversations just before I had to collect myself to speak to the group. Lance was a grounding supporter that never wavered in his encouragement and belief in me. He would remind me that I was God's "bubbling brook." I gained courage from his steady, peaceful presence. I continued to picture him as God's "still waters," not just in my life but also in ministry generally. He always knew how to drain stress away, draw out the best in others, and help people approach problems with a solution-oriented outlook.

I wasn't feeling very bubbly much of the time. Though I was working only weekends and had time in between to recover, I just couldn't seem to regain energy. I felt weak, tired, achy, and constantly sick. I didn't know what was wrong, but I didn't feel like myself. This feeling lingered all summer and left a shadowy haze over my memories. I was grateful for the weekdays at home to rest.

Summer in the City was full of memorable experiences with incredible people. I recall vividly one night when participants and leaders had all spread out our sleeping bags on the church floor for the night. One pair of girls had the giggles and couldn't stop whispering and laughing, which kept the whole group awake. The other youth started to yell at the girls to tell them to be quiet. I knew that giggles could not be cured this way!

I slipped quietly out of my sleeping bag and went to the giggly pair. I told them I would be happy to sing to them and rub their backs until they felt calm so we could all rest.

Though the girls were over sixteen years old, they responded to this idea with enthusiasm and said that they wished they had someone who would care for them like this more often. One girl told me I would be a great mom someday! It uncovered a deep desire to be a parent that I hadn't acknowledged before.

I loved how the whole room got quiet and restful as I sang songs of love and faith over the group. This became my favourite way to calm groups for bedtime, no matter how old they were. I enjoyed leading youth in creating a meaningful, safe community.

But I was puzzled by my lack of energy. I would wake early to have some solo time and engage in personal care before being plunged into the day's activity, but I was draggy and headachy most of the time. My body felt heavy and tired. Sleeping on church floors was getting more difficult. My body protested with persistent muscle aches.

The last week of our summer programming was youth camp at Silver Lake. Because I'd been struggling with my health, when I saw the list of counselling teams, I realized that I was with two new staff. That meant that the director was counting on me to anchor a group and be a mentor. I told her that I might need an experienced co-team since I wasn't feeling like myself. I knew I was not at my best.

By the third day of camp, I was really sick. I ached all over and could barely walk across the site for meals and up and down hills to the cabins. I ended up taking an afternoon off in the nurse's cabin. I felt dizzy, and I was so weak.

I was also frustrated. I was crying out to God in my quiet, introverted way. In my heart, I was saying, as the leper did to Jesus, "If you are willing, you can make me well."[11] Jesus's response to the leper was immediate health and restoration. As I lay there praying, tears rolled down my cheeks. I was so sad that my body felt weak when I had such great opportunities to serve right outside the door. I delighted in my group and hated lying on this cot, immobilized. I was ready for a quick-fix solution!

Several staff came to check on me and pray for me. It was during one of these prayer sessions that I got a picture in my imagination of a flower drooping down, almost touching the ground, with weeds wrapped all around it, sucking away life and nutrients from the flower.

In a flash of understanding, I knew the flower was me. There were weeds choking the life out of me. I asked God to remove them. But then I saw how intertwined the weeds and the flower stem were, and I knew that to pull the weeds would destroy the plant. I felt as though God was revealing to me a path to health. I was reassured that healing was possible, but I saw that the results wouldn't be immediate restoration. Piece by piece, God would need to reveal the weeds and loosen their hold on my mind, heart, relational patterns, and actions. This process would be slow but would allow me to gradually flourish and blossom again if I would yield to it.

I have been grateful for having that image to live into. It's hard to see progress when it is achieved in baby steps over a long period. But that is how I have learned to step into life and peace, grace, and freedom. But I'm getting ahead of my story.

At camp, I ended up having to pick the times of day when my presence would be most helpful for my group and spending the other parts of the day resting. I wasn't used to lowering expectations of myself, but my body could not keep up with the daily camp schedule. I had to adjust and lean into the strengths of others. I was used to being strong and never needing help. This new learning curve was abrupt and couldn't be ignored. I just couldn't perform the way I was used to.

I really enjoyed the youth in my group and still remember fondly our rich conversations and fun experiences together. I particularly remember our themed progressive dinner where our group served stir-fried chicken and veggies as the main course before attending another group's Mars dessert. We decorated our main course station with paper tablecloths, screens, and low tables to eat at. We were all seated on the floor and incorporated chopsticks into our dress-up accessories. We had so many great programming moments together! My only regret was the time I had to miss because of my health.

Despite this mysterious health problem and the fragility I felt, I had a great summer.

As fall arrived, I was looking forward to moving into a room at the house of leaders from my mission experience. I trusted them; their home felt like a sheltered place to be. Being sick made me feel more vulnerable. I was looking forward to a quiet refuge, shared meals, and informal conversations together. From this safe space, I was feeling ready for my last lap at university!

CHAPTER 43

DEFINITION

A joyful heart is good medicine.

—Proverbs 17:22, NASB

During the spring of my third year, I resigned from my leadership role on the executive for Laurier Christian Fellowship and pulled back from the extra responsibilities I used to carry. I just couldn't keep up the pace. I had great visions, but I felt I was failing to follow through with the action needed to make them a reality.

My health was just not improving. What I had thought of as a flu bug was not clearing up. I didn't know what was going on.

There was no predictability to it. Some days I would get up and walk to school, but by the time I arrived, I had to call somebody for a ride home. My legs would feel as if they were going to collapse from under me. My limbs were weak and achy, and felt heavy. My brain felt foggy. Some days, I couldn't even get out of bed.

I liked my coursework and had ample time to complete it, but the days I set aside for writing essays would get wiped out from lack of focus or migraines that made me curl up in my dark, quiet room to calm the pain.

Because I had taken an extra course in the spring, I had only three full credits and my thesis to complete. I was thankful that my professors knew me. They knew I wasn't making up excuses to get extensions. They generously allowed me extra time to complete assignments. One of my closest friends shared all my classes. Shannon had been my prayer partner and was a leader on Laurier Christian Fellowship executive with me. Her excellent note-taking carried me through lectures I missed or couldn't follow because of brain fog. I used the photocopier in the library often that year.

For my honours thesis, I decided to study the holy sonnets of John Donne. Their violent imagery was unusual for religious themes, yet they conveyed deep insights that I found compelling. My thesis advisor was patient, caring, knowledgeable, and encouraging. She was the perfect match for me. Unfortunately, my brain could not always focus. I would often start talking with her at our scheduled meeting time, and she would recognize the fatigue in my eyes and speech. She would then suggest we meet at another time when I felt better.

My health was puzzling. Why wasn't I getting stronger? My doctor had little to recommend. My symptoms had no clear cause to guide treatment options. He suggested more rest and reduced stress. I was already living a very reduced load.

By January, I put in a formal request to defer my thesis work until after my other classes were complete, since I was struggling to keep up. This meant I wouldn't graduate with my class, but I had a chance to maintain a level of excellence in my studies.

Lance and I were in a great space relationally. My year of tears and risking vulnerability had built a level of trust and interdependence that kept us growing together. We kept up our rhythm of weekly Lance-and-Peg days.

Lance and I are both visionaries and liked to imagine how we would create a unique home culture together when we got married someday. Whenever we would dream about the future, Lance would say, "But I'm not asking you. You'll know when I'm askin'." We were secure in our partnership and often talked of our future together, but Lance didn't seem in a hurry to solidify any plans.

When Christmas of my final university year came without a proposal, I started to wonder when our someday would arrive.

I was talking to Shannon about it over lunch one day. I asked her to pray that I would find contentment in the present and not always want more. I felt ready to start making plans for a future with Lance. I was graduating soon. It felt strange to imagine living back at home after four years of living away at school. I wanted to start our next chapter of life together. Lance had already graduated two years earlier. I wasn't sure what he was waiting for. I was trying not to be anxious about it. After Shannon and I prayed together, I resolved to live in the present and enjoy this stage of our relationship, instead of yearning for the future.

Lance and I had a date day on our calendar, and he invited me to his parents' house. The night before, he'd had some guys stay over, and they had wrestled. Lance laughed as he told me about his fat lip from contact with an elbow. I was just happy to see him. Our kiss of greeting was careful and lopsided to compensate.

I had to bring along some homework, but Lance assured me that we could have different workspaces before we hung out. I was sitting in his parents' sunroom, studying for a midterm and jotting notes, when I started to hear strange sounds from the next room. I heard scissors cutting Bristol board, tape unrolling and snapping off. My curiosity never fully distracted me from my work, but I did wonder what he was up to.

Finally, I was able to set aside my schoolwork and focus on a fun date with Lance! My new mindset made me ready to soak in the moments we had together.

Lance gave me a cute smile and told me that this date started outside.

He grandly held out his arm for me to tuck into. Then he led us out to the car, where we had spent so much time getting to know each other. As we settled inside the Toyota Tercel, he handed me game cards with the word "Before" on the back. As I turned each one over, they revealed some of our favourite ways of connecting during our car rides to and from events: "Loving Working Together", "Admiration + Respect + Care + Dreams." There was also one of our shared verses from Jeremiah 29:11: "I know the plans I have for you declares the Lord, plans to prosper you and not to harm you." We reminisced about the first time we had a planning meeting at my dorm during the ice storm, and the attraction we both felt when our hands touched. I still felt the electric warmth as I took his hand when he opened the car door for me.

Then Lance led me into the darkened house. He lit a candelabra and took me to our first destination. He had set up stations around the house. A small table for two in the corner of the sunroom had a sign taped to the table: "Tim Hortons." I smiled as we reminisced about our first relationship talk, during which Lance admitted to having feelings for me. We talked about our determination to pray and wait for the right timing. A card at this table said, "There's one more thing … First Long Hug"; another bore the verse we clung to in the confusion of that time from Psalm 27:13–14, NIV:

> "I will remain confident of this:
> I will see the goodness of the Lord
> in the land of the living.
> Wait for the Lord;
> Be strong and take heart
> and wait for the Lord."

On the table were also letters we wrote to one another during the intense few days following Lance's reveal.

I couldn't believe Lance had gone to the trouble of making such a fun date! I was delighted! We were reliving our shared story!

The candelabra moved with us to illuminate the next station: "6 Month Wait" was on the card in the living room. Again, game cards and letters we had exchanged were on the table to relive and enjoy. The cards said, "Waiting, wanting God's best!" "Sneaking time together, letters" and "First Kiss."

We moved to the kitchen for the next station, "Lonelm Days," where the cards said, "Sept 5, 1990 - O.K. I need you", "Bubbling Brook/Still Waters" (our way of understanding the inner world we each carried inside) "Intimacy ... learning about God's love," "Prayer Journals," and "I love you - 1 Corinthians 13."

Lance realized this was going to be a long, lingering kind of date, and he hadn't planned on dinner. So we ate at the "Lonelm station." He remembers grilled cheese; I thought we made pizzas. But what we ate is not important. The reality of our shared inner world is brighter to me than the externals of that moment. Lance said it made sense to eat at this part of our story, since we shared a lot of meals together at Lonelm when we were first dating. This table was covered with clip art cards and coupons from fun dates we shared. We relived it all, and I was even able to laugh about all the tears I shed as I learned to share my deeper struggles. My heart was singing, "Best date ever!" Lance knew me so well.

The "Summer 1991" area was next. The cards read, "Recognizing our Foundation," "I love you," and "We are home," recognizing that being together was home, which made the actual place much less important.

The "Fall '91" station had game cards highlighting lessons and growth from that time and the verse "Though the mountains be shaken, and the hills be removed, yet my unfailing love for you will not be shaken" (Isaiah 54:10). This was meaningful, as it nestled our love for one another in the bigger, unfailing love of our Creator.

The next station was "The Future." It held our shared visions and dreams about creating the life we wanted, the kind of parents we wanted to be, and the kind of priorities we wanted to live. "I will love you" is a choice for the future. The last card said, "No more worst part of our relationship," which we always felt was the parting at the end of each time we were together!

What an amazing date! Lance ushered me with the light of the candelabra and my hand tucked in his to the couch in front of the fireplace for our last stop.

The couch was labelled, "The Present." I couldn't imagine what was left to talk about and celebrate! We had spent hours remembering together all that made up our relationship story!

He lit a fire in the fireplace and then settled down beside me. I was relaxed and content to snuggle in for the rest of the evening.

One more time, he handed me game cards. The first one, when I flipped it over said, "You'll know when I'm askin'." Goosebumps!

The second card said, "I really love you!" Warmth poured through me.

The third card said, "I'm askin'." My tight throat made it hard to speak.

Since I had coached myself not to think ahead but to enjoy this stage of our relationship, the proposal took me completely by surprise! I couldn't respond right away. I looked at Lance, and for once he was the teary one. He opened the Bible he had beside him and asked me to open it to the bookmark and read the highlighted verse from our study in Hosea 2: "I will betroth you to me forever; I will betroth you in righteousness and justice, in love and compassion. I will betroth you in faithfulness, and you will acknowledge the (goodness of) the LORD." Taped inside the Bible was a ring. Lance asked me whether I would marry him. I can't even remember speaking. The emotions welled up, and everything in these few moments is hidden in a soft blur of memory. I know I said yes and leaned in for a careful, lingering kiss to avoid his sore lip. Then he slipped the ring onto my finger.

I loved the ring Lance chose! It was so simple and elegant, and I was surprised, since we had never looked at rings together. Yet he chose it perfectly for me. Lance is not materialistic. He told me later that he had never thought about jewellery or been to a jewellery store before.

We cuddled into the warmth of the couch to enjoy the fire and talk. Our future was clear. We would be married as soon as we could make a plan that made sense within our families.

We started planning our wedding party and making phone calls to share our news that night. My family knew before I did, since Lance had fit in a visit with them to tell them his intentions. Everyone we talked to wholeheartedly celebrated with us!

The time would soon come that we wouldn't have to go our separate ways every time we were together. Home for my heart was already Lance; now home could be ours to create together! When Lance dropped me off at my place that night, I lay awake, dreaming happily of the brightness of our future.

CHAPTER 44

ADJUSTING

> Chronic fatigue syndrome (CFS) is a complicated disorder characterized by extreme fatigue that lasts for at least six months and that can't be fully explained by an underlying medical condition. The fatigue worsens with physical or mental activity but doesn't improve with rest.
>
> —mayoclinic.org

With the big question about the future settled, I was able to focus my energy on giving my best to school days and ministry commitments. My health was still a daily puzzle that couldn't be counted on. I had high and low days and fitted life to my new limitations. I was grateful for my classmate Keri, who often drove me to classes to help me conserve energy to attend.

During my last year, Lance and I saw each other as often as possible. By spring, I had finished my classwork and maintained my grades, but I still had my thesis paper to work on before I could graduate.

In May, I had an appointment in Toronto with a doctor who

specialized in fatigue disorders. Lance drove me to her office. The waiting room was full of soft leather benches to allow patients to lie down if they needed to—a nod to the kind of patients she saw.

At the visit, she took a comprehensive history and then thirteen vials of blood for testing. When the results came back, she confirmed the diagnosis of chronic fatigue and immune dysfunction syndrome (CFIDS). Though this was a relatively new disorder, I matched her other patient profiles. The bloodwork had uncovered an unusual virus that seemed to start the cascade of symptoms when my cleansing and immune systems became overburdened. I walked out of her office with a diagnosis and a list of supplements to buy. I started taking a handful of vitamins each morning: evening primrose oil, vitamin B6, vitamin B12, zinc, and others my mind can't recall.

In 1992, there was little known about CFIDS other than the fact that those who suffered from it didn't generally regain health. My adult life was just beginning, and I'd been handed a life sentence of chronic illness.

Since there were no treatment options and recovery was not expected, I would get depressed anytime I read about chronic fatigue syndrome. So I stopped reading about it. My diagnosis didn't define my future. I trusted that God could lead me to a purpose beyond lying on the couch for the rest of my life. My flower image of gradual healing became a symbol of hope. I would learn to tune into the weeds of dysfunction that needed to be untangled and released.

I could still do gentle activities within my new limits. I had already started knitting a sweater for Lance. I had applied and been accepted to Teacher's College for the fall term, but Lance encouraged me to see whether we could defer it for a year so I could just take a year off to rest and heal. I was amazed when the university was willing to extend its offer to the following year. It was a relief to think that we could take the pressure off for a while to see whether I could begin to feel better.

Wedding plans were happening. Lance and I had a family

meeting with our parents to talk about what we were envisioning. We kept hearing the line "They say that ..." being used regarding what is normal for most weddings. Finally, Lance asked, "Who's 'they'? And how did they get to decide what our wedding should be like?"

Lance and I are intuitive. We only wanted things in the ceremony and reception that were meaningful to us. When we embraced a tradition, we wanted to highlight the reason for it. For example, we wanted our wedding party to not just look lovely but also to be involved in parts of the service as our dearest friends and supporters. We organized a retreat time together to enjoy one another's companionship before the wedding day.

We had a spring schedule filled with wedding showers hosted by caring friends and family. It was so lovely to be surrounded by so many supporters to cheer us on, offer wisdom, and bless us with items we would need to begin our new life together.

That summer, I was hired as director at Ryerson Camp. My limits seemed to match the strengths of my directing team and allow room for them to grow into higher levels of leadership. It was a fulfilling experience despite some challenges. I came home exhausted but satisfied with the efforts of our amazing staff team to create beautiful memories for campers.

I hadn't finished my thesis before moving down to camp, so now I had one week to finish and submit it. This task had to move to centre stage in my brain space. I worked hard to pull all the loose threads of my research and insights together into something cohesive. I found it difficult to think of school when our wedding was just a month away!

The first draft of my paper was dashed together. My new thesis adviser was a professor I'd enjoyed many courses with before. He looked over my paper and called me into his office to talk. He said he could give me my credit and let me graduate, but he knew I could write better than this. His preference was that I revise my work, either by including more research or by making my arguments and connections stronger. I got a little teary when I thought of starting back at the research phase. I told him that I was getting married in a month but would be happy to take another stab at revision.

So I went back to writing while Lance and Mom took the lead on wedding details. There were so many pieces of our future to fit together.

One of our groomsmen from Waterloo let us know of a vacancy in his building for September. Renting the two-bedroom apartment happened smoothly. By renting one month before our wedding, we had time to fix it up.

As we moved my desk to the new apartment, Lance found a bunch of cheques sitting in a drawer. He asked, "What's this?"

I was startled to see several cheques sitting in envelopes from award assemblies in high school. Winning the top average in my grade in high school a few times meant more to me than the money. The cheques were several years old. Book smarts didn't always translate to life. I asked him whether we could still deposit them. He assured me that they would be expired by now. I was a little embarrassed by my lack of adult organization and priorities. Camp always came right after each of my school years and must have taken all my focus. Oops!

The crazy thing was that Lance and I had no work lined up for our new future together. I had already decided to take the year off to focus on getting better. Lance had talked to me about stopping his work at a group home where his long shifts were about policing behaviour instead of the fun programming and creative ministry that suited him so well. He was in the application process for a church ministry position, and we were both hopeful about that opportunity. Our faith was bigger than our fears as we looked forward to our next chapter.

It would have been helpful to have those award cheques in our bank account. But Lance was characteristically gracious and didn't make me feel stupid about my blunder. We shared a laugh about it, and he commented on appreciating that I wasn't materialistic, since he wasn't sure we would ever own a house of our own.

We were given a sectional couch, and we bought an oak dining table and chairs from money that was raised by the Hudson clan at one of our wedding showers. We were impressed at how the apartment was taking shape. It was starting to feel like a place that could hold all our hopes and visions. We planned to have our wedding night in our apartment so that our first memories of our new life together would be rooted in our home rather than in an impersonal hotel room. Besides, we didn't need glitz and glamour. Our tastes were simple and just included being together and creating the kind of life we had talked about for so long.

Lance and I spent an afternoon crafting our vows from our study of scriptures about marriage. Lance's Dad worked on drawing the invitation cover. I was waiting for inspiration to write a wedding song to sing to Lance. It came unexpectedly from a movie night with my family during which we heard a Bryan Adams song featured in the movie we watched—*Robin Hood: Prince of Thieves*. I hurried to my room and scribbled down the lyrics in about twenty minutes. Things were gradually coming together!

As we prepared the guest list for the wedding, we realized we wanted to share our special day with everyone! My whole camp staff was invited to the ceremony, along with almost six hundred other guests from different parts of our lives. We trimmed the dinner reception guest list to 350, and my mom and Lance recruited help to cater and serve the meal. The Hudson side of the family alone was hard to trim down to 100.

We made an event out of addressing and stuffing envelopes with family and friends to get the invitations in the mail. Another evening was spent crafting table centrepieces with friends. Decorations for the hall were delegated to a different team under Lance's sister,

Laurel. There were so many details where I simply gave input as Mom and Lance coordinated the efforts to make them happen.

When I would feel bad for not helping with the wedding plans, Lance would smile and say, "Just get Donne done. That's your focus right now!"

Though my mind and heart were ready to have schoolwork behind me, I'm glad I made the extra effort to improve my thesis even while we worked on the apartment, organized wedding details, and spent time with family. My professor was right about the first draft being sloppy. As I reread my rough draft, I could almost taste the desperation to be finished! But I have always cared about excellence and doing my best, so I was happy to get my final draft in and hear his positive feedback alongside an A-.

Donne was done—just a week or so before our wedding day!

CHAPTER 45

ALMOST

As sure as seasons are made for change,
Our lifetimes are made for years.
So, I ... I will be here.

—Steven Curtis Chapman, "I Will Be Here"

The rehearsal dinner with our families was lovely and quiet before the happy chaos of our rehearsal. We had involved so many people in our ceremony that the church was lively, with many groups coming together as a community to celebrate with us. Our minister was a little overwhelmed with the task of leading everyone.

Lance and I had learned at Steph's wedding in the spring that we didn't want to worry about any details on our wedding day. As a wedding couple, we just wanted to enjoy our guests and live in the moment. We had Blair, my assistant director from camp, be our wedding coordinator. He stepped into the role that night as he helped everyone figure out where to go and what to do.

Eventually we got the pre-service musicians ready to rehearse, the band set up, and the choir gathered. Our parents were in position, and our wedding party was ready to stand with Lance or walk down the aisle before me to the live music provided by friends. We had two ministers sharing a reflection and words of wisdom for us. We finished the walkthrough with everyone feeling confident about his or her part. The musicians lingered to rehearse, while the rest moved downstairs for a bite to eat and a chance to visit.

At the end of the rehearsal, Lance drew my attention to my sister, Kath. She was sitting alone in the middle of the church. I made my way to the pew where she was seated and asked her how she was doing. I was so glad for the years of safe honesty we had practised together that made heart conversations natural. She said that she felt as if she were losing me. Things were never going to be the same. Home would never again be under the same roof.

I assured her that she would always be a part of "home" for me, and that my heart would always hold a place that was hers and hers alone. I also promised that we would stay connected. I told my sister I loved her as we embraced in a lingering kind of hug that I find comfortable only with my closest people.

I reminded her that I was looking forward to our sleepover with all the bridesmaids at my parents' place that night. I always slept well with Kathy in the other half of a double bed. She was a safe place—a little sister who made me feel protective and smart, and who understood my humour and lived and sang in perfect harmony with me. I was grateful for a soon-to-be husband who understood and encouraged our bond and who was perceptive enough to notice that Kath was struggling.

After enjoying our friends and family, Lance and the guys left for his parents' house while the girls came with me to my family home. We were aware that after tonight, we would be making our own home together!

The girls didn't take long to settle into the living room in our pyjamas for a chance to talk and pray before bed. I filled them in on some of the funny and touching stories that led Lance and me to this big day. Steph passed me a beautiful letter she had written to mark the importance of this transition. I had been a bridesmaid at her wedding in the spring, so she had a few months of marriage wisdom to share.

We said our goodnights, and everyone headed off to bed. Kath and I talked for a while in the dark before I heard her even breathing and knew she was asleep.

It was late, but I had only partially memorized my vows and so kept playing them over and over in my head. Body aches and a busy mind meant that it took a long time to fall asleep, but I did finally get a few hours of slumber. We had a strict shower schedule that was necessary to get all of us through the bathrooms. We planned to meet the guys over at the church for a time to reflect, worship, and pray together as inward preparation before focussing on the externals of the day. Lance and I led our wedding party in a foot-washing time as a symbol of the kind of service and support that characterized our friendships. It was a deep and meaningful hour together before it was time to get groomed and ready for the afternoon wedding.

The October day was unusually balmy. My friend Deborah had agreed to come and do hairstyling at my mom's house. I was in a phase of spiral perms, so my hair was curly and full as Deb gave it shape and secured my veil in place.

Once the veil was on, it felt funny to be wearing my sweatpants. But putting on the dress would be a last-minute thing. It was fun to get ready amidst the laughter and camaraderie of dear friends. I was so fortunate to have such kindred spirits to share my joy in this special moment of my life.

Only when I put on the dress did I really feel like a bride. Up until that moment, being a bride was an abstract idea. Wearing the dress united my hopes, dreams, and longings with reality. "I am a bride. Today I am getting married—for real!"

My health was still shaky, and the lack of sleep only increased the body ache that was now normal for me. But nothing could take the joy out of this day. However, I was starting to get a little nervous about being the centre of attention with so many people gathering to celebrate us.

To calm me, Kathy and the girls started to sing. The lively worship song captured my feelings perfectly as gratitude rose in me. It was amazing to find myself full of confidence, peace, and joy after so many years of struggling with fear and shame. I recognized God as the author of this beautiful, safe place I had landed and a future that looked so bright! My heart and voice were united with these dear friends who had walked beside me through so much. The joy of the song was perfect for the moment.

Our friend Gayle offered us the gift of being our photographer. She came to the house and took beautiful candid and posed pictures. Mom shone as hostess. She made sure all of us had enough to eat and that every need was met. She made the juggling of many details look easy. Dad just tried to stay out of the way of all the girls cycling through the bathroom.

Lance's dad showed up with his freshly washed car, ready to escort us to the church. It was almost time!

The girls and I waited in a basement Sunday school classroom as guests arrived above us. A calm quiet seemed to come over all of us as we connected without words and listened to the people arriving overhead. My sister reached over and squeezed my hand.

My brother and Lance's sisters were part of the ushering team helping people find their seats. Laurel escorted Lance's mom while Steve walked Mom up the aisle to the front of the church to light the candles on either side of the unity candle before they were seated in the front row designated for family.

Then it was time. My bridesmaids and I went up the stairs to the back of the church. I had chosen to have no train on my dress so I wouldn't worry about tripping. It was enough of a stretch to wear a long dress. We stood behind the doors and listened to our friends leading worship songs at the front. It was the perfect way to settle my heart—to reflect on the journey that had brought me to this day and thank God for the gift of my partnership with Lance.

I watched from behind as my dear friends and sister took their turns walking down the aisle with a pause for the photographer at a designated place. Then it was my turn! I stepped into the room on my dad's arm and locked eyes with Lance.

Suddenly the crowd of friends and relatives stood to welcome me among them. Lance was in the middle of a double-aisle church. Our brief connection was blocked by a sea of people. We couldn't see each other again until I reached the front of the church.

As soon as I saw my groom, my nerves settled. I had no reservations about Lance. We were ready for this important step with so many of those we loved there to witness it. We joined hands, the crowd was seated, and the wedding began.

CHAPTER 46

WEDDING DAY

You double my convictions, breathe hope in my despair
Bring vibrance to the colours and soft music fills the air.

—Peggy Wright, "Just to Say"

Lance took my hand, and we sent an admiring look to one another before we turned to listen. We had asked our parents to come to the microphone and pray for us. It was lovely to hear both sets of parents voice their support and care.

A few members of the wedding party spoke about our friendship and prayed for us. We chose scriptures to be read that we wanted to carry into our life together.

Then Lance leaned over to me as Drew and Duncan grabbed their guitars to offer an original song written from thoughts Lance had sent them. "This is as close as I'll ever get to writing a song for you," Lance whispered in my ear. Their song was about singing in the eye of the storm as our partnership, together with God's love to hold us, formed a cord of three strands that would remain unbroken.

We soaked in the passion and beautiful insight of the song as the words matched the conviction in our hearts!

The ministers each shared a reflection with us.

Then it was time for our vows!

I handed my bouquet to my sister. The minister held the microphone for Lance as we joined hands. Lance gazed deeply into my eyes as he sincerely spoke these memorized sentences:

"In the presence of God and before these witnesses I, Lance, declare my love for you, Peggy, and take you to be my wife, my life-long companion, my partner. You are God's best for me, and he uses you to meet many of my deepest needs. I cherish you and promise to seek God's best for you day by day and to walk with you faithfully wherever God leads. I promise to love you as Christ loves the church by selflessly supporting and building you up to become holy and radiant in your relationship with God. In serving you, in praying with and for you in God's word, and in working together for God's kingdom, I know that our love will not fail, because God is faithful. Through God's perfect love and power, I will love you and we will know the fullness of life in Jesus Christ."

Throughout his vows, Lance blinked away moisture that he later insisted was from lack of sleep. But it was touching for me to see his sincerity and love as it reflected the heart I had learned to trust and depend on.

Then the microphone shifted to me. I read my vows, not trusting my memory when my brain could still be foggy—especially on such an important day!

"In the presence of God and before these witnesses I, Peggy, declare my love for you, Lance, and take you to be my husband, my life-long companion, my partner. You are God's best for me, and God works through you to display His tender love and steadfast truth in my life. Today I give myself to you to be your wife. I cherish you and promise to seek God's best for you day by day and to walk with you faithfully wherever God leads. As I grow in my relationship with God and actively pursue His will, I will daily seek ways to encourage, support, and enable you. When you rejoice, I will share your joy. When you are weak, I will comfort you and lead you to God's throne of grace. When you fail, I will stand by you, uphold you and continue to always believe in you. Our home will be a refuge of unconditional love built on the foundation of God's perfect, faithful love. You are a treasure entrusted to my care, and I cherish you, Lance. Through God's perfect love and by His power, we will see God's promises unfold and taste the fullness of life in Christ Jesus."

As the minister shifted the microphone away from me, Lance got a determined look on his face as he leaned over to the minister to explain that he had forgotten an important line in his vows.

He turned back to me and said loudly for all to hear, "And *also* ..." The whole church erupted into laughter. Undeterred, Lance turned to the crowd and said, "I don't want to go through the rest of my life regretting that I didn't say this."

After a short pause, he looked into my eyes and said words that were so important to speak in light of my chronic fatigue syndrome diagnosis: "When you are defeated or overwhelmed, I will comfort you, when you are sick or weak, I will stand with you because I believe in you and the love I promise you today is unconditional."

There were a lot of moist eyes when he finished!

With the exchange of rings and confirming words from my minister, we were pronounced husband and wife! We sealed it with a kiss before I took the microphone and sang the following song, which I had written for my new husband!

JUST TO SAY

I look into your eyes and find freedom to fly.
You strengthen my frail wings with your acceptance and life.
You draw my attention to the one I see in you:
My Maker and my Father, who embodies the truth.
I need you.

Look into my eyes and see a heart that believes
God's best for you. I'll stand by you
With eyes fixed on eternity
Together we will live, daily we will die.
His unfolding promises will be our reality.

CHORUS:
I'll fly with you to the places where He leads
I'll lie with you; in green pastures we will feed.
I'll die with you; God's best we will receive.
Together we will celebrate the love that grows inside.
I need you.

I look into God's eyes, and He looks right through me.
He knows my heart, my deepest dreams, and brought you to me.
You double my convictions, breathe hope in my despair,
Bring vibrance to the colours, and soft music fills the air.
I love you.

After lighting the unity candle, Lance took my hand and led me back to the front of the church, where we stood together to enjoy the beautiful harmony of the hymn "'Tis so Sweet," sung by our talented friends who formed the choir. Lance and I soaked in the layers of sound that sang of the sweet place we had landed together.

My years of struggle and shame were temporarily lifted from

me as I stood with my new husband, the two of us looking ahead to the promise of our life together. When we looked back over our relationship, we saw God's goodness and care again and again. My mind wandered back over milestones we had travelled together: The "Tim Hortons confession," the trembling admission of "I need you," the ponderings about how our visions for our lives fit together, and the sure foundations we had found by looking for the fruit of God's movement in our relationship. We couldn't help but trust that God would continue to lead us into sweet places in the days ahead.

After we signed the register and shared communion as a couple, our friends Pat and Toshi sang a song that I had often sung with each of them.

Rather than a recessional, Lance and I decided to focus on connecting with loved ones. We started with a round of hugs for our families in the front rows.

We were married!

It felt wonderful to celebrate the moment by enjoying our friends and family who had gathered from near and far to share this moment with us! We rode the rest of the reception like an exhilarating wave.

CHAPTER 47

TIME TO REST

Solitude does not pull us away from our fellow human beings but instead makes real fellowship possible.

—Henri Nouwen

We loved the honouring speeches, funny anecdotes, and awesome music at our reception. The dinner was largely a labour of love from many camp friends who cooked and served a meal for our 350 guests. The programme ended, and tables were moved aside to create space to dance or visit.

The band set up for a camp theme night–style dance party. They started with a song titled "Lance and Peggy's Wedding" as they improvised lyrics to fit the occasion. Lance and I spent the evening circulating around the room trying to visit with all those who had travelled a long way to be there.

Lance and I did spend a few moments on the dance floor, but Lance was doing it for my sake. He really didn't like dancing. My sister and bridesmaids were a lot more exuberant! I loved seeing Kathy's joyful abandon as we danced together! Our photographer captured an amazing photo of Kath that we decided to have printed in a poster size to give her for Christmas!

Before we left the reception hall, I was going to change out of my wedding dress into normal clothes. But Lance asked me to wear the dress home so he could enjoy it.

The car ride gave us a chance to begin to debrief about our day and replay all the conversations and special moments we had experienced. I began to feel my adrenalin begin to calm. I'd been on a high-performance level all day.

Then we were home!

We were both exhausted yet happy to be alone. I felt a little self-conscious as Lance held my hands and moved me to arm's length to enjoy just looking at his bride for a moment. He helped me take the veil out of my hair and removed the hairpins. We laughed at how many there were.

Lance wanted to assure me that he didn't want to be like men in my life who cheapened me with their attention. He saw me as beautiful, and my sense of being the ugly duckling began to fall away from me.

I felt so different with Lance. He saw me, understood me, and cherished me. When we were ready for sleep, we lay in the dark and reminisced a little longer before Lance's even breathing told me he was asleep. I tried to match my breathing to his so that I could drift off to sleep, too.

But sleep didn't come easy with chronic fatigue. Insomnia had plagued me for months. This day had been so long and full of stimulation that it took me a while to calm my mind. I defaulted to my habit of replaying the day until I finally drifted off.

We slept much of the next day away. We had reservations at Pretty River Valley Farm Inn in Collingwood and could check in any time after 4:00 p.m. But nothing in us wanted to rush. We were on holiday! It was dark when we drove on the hilly gravel roads to our destination.

Our suite was lovely. We laughed that we would never find each other in the king-size bed. The fireplace in our room and jets in our bathroom tub felt decadent. There were comfy reading chairs by the fireplace. We were ready to soak it all in.

I could feel the ache in my whole body as the penalty for pushing hard the day before. I also had symptoms of a cold. But it felt wonderful to have no pressure. The only time constraint we had to structure our days around was the complimentary breakfast.

The next morning, we pulled open our curtains and stepped out the french doors to see the rolling hills of October's splendour. "Lance, look at where we are!" I breathed. The dark night had veiled the beauty of this place.

We had to speed up our morning a little to make it to the dining room in time to enjoy breakfast before it was cleared away at 10:00 a.m. We quickly dressed and moved to enjoy the hearty country spread. When we finished eating, we went back to bed for more rest. Lance seemed to be as tired as I was.

In the afternoon, we took our time reading the cards from our wedding day gift basket. They were full of heart-warming encouragement and inspiring thoughts. We were humbled by the generous monetary gifts that helped fund our honeymoon. We decided to go out for dinner every night. It felt so decadent to drive into Collingwood and try a different restaurant every day. The weather reflected our mood, as it remained warm and sunny all week long.

One day, we sat on the pier for a picnic surrounded by water and blue skies. The seagulls quickly found us and started begging. We shared a taste of our meal with them before taking a walk down the waterfront. We explored the quaint main street shops and bought some designer chocolates at the sweet shop, as well as cute gifts for family members.

By day three, my cold had turned into a familiar sinus infection. I didn't yet know any way to clear it other than seeing a doctor for an antibiotic. Lance and I drove to the hospital's emergency department, where I wrote my new last name for the first time: *Peggy Wright*. I started writing the *H* for Hudson and had to turn it into a *W.*

With the antibiotic in my system, the congestion gradually cleared from my sinuses. I would make terrible sounds from the bathroom as I worked to cough up and blow out the thick mucus. Lance would call from the other room: "I love you! You know I still love you!" His comments as I honked unromantically made me laugh. Lance knew just what I needed to cast off self-consciousness!

Every day I slept at least twelve hours. I still had achy muscles and a headache, but it was luxurious to have no pressure to perform, work, or do. We enjoyed giving each other massages.

We had been given foaming bath soap, so I decided a soak in the tub would be a good way to soothe my soreness. I put some bubble bath in, filled the tub with water, and then turned on the jets as I climbed in. What I didn't know was that bubbles and jets don't mix. The suds started to take over. They were climbing higher and higher. I turned off the jets and called Lance in to see the craziness! I started drawing on the tile wall with the bubbles. There had to be some way to use them up!

Each day was a gift of laughter, rest, reading, and exploratory walks through the woods around the inn. There was a larger hot tub available that we visited a few times during our stay to ease our sore muscles, but the chemical smells were hard on my sensitive lungs.

The week was designed to melt away tension. It was perfect: beautiful, unhurried, quiet, restful, and fun! It was everything we hoped for to begin this new chapter. Lance was someone who could share with me the refreshment of solitude. Quiet companionship was the perfect way to refuel.

As the week came to an end, I was getting excited to nest and settle into home rhythms together. I had loved choosing colours and designs for our gift registry, and now it was time to make the apartment ours! But first we had a date for Thanksgiving with both our families!

CHAPTER 48

❦

THANKSGIVING

I would maintain that thanks are the highest form of thought;
and that gratitude is happiness doubled by wonder.

—G. K. Chesterton

We landed at our apartment late in the day and unpacked. I was looking forward to creating a feeling of home in our sparsely furnished space.

We had arranged for both our families to meet for Thanksgiving at Lance's parents' place so we could debrief about the wedding and open our gifts with our loved ones. It was a joy to see everyone. We shared silly stories with family as we distributed funny gifts we had found while meandering on the main street of Collingwood.

The meal was delicious! Lance's siblings enjoy cooking and experimenting with flavour. I remember being delightfully surprised by the peppery kick in the mashed potatoes. As we sat around the table catching up on how everyone was doing, we took a moment to each speak of something we were thankful for. Our gratitude multiplied as we shared our thankfulness for family and friends, life in Canada, health and safety, great food, and opportunities to learn and work. We were so aware of our blessings!

We were surprised and moved by the generosity of our guests when our family called our attention to the mountain of gifts waiting in the basement for us. It never occurred to us that we would begin our life together with so many home comforts!

After dinner, we all went downstairs and formed a semicircle. As we opened gifts, every family member had a role in keeping us organized. When we had doubles or triples of objects, we would ask who wanted the extras for Christmas gifts so that we could be generous even without an income. It took a long time to open and appreciate the care that went into the amazing gifts from our friends and family! It was overwhelming in the best way!

I looked forward to what the objects symbolized: the meals we would cook for guests and each other, the vision of our apartment with pictures on the wall and pottery mugs on a mug rack, bedding, curtains, and even a bookcase to make our space inviting! Our spare room would be ready for friends and guests. We wanted to keep a room in our house that was God's space to fill as it was needed—especially for youth who needed a safe space for a short time.

Our family helped us load the gifts into a few cars to bring them to our apartment. My nesting instinct was high! It was time to make our dream of creating a home together a reality!

CHAPTER 49

TRANSPLANTED

If you concentrate on finding whatever is good in every situation, you will discover that your life will suddenly be filled with gratitude, a feeling that nurtures the soul.

—Rabbi Harold Kushner

The next weeks were full of decisions about where to put all our lovely new things. Lance gave me complete decorating control while he took charge of organizing the office. I loved having the ability to arrange things to my tastes and preferences. I found that when I wasn't deferring to someone else to make peace or gain approval, I actually did have a mind of my own. I spent hours poring through IKEA catalogues to see what colours and styles I liked. My tastes leaned more towards clean lines and light colours with bold accents rather than the ornate country designs I had grown up with.

I wanted to create a sense of permanence after being a student and moving every few semesters. We would even do something I never did as a student: put framed art on our walls. Lance was puzzled when his new drill wouldn't penetrate the concrete walls.

So our friend Trevor helped us use a bazooka-sized drill to mount our mug rack and wall art. We were learning homeowner skills! Lance jokingly told me to refer to him as Sven as he assembled IKEA furniture. My parents gave him a tool belt that Christmas as a nod to his pride in learning handy skills!

Our apartment held our hopes for what life could be like. This was our experiment in creating a grace-filled lifestyle. There would be no blaming or shaming. When we forgot this ground rule, we would apologize and make things right. We would be honest and continue to build on the foundation of mutual respect and trust. We would find daily rhythms that prioritized spiritual growth, reflection, conversation, and things that fuelled us. We wanted to find fresh expressions for love each day and not rest on yesterday's love. We didn't want to leave any questions in our minds about our foundation together.

When my energy was low, we referred to it as a low day. When I felt ready to tackle projects on a high day, we would enjoy it and not worry about losing ground again. When I felt pressured to put a positive spin on my health to please others and claim a recovery that wasn't true to my experience, Lance kept me honest. He would just quietly shake his head, and I would realize I was trying to make my discomfort smaller for someone else. I would then retract and say that I just had good days and low ones. That was the pattern of chronic fatigue and immune dysfunction syndrome.

Lance was such a gracious person to live with. He would head out to a meeting or a ministry task; Youth Eventz was still going strong, and Lance was in the centre of making things happen. When he would return, I often hadn't moved off the couch. I would immediately feel guilty about my "laziness" and unproductivity. But Lance started to help me reprogram my thinking with his responses.

"I'm sorry. I haven't done anything today. It's a low day," I would say as he came in the door. It was glaringly obvious to me that there was no supper started, no tidying done, no evidence of my having been at home all day.

He would jump to my defence: "You are doing something. You're healing! Remember, that's your full-time job right now."

This was a year to learn to stop striving, achieving, trying to please, and earning approval. The safety and unconditional love of our marriage was teaching me to be at rest instead of hustling for my worth. I needed to detox from my perfectionistic "shoulds." I was learning that my value and worth didn't rest in checking boxes on my to-do list or fulfilling my inner critic's or others' expectations. I knew I had to learn to just be a child of God who was delighted in for who I was, not for what I could do. Lance was reflecting that kind of love to me. He was helping me to internalize gracious acceptance.

I remember in the quiet of one afternoon picturing myself as a little girl running around to perform tasks to please God, my Father, while he just watched and waited for me to come and sit with him and enjoy the gift of being together. It was a snapshot of how I lived my life. "Be still and know that I am God" (Psalm 46:10 NIVSB) was a verse that became important for me to internalize. It was my relationship with God that fuelled my faith, and stillness allowed me to listen for the nudges and wisdom that came only when I wasn't busy and distracted.

Performing had become a default way of being. I was so keyed up inside that my mind raced with thoughts and my body had a hard time relaxing. I needed to learn to enjoy the stillness and stop tuning out signals from my body and emotions. I had to learn to stay present and shift my mind and body out of constant stress mode.

I read a book by Archibald Hart titled *Stress and Adrenalin*, in which he clarifies the role of stress to create excessive wear and tear on our bodies.[12] He emphasized the need for daily times of low arousal of the adrenal system. As his book suggested, I would lie on the couch tightening and relaxing every muscle and fit in a twenty-minute rest every day to let my body dial down. When I was at peace, my brain would settle into deeper clarity about what was important and where I should focus my limited energy.

When we went to bed each night, I loved talking to Lance in the dark. It was a time when I felt peaceful. I told my sister it was like having a sleepover every night with my best friend! My thoughts would become sharper when there was no other stimulus. When I relaxed, I would get chatty as my habit of processing my day kicked in. I loved having someone to process out loud with.

Lance would often be more ready for sleep. Eventually, he would say, "You can keep talking if you want, but I'm going to turn over now." That was his very gracious way of asking me to be quiet and go to sleep. Even when he asked me to stop talking, he protected my sensitive feelings. I so appreciated his kindness.

Early in our marriage, we decided to take turns reading aloud to one another. Night after night, we soaked in the adventure and insights from the Chronicles of Narnia. We would cuddle under blankets and take turns reading a chapter aloud, sometimes using different voices for the various characters. I loved sharing the world of stories together!

I flourished in this beautiful life I'd been transplanted into! It was easy to greet each day with an open heart.

Lance and I delighted in having my sister, Kathy, come for weekend visits. She often brought along a friend. I loved living in and offering others a safe space where judgement was not part of the language or culture.

One day I dropped a ceramic gift we had been given, and it shattered. I froze. I started calling myself names like "klutz" and "stupid," and feeling ashamed that I had ruined something of value—especially something new from someone we cared for! Guilt and self-condemnation hit instinctively and immediately.

But Lance heard the crash and came to see whether I was all right. He reminded me that things are just things and can be replaced. He was just glad that I wasn't hurt. In his eyes, *I* was the valuable!

He interrupted the critical voices in my head that shamed me for my failure, told me that I shouldn't own pretty things since I would just wreck them and told me I was damaged and never enough.

His words were simply "Oops! I'll grab the dustpan and broom." That was it!

No guilt messages here—just a mess that he was happy to help me tackle. He cleaned up after me and had me just sit out of the way of the broken glass. He didn't even lecture me with a message of justice—that I should clean up my own messes. He met me with grace—a lesson he learned long ago and seldom forgot to live and extend.

And so I was learning the rhythms of grace: of listening to my body's signals and allowing space to feel my feelings and decode them. Lance wanted to hear my inner world and hold space with me to grieve my losses and to feel sad when I realized that shame was still the dominant voice in my head. He let me process and untangle the places where weeds had been choking the life from me for years.

Our little basement apartment was a whole new spacious world to breathe deeply in. It was a place where I could begin to gather the pieces of my personality that I wanted to recover. It was also a place of shedding. This year off was just what I needed to relearn healthier patterns—to embrace ways of thinking that weren't stress-inducing and energy-depleting but rather were restorative. I didn't know where this life of grace would lead, but it felt very healing. I could feel myself blossoming as I nourished my true self and opened my heart to grace.

I wanted to share this kind of environment more widely, but chronic fatigue was teaching me to be patient and to listen to my limits. A small world to heal in without a lot of demands and voices was just what I needed in this season. I still wasn't aware of so many of the weeds that were choking the life out of me, but I was ready to learn. I was open to God's Spirit to lead and guide me to places of health and abundant life.

In this gracious soil of shared life with a partner I could count on, I had found what I needed to deepen my roots and grow stronger as I stretched towards the light.

CHAPTER 50

THE MILK PITCHER

Grace covers over a multitude of differences.

—paraphrase of 1 Peter 4:8

We had six months during which neither of us had an official job. It was a blessing to have a time with so few demands on us. Lance was still volunteering full-time hours with Youth Eventz, coordinating ministry initiatives around Southern Ontario. We had some savings and family member support that kept us afloat financially until Lance got the Christian education job at First United Church in Waterloo.

Our apartment saw our best moments and our growing pains as we learned the delicate dance of partnership.

When we started dating, Lance's question was, "Do you need me?" Learning to allow ourselves to need each other pushed at the independent spirit we both had. Working out how to communicate well, depend on each other, and make decisions together was part of the growth curve of becoming a unit.

In the safety of our relationship, I felt free to explore my tastes and preferences while I learned to separate my own ideas from my natural impulse to accommodate and please. I realized I had always found life easier when I deferred to others. Making others happy had often been enough to make me happy.

But in our new home, I was emerging. I loved having free rein in design choices and organizing where things belonged. Lance encouraged me to arrange kitchen cupboards and furniture to please my tastes and sense of "rightness." I experienced ownership at a whole new level!

Then came the milk pitcher incident.

I saw an empty milk pitcher in the fridge and heard an old blame tape coming out of my lips, saying, "Who left the empty pitcher in the fridge?"

There were only two of us in the apartment, so I admit the question was more of an accusation than a real question.

Lance's answer was "There is more than one way to do things, you know!" The tone!

My lips closed in a tight line as I put down the pitcher by the sink to be cleaned while he explained that he thought the pitcher could be chilled to prepare for the next milk bag.

Lance seldom used that tone. I felt chastised for being too controlling. Had I gone too far in dictating our household? Was my exercise of ownership too powerful and domineering? The correction triggered old insecurities and self-doubt. Had I crossed a line? Was I still lovable? Did Lance still enjoy sharing our space and life together? You can see how quickly I added to the stress load I wore as my thoughts escalated!

I was ready to withdraw. We could both feel the tension in the air. My respect for Lance held me still for a moment longer—long enough for him to bridge the distance. He never could leave me alone when he knew something was wrong.

He quickly recognized that it wasn't really about the milk pitcher.

He started asking questions to unravel my headspace as we sat down together. What messages was I telling myself?

We gained respect and understanding through our dialogue. I apologized for being annoyed and sounding the blame alarm. He apologized for his angry tone and for triggering my shame response. Fortunately, we never lasted long in an argument, because we both hated tension and distance between us.

Our apartment was witness to the joys and tensions of learning to navigate the path between independence and interdependence. We were learning to carry our own load, but also striving to make the load lighter for each other. We were growing in making marriage math work: 1+1>1.

CHAPTER 51

LIVING WITH LIMITS

*Our inner child is not an end in itself
But a doorway into the depths of our union with our
Indwelling God, a sinking down into the
Fullness of the Abba experience, into the vivid
Awareness that my inner child is Abba's child, held fast by Him,
Both in light and in shadow.*

—Brennan Manning

Being sick with chronic fatigue took some major adjustments. I wasn't sure whether this was a time to live in joyful acceptance of this season of rest or whether this was something I had to learn to fight. If I was to fight it, how? I had no idea what to do. Throwing supplements at CFIDS was not creating any changes in energy, pain level, allergies, hormone imbalance, or my weak immune system. The doctors I talked with had no other medical options.

Our camp community surrounded us with care. They arranged a prayer evening for healing. I was so grateful to friends who longed to see God move to bring life and peace to my body. They weren't aware of the deeper layers of dysfunction, trauma, and emotional pain, but it was refreshing to be surrounded by their compassion as they aligned their faith with my desire to heal. We spent the evening sharing scriptures, praying, and laughing together! I was grateful for them and shared the flower image I'd received to help us all see divine healing and care in the slow journey as readily as we recognized healing in an instant, miraculous fix. That night was such a gift for my heart as I felt the care of our camp and Youth Eventz community!

In my sickness, I feared being a burden instead of a partner to Lance. I was figuring out a path for living as a sick person while still contributing to making our home inviting. I still wanted to offer a healing space for others as we continued to care for the people in our lives. I had to maintain a strict discipline of rest in our little apartment even while I needed a sense of purpose in this year off from school and work. I focussed on creative hobbies that helped me feel that I could still contribute and add beauty.

Stress was damaging to my body. Any time I pushed myself, my body pushed back, needing days and even weeks of recovery. I had a very sensitive system that needed low stimulation and peace to calm my overactive fight, flight, or freeze mode.

I still wasn't sure what God had in mind for removing the weeds from my life. I had identified a few unhealthy patterns, but I wasn't sure how to break free from the trauma responses that were normal for me.

Did I lack the faith to heal? Was I afraid of change—of stepping into the unknown and making things worse? Was I afraid of what might happen if I opened the door to past hurts? The quiet days alone left me time to think, pray and reflect.

I found a continuing anchor in Psalm 27:13–14: "I am still confident of this: I will see the goodness of the LORD in the land of the living - wait for the LORD, be strong, take heart and wait for the LORD."

I was starting to understand that some versions of the weeds of self-contempt and condemnation grew from the shame of abuse. My default reaction was to work hard at pleasing and trying to earn love. Fear of failure linked to perfectionism made it hard to serve without anxiety. I was also growing more aware of the fear and hypervigilance that kept me tense as I approached the world outside my door.

I wanted to find the peace to rest in God's acceptance rather than striving to prove my worth. I prayed to move into a healthier identity, and for God's love to fuel my service. I wanted to quiet my anxiety by learning to trust in God's goodness and protection instead of mentally trying to prepare and brace for harsh realities. I wanted to turn down my highly sensitive system and let go of my hypervigilance, but I had no idea how to uproot and replace the weeds that had grown in my patterns of relating to myself, others, and God. And daily there was pain. It took a lot of energy just to stay positive and try not to be a burden to anyone around me.

I would cry and write in my journal when my motivation was sapped and my strength was gone. My heart was sad as I struggled to pray in a place of pain.

> What was I made for, God? How would You desire me to be? I want to be useful. I need purpose. I want to ...
>
> Oh, make me content, God. Quiet the churning and pour out your grace.
>
> While saying I don't need to *do* anything; I feel so pressured to be headed somewhere—to do something meaningful.

When I was back at my high school for Kathy's graduation, the teachers all looked at me expectantly as one of their star students. They were anxious to hear about what I was doing now. When I explained that I was taking time off to heal from chronic fatigue syndrome, one of them said, "I'm tired all the time too! I would love a year off."

Sigh. No one wanted to feel like this!

> Please bring peace ...
>
> God, it's hard to care about anything right now ...
>
> I'm just tired—so tired.
>
> I feel helpless—powerless to do anything but weep. Oh, I hurt, I ache. Hold me. Take my pain, Jesus. I want to leave it at the cross. Can I?
>
> Your ways are mysterious. But I am thankful for the promise from Psalm 139 that there is nowhere I can go where You are not still with me: "You have laid your hand on me. Such knowledge is too wonderful for me - too lofty for me to attain ..."
>
> What You choose to leave as a mystery is in Your hands. You know best; make me content simply with what I do know! You are here, now, with me in my anxiousness. You soothe my raw edges, comforting and quieting me. Thank you that you are love personified. I trust You because You know me best. I trust You to stay here beside me.

> Lance—the best part of life right now is his partnership. Thank you, God. You have not forgotten me. In your time ...
>
> Please sustain and keep Lance always in your care and provision. I love him, but You love him more. I trust You with us both.

Though my body was weak, my spirit still longed to live out my ideals. I started reading books and scriptures about healing. I was asked to share my thoughts in a few different settings. So I put together a written reflection to share my conclusions with others. I was certain that God didn't work in formulas but instead offered to be present with us in the midst of suffering. The gift was God's presence to bring guidance, freedom, hope, and joy whether we attained physical healing on this side of heaven or not.

> God, I want to be Your bubbling brook, to be pure and clean, to bring refreshment to the thirsty in this dry, parched land. I can only be a bubbling brook if I am connected to Your spring of life. You are my source. I want to have Your goodness and love pour through me.
>
> I submit to You the care of my body. Show me how to care for this temple of Yours to keep it fit for You. Take my health, and my basic needs, and fill me with Your Spirit of life. Show me how to walk free.
>
> I submit my soul, my mind, and my emotions, and I ask for your protection. Give me the wisdom to feed my thoughts well and reject what isn't true.

> "Finally, whatever is true, whatever is noble, whatever is right, whatever is pure, whatever is lovely, whatever is admirable - if anything is excellent or praiseworthy, think about such things" (Phil. 4:8).

In my weakness and pain, I seemed extra sensitive to emotional cues. I could only listen to music that was uplifting or helped me focus my mind in healthy places. Depressing or angry songs exhausted my spirit. I also had to be careful what I watched. Anything that fed me fear or heightened my sense of tragedy and cynicism would leave me with long nights lying awake with muscles aching, head pounding, and images of shadows pressing in on me.

One night, I woke up with my heart pounding from a familiar nightmare. I was hiding from a shadowy figure who was searching for me. As the threatening male figure got closer, I tried to cry out for help, but my voice wouldn't work. Then I felt a hand clamp over my mouth. I couldn't take a deep breath, and then I felt my body twitch awake! I was shaking so hard that I couldn't form a clear prayer. Lance was lying peacefully beside me, breathing deeply. I cried out frantically in my thoughts: *God, help!* I didn't want to disturb Lance's sleep.

Suddenly Lance woke, sat up, and said, "What? Peg, are you okay?"

I was amazed that God would answer my prayer by waking up my partner to be there for me even though it was the middle of the night. When I retold my dream, it seemed to dim and feel less scary. Lance wrapped his arms around me until I stopped shaking and prayed over me for peace, shelter, and protection for my mind and heart. A liquid warmth poured over me, and I was able to get back to sleep. I was so grateful to have an ally in the dark night. My inner child was learning to rest in God's care and in the safe haven we created in our home.

CHAPTER 52

ADVENTURES IN COOKING

> You go whistling in the dark
> Making light of it, making light of it
> And I follow with my heart
> Laughing all the way.
>
> —Gordon Kennedy and Pierce Pettis

Through my low days, I found comfort in reading wonderful books, watching movies on our VCR, knitting gifts for family members, and doing cross-stitch. These quiet activities could be done from the couch and took my mind off my discomfort. I couldn't rely on painkillers for relief from chronic body aches and headaches, since they could damage my organs. So I used distraction and rest.

From the couch, I often found comfort in untangling my thoughts in my journal. I was still trying to piece together a path to wellness. There was comfort in knowing that Lance would want to read my ponderings and share the journey with me.

God,

> I commit to You my future. I know that You have a plan for me and that it will fit alongside Lance! Chase away any fears about finding my place in ministry, in leadership, and in serving. I know You will place me where You want me in Your way and timing. Remove my doubts.
>
> Free me from the idea that I must carve my place or earn it or gain worth from it. You have placed me in a beautiful home beside my partner and best friend. I am so thankful for this refuge. May it be a safe place for others who walk in our door. May we all discover together that "You are our refuge and strength, an ever-present help in trouble. Therefore, we will not fear" (Psalm 46:1).

I understood that God had designed and fit together each of us for a unique role in the body of Christ, each with a different function and place. What I didn't know was what happened if someone couldn't function. Did a body part still have a place in the body when it had nothing to give? I felt like a burden.

My sister-in-law, Laurel, gave me a book about Chronic Fatigue by Dr. William Crook to try to help me find solutions. His explanation created the first piece of understanding of how I became so sick. The book explains how the physical stress load can accumulate to spark chronic fatigue. It further explains that overuse of antibiotics can deplete good bacteria that hold naturally occurring yeast in check. When good and bad bacteria are wiped out, yeast can overgrow and create intestinal dysbiosis or leaky gut, which allows food particles to escape the digestive system and end up in the bloodstream. The body sees these food particles as invaders or toxins to eliminate. This creates food sensitivities. The cleansing systems of the body become overloaded in trying to clean up toxins, which contributes to inflammation and pain. The immune system is activated and overworked and so cannot handle any new threat of virus, bacteria, parasite, mould, or toxin. Emotional trauma and stressors increase the load until a tipping point creates a chronic autoimmune condition. This was my oversimplified way of making sense of things, but it was a beginning.

All of this was new information to me. The Internet did not exist in its current form to look things like this up. But the book gave me enough understanding to help formulate my next steps. I decided that since yeast feeds off sugars, I would reduce sugar in my diet. I had been a chocolate and ice cream addict. When we had no chocolate in the house, it was time for a grocery trip. My favourite Lance and Peg dates were to the TCBY! Cutting sugar wasn't easy, but it was a promising step.

I was having a hard time with exercise. I could do short walks, but even the smallest movements would leave me sore and unable to sleep. When a brochure came to the house about a gentle exercise circuit on toning tables, I thought it was worth a try. All I had to do was lie on tables and resist the motion of the pads. It was a gentle way to keep my muscles from degenerating. Lance was supportive of using part of our modest income for investing in restoring my health.

On my high days, I could feel productive. When these bursts occurred, I would celebrate by making a nice dinner, joining Lance in a ministry outing, or reaching out to a friend.

One night, I decided to pull out the cookbook we'd been given as a wedding present to make baked breaded chicken. The recipes were compiled by a church and gifted by one of our elderly wedding guests. I was looking forward to relying on the tested culinary wisdom of experienced cooks.

I had made Shake 'N Bake chicken before, but this time, I would make my own coating from scratch! I had never considered what was in those little premade pouches.

I started measuring out the flour, baking powder, and seasonings. The recipe called for twelve teaspoons of salt. That sounded like a lot. But I guessed only a small coating went on the chicken, so maybe lots of salt was needed. So I started measuring the salt into the bag I would shake the chicken in. After six teaspoons, I just couldn't imagine needing more salt than that, so I stopped.

I breaded my chicken and put it in the oven to bake. It looked so good. I was proud of my achievement! I envisioned the happy surprise Lance would have when he came home to a nice meal and a triumphant wife!

When Lance arrived home from his new job at the church, I had mashed potatoes, carrots, and chicken ready for dinner. I couldn't wait for him to sit with me, share his day, and taste my masterpiece!

We said a quick prayer of thanks, and Lance took a bite of the chicken. He made a funny face and took the bite back out of his mouth. I quickly took a bite to see what he was reacting to.

Salt!

That was all I could taste: mouth-puckering, thirst-inducing salt.

I looked at Lance and said that I only used half of what the recipe called for. I couldn't figure out what had gone wrong. I was relying on the wisdom of the church ladies! We both started to laugh! We tried peeling the coating off the chicken, with limited success. Thankfully the vegetables tasted delicious!

I showed him my recipe after we cleaned up. Sure enough, the typed recipe read "12 tsp of Salt." We could only guess that there was supposed to be a line between the numbers. A half teaspoon of salt made a whole lot more sense!

I was grateful that we could laugh together over our misadventures. Sharing life with Lance was sweet even when it was salty!

CHAPTER 53

BOUNDARYLESS

Wherever you go, there you are.

—Thomas à Kempis

Even though I was marinating in the atmosphere and culture of grace that was permeating our new home, I still defined myself as a helper. I found joy and purpose in carrying the burdens of others. But it wasn't always clear to me when that burden wasn't mine to carry. I could plant myself in a new environment, but I was still the same person who had little practise in owning her choices.

My aunt Betty and Mom were visiting with me shortly after we had settled into our apartment. Lance was out for the evening, but I was having a wonderful time showing our home, sharing stories, and connecting. I was delighted to play hostess to these two beloved women in my life!

Then a knock came on my door.

A girl I didn't recognize was standing there. When she told me her name, I knew that this was a friend that Lance talked to occasionally on the phone. He had told me the story of how he stood up for her when she was being bullied in high school and had to appear in court as a witness. That was all I knew about Helga*.

Helga proceeded to ask whether she could stay at my place for a while, since her building was having work done and she couldn't go home because it aggravated her asthma. I felt Lance would want me to be kind and invite his friend in. We could decide to see how we could help once Lance was home.

As soon as she entered the room, Helga took over the conversation. She commanded the focus of the room, eliciting sympathy as she told tragic tales from her life. Her needs became centre stage. She announced loudly that she hadn't eaten for hours and she was really hungry.

Though I had already cleaned up our dinner meal, I started to cook spaghetti for Helga.

My mom and Aunt Betty decided they would end our visit and head home since the warm intimacy of our conversation was now broken. Before they left, they gave me a concerned look and asked me whether I was okay. I reassured them that Lance would be home soon and that all was well.

Helga followed me into the kitchen and started telling me of her hardships. My natural empathy warred with my sense of disappointment that my company had been driven away by a stranger. But politeness kicked in, and I made all the proper sympathetic sounds and responses. Helga reminded me of Lance's heroism in standing up for her as she claimed a closeness with my husband that felt a little manipulative and set off alarm bells in my mind. She was making it clear that she had a right to my sympathy and help.

I was tired and achy, but there was no room for my needs with Helga around. I was starting to feel a twinge of resentment.

After she ate, she plopped down on the couch to be entertained. I found a show for her to enjoy while I did the dishes and cleaned the kitchen for the second time that night. She didn't offer to help, and I didn't expect that she would. I was starting to feel a little anger growing in me. I wasn't good at letting myself feel my emotions, but this one couldn't help but be felt! Though I continued to serve her, I was aware of the extra load she was putting on my tired system. I felt like a victim of her dominant personality.

Before I knew it, she had convinced me that I had to let her spend the night. I was uncomfortable with this decision, but I wasn't sure how I had agreed to it. It was as if she took over my brain. I gave her my favourite new pyjamas, knowing they were the only thing I had that might fit her.

By the time Lance came home, Helga was firmly settled in my pyjamas in my favourite spot, watching a show I didn't like on our TV set, with my favourite blanket wrapped snugly around her. As I tried to explain to him how this had all unfolded, Helga interrupted us and started to flirt with my husband.

That was it! The tension that had been building in me over this demanding forced acquaintance hit the breaking point. I was frustrated, tired, and felt displaced in my own life. Somehow Lance's questions made me feel as if I had allowed this to happen. I didn't feel as though I had chosen any of it! My patterns as a helper were so entrenched that I could see no other options than the choices that had led me to this moment! It was still the same gracious space we had been working to create in our apartment, but I had allowed it to be hijacked until it didn't feel safe for me any more!

I gave Lance a look of exasperation and left him to deal with his friend while I got ready for bed.

Lance allowed Helga to use our spare room that night but made it clear that she would need to find somewhere else to live in the morning. When he crawled into bed beside me, he asked again how this had happened.

Lance would never have allowed Helga to take over our life. I still had no idea what I should have done differently. I didn't feel secure enough in my worth to value my health, needs, and preferences over a more dominant force. Lance comforted me and assured me that we would sort things out in the morning.

Helga slept late and then showered, and we gave her choices for breakfast. Lance offered to drop her off at her parents' house. She immediately protested and launched into a big explanation about why she needed to stay at our place. But she couldn't manipulate Lance. He was clear about how he was to be treated and what he was willing to give. When she was reluctant to go to her parents or her apartment, he assured her that these were the only options we were offering. He modelled ways of caring that still protected space for us.

When Lance returned from dropping Helga off, I asked why she hadn't gone to her parents' the night before. She had made me feel like our place was her only possibility. Lance retraced my decisions with me to show me other ways I could have cared while keeping control of my choices. He showed me that Helga was a responsible adult with parents and a support system and that, as a stranger, I didn't need to feel that I had to be her rescuer.

I was alarmed that I seemed so ill-equipped to run my life in a way that valued and protected my sense of safety, autonomy, and ability to make choices. Life seemed to just happen to me. I needed to find my voice and advocate for myself. And I needed to learn how to say no.

In the quiet of our home, I was trying to learn the rhythms of rest and tuning into what my body and emotions were telling me. But when I was around obvious needs or demanding people, their voices became dominant and I lost myself.

Lance assured me that we could maintain our life of privacy and peace. We could decide what we wanted to and were able to give, and we didn't need to feel responsible for someone else's life and decisions.

I captured my dysfunctions in a song about self-protection and the need to surrender the walls that were no longer serving me. My wounded heart was hidden behind the walls I'd erected as a helper, achiever, perfectionist, and performer. These looked like admirable ways of living, but they contained weeds that distracted me from growing into my true identity. They were driven by shame. The patterns were used to earn my worth. It was time to listen to the voice of my inner child and provide the nurture and protection that only I could give. It was time to listen to the needs of my heart and make self-care and healthy, authentic connection a priority.

WALLS

The light shines so brightly,
But no one's at home.
I act as the hostess, but I feel alone.
Can anyone see there's a hidden ache in me
To be fully alive and finally free?

Chorus:
It's a tyranny; this trying to please
Must not hurt others but must protect me.
Behind these walls I've built to survive,
I've lost sight of me

The frailty that I lock inside
Hides my shame and duality
I wear strength like armour, but is it really me?
Can anyone see there's a hidden ache in me
To be fully alive and finally free?

Chorus 2:
It's a tyranny, this hating to need,
Starving for truth but crushing the plea.
Behind these walls I've built to survive,
I've lost sight of me.

BRIDGE:
Building strong walls only separates me from you
No more hiding; I want to live like You.
Jesus, breathe on me, make my heart anew.

Chorus 3:
Can't you see? God's here to be
The only truth that will set you free.
Surrender your walls, step into the light,
And live authentically

In some ways, chronic fatigue syndrome was a gift. My body was saying no for me when I didn't know how to. My new limitations didn't allow me to be careless about my time and energy. Being sick was forcing me to make choices for healing.

I was relieved to learn that it wasn't unloving to choose not to help sometimes. God was the one who held all things together. It wasn't up to me to carry others. We were each to carry our own load. I enjoyed taking time to pray for people and lifting them to the one who knew best how to meet their needs. But I couldn't try to take their feelings and hardships as my burden to solve. I had to start taking responsibility for my health. No one else could make the daily choices of doing things that were helpful to my body, mind, and emotions. That was my job. There was no one coming to rescue me. Self-care was my adult responsibility.

Around this time, I was getting invitations to speak, lead worship, and attend gatherings or events. Instead of giving automatic yeses, I learned to ask for time to think about it.

As I would talk to Lance about various opportunities, he would ask me questions like "Is it in your area of priority?"

I was stunned. I had never asked this question before! Area of priority?! I had never thought about having one of those. I started to realize that I had merely drifted along, pulled by the expectations, needs, and desires of others.

It was time to learn to own my direction instead of bouncing around like a pinball, feeling depleted and weary and wondering how I got there.

This new way of thinking made me suspect that my decision in residence to see everyone that came to my door as someone sent from God might have been a way to spiritualize the path of least resistance for me. It was easier than setting priorities and taking responsibility for my choices. It was time for a change.

I decided I needed to read more about boundaries and found Henry Cloud and John Townsend's book on the subject illuminating.[13] They helped clear the confusion I had about taking responsibility for my own choices and taking on others' responsibilities as my own. I was often hooked by a legitimate need. But I would go too far in taking on responsibility that belonged to others. Without considering whether my energy and time were sufficient to be helpful, I would automatically take on the role of giver, whether that role was appropriate or not. I would silence my own needs in the mix. It was time to exercise caring by empowering others to care well for themselves as I took better care of myself. I no longer wanted to be a martyr in my service.

I had to be smart in giving my limited time and energy away. I hadn't been spending much time with my mutual friends since chronic illness had hit. I had to rework the tapes in my head, which made me reluctant to nurture healthy friendships. These relationships were like sunshine to my growth. I had to learn to carefully tend the blossom of my soul and emotions.

One boundary effort Lance and I made to take control of our time was to install an answering machine so that we could decide when we were available to answer the phone. When we were having a date night or hosting groups or guests, the phone couldn't take priority over our present company. We learned to screen calls so that we wouldn't miss urgent messages or family emergencies.

As I began to put priorities and boundaries in place, I felt increasingly able to live my life instead of feeling dominated and swept along by the priorities and expectations of others. I was experiencing a new level of freedom that put the joy back into serving.

CHAPTER 54

❦

LEARNING TO BE ME

You cannot keep abandoning yourself for the comfort of others and expect to walk in alignment with your purpose. Being anyone but yourself will keep you small and stuck in unhealthy cycles.

—Alex Elle

As I nurtured authenticity in some close friendships alongside my marriage, I learned to explore the terrain of the heart and reconnect with the wisdom of my emotions to signal the need for change.

When my boundaries were being pushed by others, my emotions would signal me with an internal alarm that something was off or unhealthy. But I often discounted my reluctance to care and serve as selfishness. But when my yes was dragged from me instead of freely given, resentment would follow. Giving with resentment made me feel ashamed of myself. I knew I wasn't loving others well. I tried to change my feelings or shut them down to live the life of service I wanted to. But, perhaps with healthier boundaries, it was time to tune into my emotions to make giving intentional and thoughtful.

I began to wonder about the role of emotions as a nudge God could use to move me towards health and peace. I needed to learn to trust my intuition more.

I picked up a book by Dan Allender called *The Wounded Heart*.[14] It became a door to begin to unravel the impact of childhood sexual abuse on my relationships. I was often confused by my ongoing struggle with self-doubt and insecurity, which led to erecting walls.

The more I read, the more I began to gather pieces of a puzzle about my triggers, reactions, and patterns of relating. I was a classic "Good Girl" who turned confusion, anger, and blame from being abused inward. I condemned myself. Allender called this self-contempt. According to the book, the "Tough Girl" has contempt too but turns it towards others. And the "Party Girl" alternates between self- and other-centred contempt. All of these are self-protective patterns to keep people from getting too close to a wounded heart. They are all forms of self-protective walls.

As I was reading stories of how others were healing from trauma, a statement in the book jumped out at me. It said that some people find it healing to talk to their abusers about the consequences and damage of abuse. Only one of my abusers was still in my life. The man still attended family events and was part of our inner circle. I couldn't shake the thought, but I was convinced there was no way I could ever talk to him about what had happened. I hated hard conversations. Going to the root of my emotional pain with someone who had sparked it seemed completely unrealistic. I dismissed the idea at first.

The Wounded Heart caused me to look more deeply at what my body and emotions were trying to tell me. I was learning how much I dissociated from my body's signals and shut down my emotions. What I didn't realize was that burying my feelings prevented them from leaving. They got stuck in the form of body symptoms, tension, and nervous system reactions. My feelings of being in danger kept my nervous system on high alert, ready for a fight, flight, or freeze response. Freeze mode is a normal reaction of the nervous system for a child who doesn't feel he or she has the autonomy for fight or flight. I gained compassion for my younger self and recognized that I still regularly felt stuck in freeze mode. I lived with a steady feeling of helplessness. I had no idea how to get unstuck.

Alex Howard, author of *Decode Your Fatigue*, compares processing our emotions to digestion. We need to taste or name our emotions, extract the wisdom or nutrients from them, and then let them pass through our bodies to be released. I needed to learn how to digest my emotions so that they didn't get stuck in the form of body symptoms. This was the beginning of a long process of tuning into my inner signals and valuing my emotions.

Lance was so supportive as I learned to process feelings when they hit. He offered the gift of staying present with me. He asked insightful questions that helped me look deeper. He didn't minimize my feelings or try to talk me out of them. We both learned that if we just gave them space to be felt, they would gradually lift. Allowing tears or processing feelings and thoughts in our safe relationship became a great release.

We also learned that this kind of emotional work didn't fit well at certain times of the day. Emotional energy is even more exhausting than physical exertion. I learned to have boundaries with myself as well as with my partner.

Late at night was not a good time for me to explore hard emotional terrain, since I felt more fragile when I was tired and it often kept me awake as my mind was processing.

I also wanted to be sensitive to Lance's energy and choose times when we could both be fully present. For instance, talking while he watched a hockey game was not cool or fruitful for either of us!

When emotions surfaced at inconvenient times, my journal was such a helpful place to process and put words to what I was feeling. I could share it with Lance or a good friend when the timing was right for this level of sharing. Knowing this helped me to release it onto the pages and know that I didn't have to keep replaying my thoughts and keep my emotions stuck inside. Just naming and writing about my feelings often brought about a sense of peace, allowing the emotions to pass.

I needed to keep learning that emotions aren't good or bad. They are signals that need investigating, like the lights on a car's dashboard. Anger alerted me that a boundary had been crossed—someone was pushing me to give something I didn't want to give or trying to manipulate or pressure me in some way. Sometimes I allowed others the dominant emotional space in our relationships and my pleaser side felt talked into promises or actions but then resented it. This awareness led me to acknowledge the dynamics of relating that needed to change. I was allowing anger to be a healing clue.

Sadness was a clue to losses. The loss in question might be the loss of a friendship, the feeling of being silenced or disregarded, or my neglect of my soul's needs. To heal, I had to take on the responsibility of caring for my physical, emotional, and social needs so that I could fuel up and give out of that fullness.

I had to form the habits to make sure my body was nourished, hydrated, and well-rested, and I investigated symptoms for clues about how to support various body systems that needed attention.

I realized, too, that only I could make choices about how to use my time.

Loneliness from the isolation of chronic fatigue could improve only if I was willing to reach out and be vulnerable with my friends. We are all wired for healthy connection. In my desire for mutual friendships, I easily talked myself out of calling friends. I would tell myself that they would be too busy to talk to me or that they already had lots of friends and didn't need me in their lives. But that was really the influence of my fear. I didn't want to be vulnerable to rejection or confirm that I wasn't needed or wanted.

I was reminded that mutual friendships are marked by the

exchange of respect for one another's needs and emotions. I had some relationships that were too draining to sustain in my recovery, so I stopped fuelling them. But I also had amazing friends that I could process with, and we could pray for and encourage one another.

Lance and I recognized that my default was still to perform and help while tuning out headaches, fatigue, emotions, and symptoms. But then I got overwhelmed easily. So, for a time, we came up with the rule of "one thing." I could commit to only one thing each day. Any more than that and I couldn't ensure I would be up for it. I wanted to avoid feeling unreliable. If I did push through to do more, I would spend days recovering.

As an introvert, I needed rest and silence so that I could tune into my internal voice. I learned in university from the Myers-Briggs Type Indicator that I am an INFP (Introversion, Intuition, Feeling, Perceiving). I had always ignored my natural personality preferences to defer and please or to do whatever needed to be done. But living with another introvert was freeing. Lance and I both refuelled by being alone. I didn't feel pressure in our relationship to always keep a conversation going, play hostess, or be entertaining. Nurturing our internal world was something both Lance and I valued.

When we took holidays together, we loved to bring along a bag of books each so we would have many options to choose from. One of our favourite ways of relaxing was to read together in silence and enjoy the quiet companionship. But I also loved the exchange of ideas that happened naturally as we shared aloud something we were reading. Our inside reflection time always enhanced our conversation and connection. I delighted in learning about Lance's inner world and sharing mine with him! This was one of the joys of our partnership.

When December arrived, we bought a five-foot artificial Christmas tree for our apartment since I have a lot of tree allergies. We kept things simple. I made poster art for our fridge, we had a collection of ornaments from both our parents, and we made gifts for Christmas. I created an illustrated guide to "Lance's Endearing Eccentricities" and finished the sweater I had been knitting for him.

Lance surprised me by making one of my dreams come true. He had arranged to have friends record the songs I had written so that they wouldn't be lost or forgotten. I was stunned by such a generous gift of time and care from musicians I respected and trusted! My partner knew me well!

Lance arranged for my sister to sing harmony vocals, and our friends volunteered their time in exchange for meals to make this project happen! The shape of it changed over time, and it took a couple of years to complete as Lance coordinated the efforts. I will be forever grateful to our friends Pat, Dave, Duane, Roger, Gord, and Kevin for their thoughtfulness and musical sensitivity that turned my bare melody lines into fully arranged songs! It was beautiful to me that Lance used his gifts of leadership and coordination to bring life to a long-held desire. He was in tune with my emotional world, which allowed him to nourish my belief that, even with chronic pain and fatigue, I had gifts to offer. He helped me find my voice again.

CHAPTER 55

CLEANSING

> But in the end, it's only a passing thing, this shadow.
> Even darkness must pass. A new day will come. And
> when the sun shines it will shine out the clearer.
>
> —J. R. R. Tolkien

I remember asking God whether I needed to focus on physical, emotional, or spiritual weeds that were contributing to my illness. My attention would be drawn to different priorities at different times. I felt gently led into new illumination, as I was ready for another healing step.

A friend from Laurier had heard how sick I was and sent me an educational video about a digestive cleanse. I was impressed by what the doctor was saying about the villi of the digestive tract getting coated with white flour and sugar residues that would prevent the absorption of nutrients from food and supplements. Though I had been taking the recommended supplements from the specialist for two years, I felt no different. I wondered whether I wasn't absorbing the nutrients that I was taking every day.

This knowledge, alongside the book I read about yeast overgrowth, convinced me to work on gut health. Unburdening the body's cleansing systems made sense to me as a great place to begin restoring healthy function.

Lance and I decided to both do a three-month digestive and parasite cleanse. My efforts at cleansing could be undone by close contact with my partner if he didn't also rid his body of pathogens. I was amazed at how much impact this had on my health. My body felt lighter, and it seemed that my brain fog was lessened.

After a three-month cleanse, I felt well enough to make some other dietary changes and met with a friend who is a nurse with a special interest in nutrition. Linda showed me various vegetables and their benefits as she encouraged me to include them daily to round out my nutrient intake. So I, who had always made dramatic faces in resistance to trying new foods, was willingly stepping into adult choices to eat for health and not just for pleasing my taste buds. It was a learning curve!

After our first two years of marriage, my sister started university at Laurier and moved into an apartment across the hall. It was wonderful having her so close! Though he had always been the youngest in his family, Lance was a natural at being a protective big brother.

Since our marriage, we had often enjoyed hosting Kathy and her friend Andrea for sleepovers. They were great company! We would often laugh so much during our visits that we would have to go into separate rooms to get ourselves back under control. Andrea awarded us a membership paper to the "Society of Childlike Grownups" for those who approach life with a sense of wonder. We proudly displayed it on our fridge.[15]

Kathy became my exercise buddy to keep me motivated and accountable. We did gentle cardio, resistance moves, and stretches to gradually reverse the prior downward spiral of my health.

Lance and Kathy were both my safe people. Lance's confidence and playfulness were so good for me and Kath. We both hated being embarrassed, but Lance was quick to turn the story around to help us see the humour in it. He helped us laugh at ourselves instead of trying to hide in shame. If Lance had something embarrassing happen, he saw it as a chance for some slapstick acting. If he was going to fall, he would exaggerate his movement and turn it into a comedy sketch. He was great at making us laugh!

Lance and Kathy both were good at delighting in me and making me feel special. Kath and I found it fun to perform for each other, sing together, and look for ways to make each other smile. An appreciative audience of safe people allowed me to remember how much I enjoyed speaking, singing, and exploring creative expression!

Lance and I often hosted planning meetings, groups, and friends in our apartment space! Our extra room was a haven we enjoyed sharing. We loved having our home be a safe channel for creativity, compassion, and insight to flow. Grace was teaching us that our mistakes don't define us; they are just a place to grow from. Despite chronic fatigue, life was joyful, peaceful, and rich!

From this place of safety and efforts to heal, I was gradually growing in my conviction that my wounded heart would begin to open to light only when I was honest about the damage done. Part of that journey, I feared, would involve breaking the power of secrecy in my life. I had to stop hiding and pretending in my close circles. I feared this would involve talking openly to my first abuser and being open with my family. Both of these thoughts terrified me. This step might not be necessary for all who seek to heal, but I was following a conviction that grew in me steadily for over two years that this was part of my path forward. I decided to seek help.

As I was praying about this, I got an image in my mind of my first abuser shrivelling and withdrawing from the world into the shadows. I was convinced that if we let the light pour in, it could bring healing and allow us both to become more of the people God intended us to be. Hiding wasn't bringing about health and wholeness for anyone.

I decided to go to a counsellor to prepare my thoughts and build resilience for this monumental shift in my primary emotional system. I was nervous as I was ushered into a small office space and introduced to Lorraine, who offered a soft-spoken, caring presence.

Her question to start us off after general introductions was "So what brings you here?"

I blurted out, "I want to be authentic."

Did I mention I was nervous? I had never done this before.

She asked me to elaborate.

I told her how for so many years I had felt splintered, often robotic. I had the ideal self that I projected to the world and my wounded self that I was learning to listen to and honour. I felt that the only way to feel whole would be to bring both parts of me into my primary relationships. Secrecy was draining me, and I could be so easily hurt or triggered by comments that were made without awareness of my deeper struggles. The silencing of my wounded self was making that part desperate to be heard. I had started to feel as if no one knew me unless he or she knew the full story. But that level of sharing is not always helpful or appropriate. I would sometimes blurt out to a friend that I had been abused as a child, but I would then feel raw and exposed. The reactions I got weren't always helpful to my healing process. I had to learn what authenticity looked like in different relational spaces.

I told her of my conviction that I needed to break the power of the secret. I wanted to be honest about the damage abuse had caused in my life with the one who was still connected to my family circle.

After several sessions with Lorraine, I found words to articulate what I needed to express. I found it comforting to be in a counselling session where we both focussed on what was going on in me. My energy could be focused on my own journey instead of trying to make someone else comfortable. I so appreciated her gift of insightful questions, guided processing, and help in recovering my truth.

I wrote a letter to the man and then gathered up my prayers and courage to contact him about meeting with me. Lance would be by my side as a support. There were a few close friends I asked to pray for me through this emotional process.

Several times my plans to set a date for this meeting were foiled. This created an emotional roller coaster to ride, as I would work up my courage to make the phone call and then would have to calm the adrenalin rush to put it all aside to try again.

Lance reminded me to approach the meeting with self-care and time for emotional preparation. The meeting was definitely my "one thing" for the day. Lance was great at being "still waters" to steady me as I figured things out. I was learning to listen to my body signals to recognize and reduce stress responses.

When I finally did reach my abuser, I kept the call brief as I told the man I wanted to discuss some things that had surfaced in sessions with a counsellor. We set up a meeting place and time. He agreed to come.

Then the churning in my stomach increased. I allowed myself distractions of fiction books and movies to manage the stress load. I had done the preparation, so I couldn't let myself keep trying to imagine how this meeting would go. This meeting was necessary even though I couldn't control the outcome. This person was still part of my emotional system, and I couldn't continue pretending a closeness and ease that I didn't feel. I had to stop suffering in silence. I needed to break the power of the secrecy that made me feel as if I were acting all the time. I still felt as though I were carrying a secret bomb around that I needed to put down. I couldn't camouflage it any more. I was counting on the wisdom that truth would set us all free (John 8:32). My heart had to find rest in that.

CHAPTER 56

MEETING IN THE PARK

What is denied cannot be healed.

—Brennan Manning

As the day arrived, Lance freed up his afternoon and drove with me to the park where we had agreed to meet the man. We were five minutes late. As we raced to get there, my stomach was in knots and my head felt like a balloon. My whole body ached, and I was grateful that I had prepared a written letter to guide us through the meeting so I didn't have to rely on my foggy brain to express my thoughts clearly in the moment.

It was a wet, drizzly day, and after a wave of recognition and general hellos, we were fortunate to find a picnic shelter available. As we walked to a table, I was thankful for Lance's ease of manner and conversation. We placed ourselves with Lance beside me across from the man.

I didn't want to waste time and energy on meaningless pleasantries. I explained that I had formed my thoughts into a letter in preparation for this meeting and said it might be easiest if I just read it. I asked whether he would listen without interrupting me until I finished reading it to the end.

Here is a summary of that letter, with less detail:

> I feel like God has challenged me recently to find freedom by facing my past honestly.
>
> Memories that hurt ... these are difficult to communicate.
>
> When I would come to you as a child needing security and comfort, it was confusing when you would touch me inappropriately.
>
> I began to hate my body and my needs because they betrayed me. I felt dirty, unlovable, and shameful. I couldn't talk to anyone about it because, despite how you wrongfully acted, I loved you and didn't want you to be judged or cut off from my family.

As I read the opening paragraph, I could hardly believe I was reading this letter to my former caregiver. The rehearsals ahead of time with Lance, Lorraine, and Kathy strengthened my resolve as they each affirmed that what I was saying carried the tone of truth without shaming. I wanted to be heard, not to create further damage.

For two pages I read without looking up. I was afraid to meet his gaze, as I didn't want to be impacted by how he was reacting. Here is the substance of what I needed to communicate:

> Each time it happened, I would try to clean myself off and gather myself together so that I could carry on pretending. I tried hard to act normal around everyone, but when that became too hard, I would

withdraw to be alone. I felt cut off from my family in my silence, fear, and self-contempt. I felt like I carried a bomb that could destroy us if I stopped carrying its weight.

I lost my trust in you. I hoped you would make good choices so that I wouldn't have to carry the responsibility.

I was determined to forgive you for abusing me and have done so at different times in different ways. I thought that once I forgave you, I could then move on with my life and put the past behind me.

There were a few things wrong with this way of thinking. I minimized the effect that these incidents had on shaping my identity and relationship patterns. And no matter how I longed to move past them, the memories have continued to be a source of pain and shame, as they are easily triggered.

I need to take time to share with you my understanding of how this has influenced me, and my sorrow, so that forgiveness and healing can be much deeper than my search for a quick fix has allowed. Because we have never spoken of it, I feel that the only way to break the power of the secret to continue to damage and prevent healing is to talk with you about it. That is the reason for this meeting and this letter.

One of the most pervasive influences these events have had on me was shaping how I perceive myself and relate to others. My sense of shame and unworthiness developed after your treatment of me. You undermined my God-given dignity by treating me as an object to be used instead of a person to be cherished, encouraged, and protected.

This developed in me a need to prove my significance to myself and others. I'd lost any sense of my inherent worth. I gave away power in relationships because I felt others mattered but I didn't. I felt as though it were my job to please and fulfill expectations. Servanthood became martyrdom as I denied any access to my true feelings and needs. I shut them down to function. I took on roles like the Achiever, the Pleaser, the Good Girl, and the Helper to try to achieve a sense of value—to feel successful and liked. Rest felt lazy and was tolerated only when my body was physically ill. Intimacy was too risky and so it was easier to impress people and look loving than to be myself. I didn't like me, so why would anyone else? I realize that the patterns weren't a product of the abuse alone, but the abuse certainly reinforced them as a way to find worth. It also made me afraid of failure and of disappointing anyone.

Being liked and respected became more important than being authentic. I felt the pressure of expectations and felt little control over what I gave or withheld—I never had that power with you. I worked hard to please, and that was disastrous with unsafe guys in my life. I figured that as long as a boy only did as much as my abuser, it wasn't really a violation. I felt ugly and unworthy of a healthy relationship and so fell prey to dating someone that made me feel attractive and needed me. I'm grateful that God rescued me from making a bad choice in marriage!

I cried to God in my loneliness and confusion but felt unworthy of one so pure, and my heart felt beyond love. And since I had so dissociated from my emotions, I just couldn't feel loved.

Having a secret to contain made me feel as if I had the power to damage or protect my family. This was a huge weight of responsibility for an adolescent. I have upheld the family's narrative of my perfect life to keep the peace, but the consequences have fallen squarely on my health. I have confided in a few friends over the years to have an outlet, but my relationship with Lance has been my first relationship to offer the security and stability to honestly process and listen to my wounded heart.

When I made eye contact a few times, I met a remorseful, sorrowful gaze. I gathered strength from the fact that he neither made excuses nor shrank from taking responsibility.

I now hunger for honesty in all of my life and relationships.

Because my family doesn't know about the abuse between you and me, I often negate their encouragement and support. They are encouraging the ideal me. I have to hide from them my deepest struggles to protect your relationship with them. I often live in half-truths because they are unaware of any sexual abuse in my life. They are puzzled by my illness and the mindsets that have been driving me. It's hard for me to explain my lack of self-worth. I long to be free to talk openly to my parents.

At the same time, I respect that your relationship is full of complicated balances, and so I want to leave the responsibility of sharing the truth with them to you. My hope is that by opening this door, the truth will be freeing for all of us.

This meeting is about being heard and acknowledging the truth to allow healing to begin between us and as individuals. Don't feel pressured to respond in any particular way right now, but I want to also give you the freedom to respond if you wish. It may be necessary to schedule another meeting to continue to move forward to embrace truth and restoration.

I do want the best for both of us. I hope for freedom to be unleashed in all areas of your life, even as I pursue the same in mine.

Sincerely,
Peg

    The man shuffled in his seat a few times as I was speaking, but I didn't expect a response after I finished sharing. I left airtime for it if he did wish to speak.
    He surprised me by saying that he had thought about this a lot. We had been playing the pretend game so long I had never had any

clue that he acknowledged what happened at all. There was only my imagined interpretation of a certain look he gave or a phrase that was ambiguous. We had a strange subtext under so many conversations.

He said he knew that he had damaged me, but he had prayed that it was less severe than it really was. He acknowledged the abuse's effect on my self-esteem and affirmed that this search for understanding and truth was needed for healing.

He justified his actions in a small way by saying that he never learned with his family how to communicate love, implying that his inappropriate touch was a loving expression and he was a victim. I would have to unpack that later. He knew that he had overstepped the boundaries of our relationship and had feared doing the same with Kathy and so had withdrawn from her. He wondered aloud whether he should have approached me about this sooner to apologize.

I couldn't say whether that would have been helpful or not, but I knew that this meeting was necessary now for my health.

After apologizing, he asked what else he could do to repair the damage. I told him that I didn't know what would help beyond this point because all my focus had brought me only this far.

I was careful to say that I wanted to find true healing and would not settle for a quick-fix solution. Lance suggested to the man that perhaps telling my family the truth might help me to live more freely at my family home. The man thought that his relationship with my family could withstand the truth, and he sounded willing to talk about it sometime when the timing seemed right. Lance had recently been studying emotional systems and spoke of the potential for the truth to shift the dynamics to bring new freedom to the whole family. The man seemed to capture this vision beyond the pain and potential cost of honesty.

At this point, I felt we had said all there was to say, and I sensed that it could be dangerous to linger since my impulse was to console or comfort my abuser's obvious display of remorse. That didn't feel appropriate, and I didn't want to go back to shrinking and minimizing the damage.

When I suggested we walk to the cars, the man suggested that maybe we could pray together before we left.

This felt okay to me so long as we first talked about the danger of prayer making us feel that all was now restored and resolved. There was still hard work ahead of us. Though the intimacy of prayer was a little uncomfortable for me, the prayer itself seemed fruitful and good. My abuser prayed for the courage to be honest in relationships, I prayed for freedom from damaging patterns, and Lance closed by asking God to guide us and help us move towards further healing.

Lance lightened the moment by suggesting that we walk towards a washroom. We did, and we then regrouped outside. We walked together to the cars, and I flinched as my abuser came to hug me. I felt discomfort over this familiar closeness that I so often felt obliged to exhibit as a performance for others.

Every instinct then was to leave. I couldn't bear another moment. I felt wound up tight with the effort this meeting had required.

Lance and I climbed into the car, looked at each other, and exhaled deeply at the same time.

"That was the scariest thing I have ever done."

Lance's response was "Yeah! Scary as hell!"

His response seemed to capture the weight of the moment with his choice of words, since Lance never used the word "hell" to be expressive.

My head fell back against the headrest. I felt numb and extremely drained.

On the ride home, Lance and I debriefed about the experience and spoke of the man's apparent love and expression of regret. It seemed unlikely that he would initiate a truthful encounter with my family, but I was satisfied that he listened without minimizing the damage or deflecting responsibility. The future for our family and my relationship with him was still very vague. But I had taken a step towards truth that might eventually keep me from having to sustain the charade that made me live in half-truths and kept me disconnected from my real feelings. Alongside my fatigue, there was a sense of satisfaction as I allowed my faith in God's goodness to triumph over my fear. That was the bravest step I had ever taken.

CHAPTER 57

DEBRIEFING

> Boundaries have nothing to do with whether you love someone or not. They are not judgments, punishments, or betrayals. They are a purely peaceable thing: the basic principles you identify for yourself that define the behaviours that you will tolerate from others, as well as the responses you will have to those behaviours. Boundaries teach people how to treat you, and they teach you how to respect yourself.
>
> —Cheryl Strayed, *Tiny Beautiful Things: Advice on Love and Life from Dear Sugar*

As I debriefed about my meeting with my counsellor, she affirmed that I was smart to override my impulse to soothe the man's remorse. It made me wonder what made me so willing to take care of other people's feelings while ignoring my own. I realized that I did not wish to be a confidante or key emotional supporter for the man or my parents as this step towards honesty unfolded. My role as rescuer had to be displaced. I could not take responsibility for others' choices and feelings.

Relational dynamics felt as if they had shifted. Having confided a truthful perspective of myself to the man caused him to know me more than my family did. I wasn't sure how I would feel about that level of intimacy when we would all gather again. I somehow felt a little more vulnerable with the man.

I was an adult now and had begun to listen to the needs of the young girl inside me who wanted protection and care. I couldn't look to someone else to do that. It was my job to put in place boundaries that respected my inner child. I had to create the safety I craved. I needed security to decrease my body's constant stress response. I couldn't heal well with my overactive, hypervigilant nervous system.

I set up a second meeting with the man to put in place some ground rules for what I could tolerate and what I needed from him to feel safe. I no longer wanted to pretend our relationship was close. I didn't trust him. There could be room to allow him to earn back my trust someday, but I felt it shouldn't be assumed. Forgiveness would mean that I was releasing my desire to punish him, but it was not the same thing as reconciliation or restoration of a relationship. Only time and actions could show me whether his remorse and desire for healing were sincere.

Again, it felt easiest to prepare my thoughts in a letter that we could each have after I read it out loud.

Here is a taste of that letter:

> Since our meeting, I have had time to meet with my counsellor twice. This has been extremely helpful, as I have been unsure of where we go from here. Thanks for meeting with me and Lance, and for hearing my letter. It was important for me that you understand how awkward the past many years have been in relating to you. I suggested to my counsellor that I was unsure of how our meeting

would impact gatherings now that you are aware of my discomfort.

It might feel natural for you to try to ease my discomfort by trying to be close. But that would be extremely uncomfortable for me. I find physical closeness especially awkward, as it conveys a sense of intimacy that I don't feel. I have learned to distrust you in the past, and that trust will only return slowly as we live honestly and with clear efforts to heal. Right now, I need you to give me lots of time and space.

Here are some things that would make me feel safe:

1. I don't want to be alone in a room with you. I need the safety of three or more people.
2. I can give our traditional hug at the door, but any other affection (tickling, a squeeze, or massage) would feel violating.
3. I don't want to sit beside you on a couch or at the dining table.

I am asking you to respect these basic boundaries as a way of caring for me. I will only learn to trust you as you respect my need for space and time. I will need evidence that you are dealing with this area of life and not just minimizing and pretending it away.

I mentioned at the end of my last letter that it may be appropriate to give you an opportunity to respond to my letter. I have reconsidered this and feel that this could be harmful. I realized that I opened a door to a wound that has been unattended for years. My impulse was to pull out a Band-Aid for you, but I think it is important to let the wound exist in the light of God's presence to receive proper tending and care. It is up to you to take care of it. Since it is not my role to comfort or tend to it, I must not put myself in a situation where this impulse arises.

As much as I wish my family to know the truth, I don't want to step between them and you, so I am leaving the responsibility of sharing the truth with you.

Thanks for being open to beginning to live more honestly. I appreciate that you took responsibility for what happened and acknowledged my need to be heard. The future is ours to choose. I hope we can all grow in grace and truth.

After this letter, the man shared his initial reactions.

He said that the letter from our first meeting "wasn't that bad." He felt that if my course of action was set, he would just let it unfold. He said that he didn't feel my family had to know. His rationale went something like this: "You said you've forgiven me, and I know God has forgiven me. I realized that what I was doing with you was wrong, and so I stopped and said I was sorry. I've never done anything like that again. Nobody needs to know. It doesn't affect me."

At the time I was focused on listening and trying to understand where he was coming from. But I could feel myself growing flushed and uncomfortable. I knew I needed time and space to process before we talked again.

Lance was so patient at listening as I debriefed these conversations and found my path forward. I also had some amazing friends who could explore this heart terrain with me in a constructive way by asking insightful questions and standing up for my inner child in ways that were still new to me.

I was still meeting with a counsellor to figure this stuff out. It was she who reminded me that what the man did was a crime. I had every right to press charges and hold him accountable for the damage he caused. Another option she presented would be to have him pay for my counselling sessions, since I could afford only a minimal amount at a sliding-scale practice. With Lance's church salary as our only income, we didn't have a lot of money for therapy sessions.

Though I heard the truth of her words, they didn't feel like the right course of action in this case. It would feel a bit like coercion and manipulation. I wanted his responses to come from a heart change. I didn't want to punish him but to extend a grace that could open him to the work of God's Spirit. I also didn't want him to feel he had paid for the damage and could now ignore its effects. The man was mostly right about not doing anything like that again, but I also felt he had allowed himself to drift along into behaviour that was still problematic, and I wanted to be honest about what I saw.

Months passed with no movement from the man towards an honest connection with my family. I decided that I needed to use further limits for my own health. It took too much energy to keep playing the game of pretending, especially after my resolve to live authentically grew.

So I wrote another letter.

> As part of this quest for truth, I feel like it is important, to be honest with some lingering concerns I have.

At our last meeting, I was making an effort to understand your perspective but have since felt angry at some ways I feel you have minimized the past and its present effect on relationships.

First of all, it seems that you have forgotten that what you did was a crime. The time lapse doesn't clear away your guilt in the eyes of our legal system. My forgiveness feels shallow unless you realize that it means I have chosen not to publicly shame you, press charges, or seek financial restitution. Do you still not recognize the tremendous harm of your actions to disrupt my personal development and shackle me with shame and self-contempt that created harmful repercussions for years of my life? Autoimmune disorders are linked to stressful trauma, not just physical burnout. My years of sickness are part of the consequences I have paid for your damaging choices.

One of the things that concerns me is the deadening effect of your buried struggles. I see in you a resignation to a mediocre life. It's like you have settled into your imperfections and excused them by saying that they are not much different from other guys'. You stopped rising to be all you can be. You keep yourself in an isolated internal world. When I pray for you, I see a small, shrivelled version of yourself in place of the man you could be.

Your choice to quit smoking gives me hope of a "new life" for you. That you chose to do the hard thing for your health shows signs of possibility. God isn't finished with you yet, so I hope that you're not finished with you.

Another concern is that neglecting to clean the skeletons out of the closet affects your judgment as you relate to others. I see evidence that lust is still a present problem for you and not just a past one that ended when your abusive treatment of me stopped. You make inappropriate comments and jokes that have earned you a sleazy reputation. You give inappropriate attention to women, and I've heard of one incident where you clearly crossed a line. I feel like my silence and lack of pressing for accountability have enabled your inappropriate patterns.

Your behaviour and choices have consequences. You have been shielded from consequences of any kind because of my choice to remain silent and allow you time to deal with this issue and bring it into the light of relationships. I need to see that you are taking responsibility to leave lust behind and learn the high path of selfless love.

You seem anxious to retain a connection with me and my family. For any relationship I have with you to be rebuilt, I need to see you move beyond passivity and your insistence that there is no problem. My boundaries are my insurance that I will not be hurt by you any longer. And if I see any need to protect others from your lack of judgment, I will reconsider my silence so that I do not enable bad behaviour.

Evidence that will show me that you are making an effort:

1. You commit to Christian counselling to identify and work on issues.
2. Your reputation shifts as your friends see a change in your words and behaviour.
3. You seek honest accountability with at least two other men.
4. You commit time and effort to healthy honesty in your relationships with my family and in your primary relationships.

If I see these efforts, I will gradually begin to relax my hypervigilance around you. God can redeem and make new, but you have to embrace growth, not hide from it.

I have talked this through with Lance, and we feel strongly that I have to get out of the middle of your relationship with my family. I have decided to give you a deadline to talk to my parents. If you don't choose to talk with them, I will meet with them on Saturday, December 7, in the evening, with a letter to fill them in. It is my hope that you will speak with them first and make the hard choice to grow, heal and rebuild in truth. Unless I hear from you, I will arrange this meeting on Friday evening before this.

Sincerely,
Peg

For so long I had chosen to keep the peace instead of having honest conversations, so these exchanges were new territory for me. It was extremely draining. The exercise of boundaries felt so new. It was like unfolding wings I had never used and flapping them in the breeze to see what they felt like. I felt harsh, but also knew my inner child felt more secure as I lived in a more truthful space that honoured my feelings and intuition over trying to make others happy.

After this meeting, all that was left to do was to wait and see whether the man would rise to take ownership for reparation or whether he would remain passive and leave the hard work to me. I was tired of carrying the secret bomb. It was time to defuse it.

CHAPTER 58

LETTING LIGHT IN

*The decision to come out of hiding is our initiation rite
into the healing ministry of Jesus ...
We stand in the Truth that sets us free
and live out of the Reality that makes us whole.*

—Brennan Manning, *The Rabbi's Heartbeat*

Time was ticking by with no evidence of movement from the man. I had to spend long days of recovery after each of these meetings.

My days were filled with quiet rest. I kept my hands and mind busy as I spent hours knitting or doing cross-stitch embroidery as gifts for family members. Most of our Christmas gifts were labours of love, since time was more plentiful than money for me. The creativity was peaceful and suited my desire to increase beauty in the world. It was good for my neurological system to be still and creative. I read every day—some books to learn about physical health, some for spiritual refreshment, and a steady diet of redemptive stories for immersing myself in hopeful places.

I had to counteract the ongoing emotional and physical tension in this waiting time as I watched to see what the man would choose to do. Family gatherings were a mixture of the lovely and the increasingly difficult as I was aware of the hidden subtext under conversations. My parents cared so much and asked the kind of questions that reflected that, but I often had to dodge the truth since they were unaware of the trauma piece of my illness. The deadline for the man to act was looming. He still made no move to be honest about the abuse with my parents. I eventually realized it was up to me to go ahead with my plan.

The man agreed to attend if I set it up.

I knew I couldn't just drop a bomb into my family's laps without having some support in place. I also knew that I could not be their source of comfort as they were processing, so I travelled with my sister to speak with my aunt and uncle, who are my parent's closest friends. I shared with them my initial letter, which described what happened to me, to explain what I was working through. I asked them whether they were willing to be present with my parents on the weekend when the truth came to light. They were extremely caring and supportive and promised to come. They affirmed that my family needed to know so that truth and grace could do their work. They knew the man and had a unique perspective and understanding of all the people involved.

Next, I made a phone call that I hoped would shift the dynamics of my emotional system and break the hardship of secrecy. I set up a time to meet with my family and the man.

It wasn't unusual for my aunt and uncle to call about a time they could visit. They arranged to be there that weekend.

On the day of the meeting, Lance and I arrived at my parents' house shortly after the man, and my mom seemed to sense that something unusual was unfolding.

After our regular exchanges of hugs and hellos, Lance sat beside me on the couch across from the man, with my parents on my right and my aunt and uncle on my left. My mom's and dad's eyes were fixed on me. The man looked at the floor, and my aunt and uncle nodded their support. I had decided to tell my brother and his wife separately after this meeting. I didn't want to have too many emotions in the room to contend with at one time. And, of course, Kathy already knew and was praying for us.

As with each sensitive meeting before, I prepared a letter to explain the things that were important to me. I asked that they just listen and not interrupt.

This letter was shorter, since the main purpose was to admit the presence of the bomb and its impact on my health. I apologized for keeping the secret but explained why it felt necessary. The man never spoke a word during my letter. But as soon as I finished speaking, Mom jumped out of her seat and wrapped her arms around me and started to cry, saying how sorry she was that this had happened to me. She had no idea I had gone through any of this.

I awkwardly hugged her back and tried to be comforting. I had to remind myself that it wasn't my role to fix anyone else's feelings. My emotions were already disengaged to get through this. I consoled my parents with words about how I was doing the work of healing and wanted them to focus on their own process now. I was giving responsibility back to my parents to navigate their relationships. My aunt and uncle were there to debrief with them and support them.

When Mom finally sat down, she got angry. She felt that the man's past behaviour crippled us all. She asked the man what he felt.

He said he had nothing to add. It was all plainly there in my letter. He was following my action plan, and he was unsure how to proceed. He seemed more shut down than when he was with just me and Lance.

My uncle asked the man if he had any trusted male friends, since I had requested accountability as a condition of trust-building and reparation. The man thought maybe he did, but he couldn't be sure. When Mom pressed him to name some, he offered a name but then said maybe that person wouldn't work. Mom and Dad were surprised. They hadn't realized the man wasn't really close to anybody beyond the people in the room.

As someone a step removed from the emotional system, my uncle offered to be accountability support. My aunt asked whether the man would resent their questions: "You won't get your back up?"

The man agreed to try.

In response to my request that he get counselling, they discussed possibilities. A ministry couple from family camp was mentioned. I suggested my counsellor as a resource. I thought it might be helpful to have someone outside our regular community.

The man made a comment that painted me as the troubled one with the problem and stated that he was doing everything for my benefit. I felt myself getting a little angry, since it was his issues that began all of this.

I explained that I was taking responsibility for my reactions to trauma and doing everything I could to heal. I hoped that he would take the opportunity to address the dysfunction in his own life. I acknowledged that this conversation was an important step for me. I was hopeful that breaking the power of the secret would lessen the burden I carried. The truth didn't hurt me like deception and hiding did. I was working hard on getting to the centre of my woundedness to let the poison out.

I shared parts of my healing process with my family members and the man. I talked of being in a safe, honest space in my life with Lance and the support network of my friendships. My parents asked me how this had impacted my marriage. I wasn't ready to talk about that with them. It was too vulnerable a question. My purpose for meeting that night was finished. I was ready to move out of the middle of all of this. I didn't want to feel responsible for the management of all the emotions in the room. My parents were still unaware of many parts of my inner story. This disclosure was just the first step in the right direction towards authentic relationships, but it was enough for one night!

My parents and the man had a lot to talk about. I didn't want to linger there.

For over ten years, I had carried the bomb of this secret around while trying to camouflage and hide it. But on this night, I had said my piece, revealed the bomb, and nodded to Lance that it was time to go. I was leaving the bomb with my parents to figure out how to defuse it. They needed space to process it without fear of hurting me. I already felt lighter from unburdening the weight of secrecy.

Mom once again wanted to embrace me as she cried. She held me for a few minutes, trying to comfort me, but I was too numb to receive it. She told me she was sorry she wasn't there for me. I knew there was nothing to be done about the past, and I couldn't fix her sense of remorse. I shifted into strength mode and reassured her that I was in a good place now and that I wanted them to focus on navigating the truth together without me in the middle of it all.

I wasn't sure what I needed yet for the future.

Before we left, I reaffirmed to the man that I didn't hate him. I just didn't want to pretend to be close when I felt unsafe. I just needed him to respect my boundaries and do the work that might allow me to trust him again.

We all prayed for a moment at my mom and dad's request. It felt like a good place to rest my heart as we asked for God's help with the future. God had been my refuge through all the years and continued to be my safe place in that moment.

The car ride home allowed me to decompress and unpack the experience. I had to coach myself to breathe deeply and let go of some of the tension I had been carrying. Releasing tension was something I would have to keep working on. As I detached from emotions, they seemed to get stuck in body tension that I had been storing for a long time. The daily neck stiffness and headaches I experienced were making sense.

For now, my goal of breaking the power of the secret was accomplished. There was still a lot to process, and in some ways, this felt more like a beginning than an end. I wasn't sure where this was leading, but I trusted God to be gentle with us. I was counting on God to bring beauty from the ashes of our pain.[16]

I was looking forward to a time when the truth could do its work to bring deeper freedom for all of us. I still wasn't sure whether we could get through this without the truth bomb blowing up our emotional system. I didn't know whether the man was willing to put in the effort to grow or whether he would continue to be part of our family gatherings, but I trusted the light of truth and love to heal us. God had always been my "refuge and strength, an ever-present help in trouble," so I would cling to faith to calm my fears.[17]

CHAPTER 59

THE GIFT IN THE ILLNESS

> Praise be to the God and Father of our Lord Jesus Christ, the Father of compassion and the God of all comfort, who comforts us in all our troubles, so that we can comfort those in any trouble with the comfort we ourselves receive from God.
>
> —2 Corinthians 1:3–4, NIV

Gradually over the years of focussing on healing from this illness, I began to feel the gift of time I'd been given. I would never have chosen to take time off from school and work to heal the deep trauma that shaped me. Illness is one of the only socially acceptable forms of rest. Since I hadn't learned to set priorities and boundaries, my body just finally burned out and said, "Enough!" Chronic fatigue syndrome was the stop sign I needed to begin to figure out why I was so driven and emotionally fragile.

Our culture esteems hard work, independence, self-sufficiency, and competition, but I had started listening to a still, small voice that whispered of another way. I began to be thankful for the fatigue that made it impossible to live in my old driven patterns. I was learning, instead, to listen to the rhythms of grace. I'd experienced gentle promptings and insight to begin sorting out issues of identity, trauma, and safety. And in time, I felt that I was blossoming and receiving back lost parts of myself, even as I was forced to stop striving and pushing to achieve, please, and prove my worth. I felt the allure of quieter days with fewer demands and space to stay connected to the inner terrain of my thoughts and feelings. I loved to create, serve, and give out of this space.

My shame root was gradually shrivelling as I nourished the soil of my heart with healthier affirmations rooted in a love that I couldn't lose or earn. Our home became the culture of grace, where I could learn to trust God to show me how to put the dislocated puzzle pieces of my health, identity, and purpose back together again. As I surrendered my world of emotions and thoughts to God, instead of losing myself, I felt as though I was receiving back a truer self transformed by divine love. The negative emotions I had been so afraid of and had tried to smother were now being processed, digested, and let go. When I made space to acknowledge and feel them, they lost their power to hurt me. I still had lots of growing to do, but I was less afraid of the journey ahead.

Part of adulting was learning to take responsibility for self-care and choosing which priorities would direct my use of time and energy. I wanted to show up as the best version of myself, doing things that mattered to me.[18] But this best self was not just an ideal projection divorced from my inner world of vulnerability. Honest relationships were teaching me to stay present and allow growth. My wounded past became a place to rise from instead of something to shrink from in fear or shame. My personality was being recovered instead of ignored and denied. I was learning to allow God's light to shine uniquely through me.

As I gradually untangled the weeds that were robbing me of life,

I felt that my days were filled with goodness that was like life-giving sunshine and gentle rains to nourish my becoming! I sometimes had to use my boundaries to keep other people's storms from blowing in to knock me over. But I found that service was becoming more satisfying as I learned to care more appropriately. Often, people in my life simply needed to be heard, seen, and loved. I enjoyed offering validation and understanding while empowering them to care for their own needs, instead of trying to carry their loads. I started relinquishing the role of being responsible for the feelings and choices of others.

I was surprised that God was transforming my weaknesses and life lessons into fruitful ways to serve. The comfort I received became the gifts I could now offer. I was meeting so many people working through similar journeys of healing. Health puzzles were fascinating to me, and I found that the clues to healing often emerged from exploring our stories together. I also found myself working through *The Wounded Heart* with other survivors of childhood sexual abuse. We found a safe place to process, encourage, and hear one another as we each took steps to heal.

Lance's job at First United Church gave us stability and a wonderful community, though admittedly I was part of just small slivers of it. Since I slept through the mornings to get my fourteen hours of restless rest, I seldom went to church. Getting up for Sunday worship services on special occasions made me feel as if I got up in the middle of the night. I would need days to recover on the couch afterward. But gradually my sleep began to deepen as my hypervigilance decreased. Releasing the deep-rooted stress of secrecy and fear, and living in a safe, nurturing environment was an important part of shifting my body from stress mode to healing mode.

Eventually, I could tolerate more outings. I still had high days and low days, but I was able to live beyond my "one-thing-a-day" rule. These changes made a big impact on my mindset. Hope was rising. I was beginning to think that my dream of having enough health to be a parent someday might be possible.

As my body was slowly mending, so were my heart and mind. I was learning a different path that was uniquely mine. I was learning to find joy in stepping away from the push of competition and achieving society's markers of success. I was learning to quiet the voice of condemnation when I was criticized or when shame rose over my lack of self-sufficiency. My health was not stable enough to work outside the home. Healing was still my priority, and I had to work regularly on dismantling fear and self-doubt. My world had to remain small to take the pressures away, and I found that I preferred living a quieter life.

I was learning to embrace my introverted nature. I loved the prayerful rhythms that started my waking hours, even if I didn't usually get up until the afternoon. As I started having deeper, more satisfying sleep, I would wake earlier, having time for breakfast and lunch on the same day. I remember asking Lance, "What is lunch?" It had been so long since I had been awake for both meals, and I'd forgotten what people generally ate. Tuning into my needs as an introvert for rest, calm environments, and solitude was a key to my healing. I couldn't give out of an empty tank, and refuelling for me meant time alone or with my safe people doing something creative, bookish, and quiet. Sometimes I got lost in a project and could forget how much I liked people until loneliness reminded me to reach out again. Deep conversations with one or two people were my favourite way of enjoying large gatherings and parties. I adjusted the kinds of connection time I would prioritize.

With each year, I felt my health growing stronger. I had learned that certain foods trigger inflammation for me, so I cut them out.[19] This made a huge difference with headaches and body aches. The digestive cleanse had given me back some ability to move my muscles gently without penalty, but I still had to listen to my limits. It took practice to make sure I didn't tune out and push my body too hard.

By listening to my pain and energy levels, I could avoid triggering a stress response that slowed down my recovery.

Having Kathy live across the hall from us was such a special season. I so enjoyed our heart exchanges and her help in staying motivated to do gentle exercises that would strengthen me. We enjoyed the richness of being a support and a comfort to each other! Lance and I also took seriously our role of big brother and sister. It was a pleasure to help her with school, listen to her inner world and help her recognize signs of healthy and unhealthy relationships. We were unapologetically protective as guys swirled around her. We didn't want her to be as vulnerable as I had been to predators.

After opening my wounds to my family, I found our exchanges became more meaningful and helpful. Honesty made me feel more seen and understood by my parents. The wounds were given space to heal in our relationship in place of trying to protect the family from my truth. My needs had space.

I was learning to tend to the garden of my heart's needs and to admit when I was feeling neglected or choked out by my familiar weeds. This was important to my growth as I made the adjustments needed to choose a different path. I was working on authenticity instead of minimizing my feelings and presenting a stoic front. Emotions no longer scared me. I actually began to love exploring the world of the heart and welcomed relationships where we could talk openly and make sense of our experiences and how they impacted us.

I felt less pressured by my family and friends to feel better and get on with my life. We all recognized that chronic fatigue syndrome was a long-term autoimmune disorder and that trauma complicated the picture. There was no quick fix. I suspected that it would be a condition I would have to learn to manage for the rest of my life. I was hopeful that I could keep improving as I learned the best ways to work with this autoimmune disorder.[20] It was lovely to feel the support from my close circle as I embraced the patient unfolding that was part of this healing journey for me. I was finding that I could live out a sense of purpose even in this adapted form my life had taken.

My initial conversations with the man and my family were bearing fruit. Stepping out of the middle of their relationship allowed them to wrestle with their growth and healing apart from me. Releasing the truth into our emotional system was having a good effect not only on my health but on all of us.

The man took seriously the challenges to rebuild. He started to attend regular group therapy meetings where he shared my letter. The counsellor asked for a copy to use with other groups since it gave a sense of the ways childhood sexual abuse can have long-lasting consequences for survivors. I gave my permission to share it. The man chose to stay for extra sessions to continue to grow and give back. I was amazed that such a private person would agree to group counselling. I was shocked when the therapist asked him to help facilitate other groups. The man was working on honesty and accountability in therapy and with my parents and aunt and uncle. Only time would tell how truth could work to bring about wholeness and freedom.

I was amazed as I watched my parents process what had happened to me and turn it into a passion to work tirelessly and preventatively to help other young people avoid the degradation of abuse. In their retirement, my parents went to a discipleship training school with Youth With A Mission (YWAM). Their outreach trip to Northern Thailand sparked a whole new ministry to keep vulnerable children in school, protecting them from predators who seek out poor families to target for human trafficking. That is an entirely different story that deserves to be told but goes beyond the scope of this one. But I mention it because it demonstrates a redemptive beauty that rose from the hard work of forgiveness as we offered to God the painful parts of our stories. The truth seeded freedom that branched out well beyond our family circle. In fact, they called the ministry Mighty Oak Global Initiatives to explain how the seeds of compassion, education, wisdom, and grace can create in each of us the resilience of an oak tree.[21] Through partnerships with sponsors, we have seen many children in extreme poverty given the opportunity to stay in school, grow in character, and gain skills that enable them to live out their dreams of a stable future. They have become mighty oaks that have brought strength, faith, and comfort to their families and communities.

Camp ministry remained a big part of my life. Lance and I continued to serve at a sixteen-day leadership camp each summer. I focussed my limited energy on parts of the day when I could contribute most effectively. Active games were the best time for me to nap or get some planning done! To go on the canoe trip with the group, I had to pack special foods, an inflatable mattress, and a padded canoe seat to accommodate my unique needs and to keep my muscles from rebelling! I felt like the princess from the story "The Princess and the Pea"—sore and bruised in a way that made sleep impossible when I didn't have a soft place to lie down. Although I felt a little high maintenance, these adjustments allowed involvements that fuelled my sense of purpose. I was learning to be unashamed about needing to lean into the strength of others.

Like most people navigating chronic illness, I had a defining moment when I knew I was really healing! In 1998, I was able to paddle all the way back from our campsite to the A-frame in Algonquin without days of agonizing recovery. I really was getting better! I had moved from 20 per cent energy to about 60 per cent.

Our first five years of marriage were rich with a great community, unique opportunities, the beauty of our partnership, and the gracious culture we created together in our home. We loved our two-bedroom basement apartment as our first experiment in homemaking!

But I'd been considering our housing situation. I was thinking about the $425 we spent each month on rent and wondered whether there was some kind of condo we could purchase that would put our monthly payments towards ownership to build equity.

We contacted a real estate agent, and she discovered a newly renovated semi-detached farmhouse. Lance's parents helped us with the down payment. It was the perfect starter home for us. It was closer to Lance's parents and had a little backyard and a garden. We invited Kathy and her good friend Karen to live with us when they came back to Kitchener for school in the fall.

As we looked forward to becoming homeowners, Lance and I felt that a new chapter was beginning where the healing steps we had been walking together would become building blocks of lovely new possibilities—not just for us, but also for those God put in our path. We had seen such good fruit from our partnership and the path we had discerned together! In our next steps, we would continue to create spaces of grace, discover our place in God's redemptive story, lift our faces to the light, and learn to thrive in this big, wide world together.

ENDNOTES

Chapter 6: Life Can Hurt

1   Gordon Lightfoot, "Pussy Willows, Cat-tails," on *Sunday Concert*, Warner Chappell Music, Inc., 1969, 33⅓ RPM.

Chapter 8: Dissociation

2   Bryan Duncan, "Only Wanna Do What's Right," *Bryan Duncan: Holy Rollin'*, Light Records, 1986, 33⅓ RPM.

Chapter 11: Deepening Friendship

3   Life Savers, "Life Savers Tweet Tweet 1983," Retrontario, uploaded September 11, 2011, video, https://www.youtube.com/watch?v=y9VsvGYC_ac.

Chapter 14: Peggy Pedestal

4   Galatians 5:22, NET: "But the fruit of the Spirit is love, joy, peace, patience, kindness, goodness, faithfulness, gentleness, and self-control."

Chapter 25: Learned Helplessness

5   Mark Gersmehl and Billy Smiley, "Quiet Love," on *White Heart: Vital Signs*, Home Sweet Home/Myrrh, 1984, 33⅓ RPM.
6   Gerard Manley Hopkins, *Gerard Manley Hopkins: Poems and Prose* (London: Penguin Classics, 1985).

Chapter 26: Relationships

7   *Zondervan NIV Study Bible*, Psalm 27:1, 13, 14: "The Lord is my light and my salvation – whom shall I fear? I am still confident of this: I will see the goodness of the Lord in the land of the living. Wait for the Lord; be strong and take heart and wait for the Lord."

Chapter 39: Striving

8   Peggy Wright, "Our Best Defense During Cold & Flu Season," getoiling.com, September 11, 2020, https://getoiling.com/PeggyWright/blog/16577/our-best-defense-during-cold-flu-season My family has found this approach to fighting viruses has kept us from secondary infections for a few decades.

9   Peggy Wright, "Essentials for Healthy Hormones," getoiling.com, February 24, 2022, https://getoiling.com/PeggyWright/blog/31680/essentials-for-healthy-hormones

    Peggy Wright, "Ditch & Switch for Hormone Health," getoiling.com, February 25,2022, https://getoiling.com/PeggyWright/blog/31720/ditch-switch-for-hormone-health

    Addressing hormone imbalance has been a huge shift in getting to the roots of symptoms.

10 Peggy Wright, "Food Swaps to Avoid High Intolerance Foods" getoiling.com, November 23, 2020, https://getoiling.com/PeggyWright/blog/19673/food-swaps-to-avoid-high-intolerance-foods

    Peggy Wright, "Natural Remedy Kit," getoiling.com, August 5, 2020, https://getoiling.com/PeggyWright/blog/14869/natural-remedy-kit

Chapter 42: Summer In the City

11 *Zondervan NIV Study Bible*, Luke 5:12: "Lord, if you are willing, you can make me clean."

Chapter 44: Adjusting

12 Dr. Archibald Hart, *Stress and Adrenaline* (Nashville, TN: Thomas Nelson, 1988).

Chapter 50: The Milk Pitcher

13 Dr. Henry Cloud and Dr. John Townsend, *Boundaries*. (Michigan: Zondervan Publishing House, 1992).

Chapter 54: The Wisdom of Emotions

14 Dan Allender, *The Wounded Heart* (Colorado: Nav Press, 1995).

Chapter 55: Cleansing

15 Bruce Williamson, "THE SOCIETY OF CHILDLIKE GROWNUPS," Cornell University, May 8, 2014, https://www.classe.cornell.edu/~seb/childlike.html.

Chapter 58: Letting Light In

16 *Zondervan NIV Study Bible*, Isaiah 61:1–3: "The Spirit of the Sovereign Lord is on me, / because the Lord has anointed me/ to proclaim good news to the poor. / He has sent me to bind up the broken-hearted, / to proclaim freedom for the captives / and release from darkness for the prisoners, / to proclaim the year of the Lord's favor… to bestow on them a crown of beauty / instead of ashes, / the oil of joy / instead of mourning, / and a garment of praise/ instead of a spirit of despair. / They will be called oaks of righteousness, / a planting of the Lord/ for the display of his splendor."

17 *Zondervan NIV Study Bible*, Psalm 46:1: "God is our refuge and strength, an ever-present help in trouble."

Chapter 59: The Gift in the Illness

18 I created a printable document called "Four Steps to Your Best Self." You can sign up to have it delivered to your inbox from the pop-up on my website: https://getoiling.com/PeggyWright

19 Peggy Wright, "Food Swaps to Avoid High Intolerance Foods," getoiling.com, November 23, 2020, https://getoiling.com/PeggyWright/blog/19673/food-swaps-to-avoid-high-intolerance-foods

20 Peggy Wright, "Autoimmune Series #1," video, March 18, 2021, https://youtu.be/8Wcq0_LpEJg
21 Details about this awesome ministry can be found at Mighty Oaks Global Initiatives (mighty-oaks.com).